Pricing in Big Business

Pricing in Big Business / *a case approach*

by A. D. H. Kaplan
Joel B. Dirlam
Robert F. Lanzillotti

The Brookings Institution, *Washington, D. C.*

Library of Congress Catalogue Card Number 58-10077

HF
5415
.K2

Printed in the United States of America

George Banta Company, Inc.

Menasha, Wisconsin

THE BROOKINGS INSTITUTION is an independent organization engaged in research and education in the social sciences. Its principal purposes are to aid in the development of sound public policies and to provide advanced training for students in the social sciences.

The Institution was founded December 8, 1927, as a consolidation of three antecedent organizations: the Institute for Government Research, 1916; the Institute of Economics, 1922; and the Robert Brookings Graduate School of Economics and Government, 1924.

The general administration of the Institution is the responsibility of a self-perpetuating Board of Trustees. In addition to this general responsibility the By-Laws provide that, "It is the function of the Trustees to make possible the conduct of scientific research and publication, under the most favorable conditions, and to safeguard the independence of the research staff in the pursuit of their studies and in the publication of the results of such studies. It is not a part of their function to determine, control, or influence the conduct of particular investigations or the conclusions reached." The immediate direction of the policies, program, and staff of the Institution is vested in the President, who is assisted by an advisory council, chosen from the professional staff of the Institution.

In publishing a study the Institution presents it as a competent treatment of a subject worthy of public consideration. The interpretations and conclusions in such publications are those of the author or authors and do not necessarily reflect the views of other members of the Brookings staff or of the administrative officers of the Institution.

Foreword

IN AN EARLIER volume on *Big Enterprise in a Competitive System,* interviews with top executives of large corporations, company statements, and materials from many other sources provided useful background for generalizations regarding the place of the large-scale enterprise in the structure of the economy. In this monograph the case materials themselves are reviewed in detail in an effort to determine the manner in which representative large enterprises have formed their pricing policies.

Since most of the original interviews were conducted between the years 1948-51 in preparation for the earlier study, it was necessary for the authors of this monograph to go back to a number of the companies during the past two years to bring the materials on company pricing policy more nearly up to date. The Brookings Institution appreciates the assistance and the contribution of the co-operating companies, and is particularly grateful to those that made charts and tables available for publication.

A. D. H. Kaplan began work on the study of big business in 1948, and as senior author had major responsibility for the preparation of the manuscript on pricing. He was assisted by several scholars who joined the Brookings staff at intervals and participated in the preparation of the monograph. Joel B. Dirlam worked with the project from 1955 to 1957 and in the drafting of the manuscript, while associate professor of economics at the University of Connecticut. Robert F. Lanzillotti joined the study during the academic year 1956-57, on leave from the State College of Washington, where he is associate professor of economics. The contributions of Mr. Dirlam and Mr. Lanzillotti are recognized in their co-authorship of the present volume. Mr. Kaplan, however, assumes primary responsibility for the conclusions and for the use of the materials included in the monograph.

Alfred E. Kahn was with the study on leave from Cornell University during the academic year 1951-52, and participated in the review and organization of the initial interview materials. The Institution also wishes to acknowledge its indebtedness to the following consultants from a number of universities who collaborated in the initial field work: Joel Dean, Columbia; Melvin G. de Chazeau, Cornell; Ewald T. Grether, University of California, Berkeley; Clare E. Griffin, Michigan; Richard B. Heflebower, Northwestern; Neil H. Jacoby, University of California, Los Angeles; John P. Miller, Yale; Herluf V. Olsen, Dartmouth; Russell A. Stevenson, Michigan; Lawrence H. Seltzer, Wayne.

Helpful comments were made by Bert G. Hickman, Lewis Kimmel, Harold B. Rowe and Ralph Watkins of the Institution's staff.

Mention cannot be made here of the many individuals in business and in the economics profession who participated in conferences and contributed their views and criticisms. The Institution joins with the authors in extending to all of them this expression of grateful appreciation.

The early work on this study was financed jointly by the Maurice and Laura Falk Foundation and the Alfred P. Sloan Foundation. For this helpful support the Institution is especially grateful.

The views expressed herein are those of the authors, and do not necessarily represent those of other staff members, officers, or trustees of the Brookings Institution. They should not be regarded as representing the views of the supporting foundations.

ROBERT D. CALKINS
President

June 1958

Table of Contents

ix

PART II   ANALYSIS AND INTERPRETATION

Tables

Charts

PART
I / Case Materials

Introduction

THIS MONOGRAPH DEALS WITH price policy and pricing
practices, a phase of the activities of large corporations that awakens
in the general public the most lively interest. It is based on a series
of interviews with top management of a representative group of
large-scale enterprises in the fields of primary production, manufacturing, and distribution. The survey was conducted primarily for the
purpose of interpreting the general role of big business in the American economy, and pricing was considered within the context of comprehensive company policy. This approach limited the inquiry into
pricing *per se,* but it provided certain advantages, notably the insights
afforded into top management's concept of the role of prices in over-
all market operation. This management perspective is in itself significant for a thorough understanding of pricing policies; for, in the real
market setting, prices are not formed, altered, or continued in isolation.

Apart from a few corporations regarded as indispensable because
of their dominant stature, companies were selected for convenience,
because top management co-operation was assured, or because their
experience seemed especially pertinent. Twenty made their chief
executive officers and associates available for extended inquiry.
Others supplied information only in selected areas.

The officials who discussed policy with the interviewers found it
difficult to analyze pricing as a separate activity distinct from others
entering into their company policy. Pricing decisions were made or
influenced by executives from production, development engineering,
accounting, finance, sales, and public relations divisions. They were
usually considered part of the general strategy for achieving a broadly
defined goal. Hence, on the whole, the executives tended to minimize
price policy as such, or to discuss it in such broad terms that inter-

3

viewers initially found it difficult to apply the explanation to particular pricing situations.[1]

Under these conditions, the focus of this monograph on price policy—not infrequently out of the context of general company policy—does some violence to the accurate reproduction of the atmosphere of the original interviews. The alternative, however, would be to bury the pricing process in a general study of each company; the pricing decision would then be considered in the context of company policy as it is related to product improvement, distribution methods, market shares, advertising, protection of supply, divisional organization, possible impact of the antitrust laws, and the character of the executive personalities. This procedure might provide superior insight into the broad question of how decisions of all types are made by the large corporation, but it would fail to focus sufficiently on the pricing itself—an area of legitimate public concern outside the corporation.

However strongly the firm may insist that pricing is not a major area of decision, or a separable one, price is nevertheless one of the most important outward manifestations of the policy of a large corporation. Price is easily expressed in figures that are susceptible of comparison with similar data for other corporations, at any given moment or over time. Difficulties in reducing to measurable quantities differences in quality or attractiveness, or the extent of service associated with the product—which firms find it almost impossible to separate from price—tend to minimize the stress placed on such aspects of policy by those outside the company.

Accepting some disparity between the firm's view and that of the community regarding the importance and character of the process of pricing, this monograph attempts a workable compromise. It begins by presenting a series of case histories primarily from the viewpoint of management, allowing for the fact that firms rarely view pricing as a separable policy decision. It then presents an interpretation and analysis of pricing practices.

This discussion of pricing decisions will incorporate little editorial judgment other than that involved in isolating the pricing of any one product from the fabric of broad company policy. Account will be

[1] A section of the Brookings questionnaire dealing with marketing and pricing is reproduced in App. 1.

taken, however, of the related policy problems and influences to which the management itself gave weight. The reader will be given the pricing experience with a certain product, developed against its own unique background within the company. By this method of presentation of big business pricing, not all companies included in the sample can be covered, nor can the monograph give uniformity of treatment to those selected.

It was evident that most of the executives with whom the interviews were conducted did not ordinarily concern themselves with pricing details; instances appeared in which they were not intimately aware of how their products were priced. Even officers who were quite familiar with company policy in the pricing area were among those who could not illustrate the policy by a detailed follow-through of particular price decisions. The fact that in some of the companies there was a gulf between the top officials and the price makers is in itself significant. Efforts to follow up the policy statements of officials to get specific illustrations of price making in practice frequently developed the fact that it was delegated to lower echelons. The frequent lack of direct concern with pricing problems by top management as a major problem area for company analysis partially accounts for the relative thinness of materials made available for publication by some of the companies interviewed.

Economists, legislators, and the public generally would like to see pricing decisions by big companies analyzed in logical fashion, with historical comparisons of competitors' prices, cost factors, and profit margins given consistent and quantitative weight in detailed memoranda of officials involved. Unfortunately for those who would insist on fully ordered business behavior, such strategic memoranda summarizing the considerations at an important conference leading to a price decision are rarely found. Perhaps the presumed formal conference was never held. Even where the people doing the pricing tended to have certain staff information placed before them while making up their minds, whether and just how that information was taken into consideration often remained obscure. There was no document tracing the steps by which the staff information could be said to account for the price decision. Repeatedly, reference was made to the "art" or "feel" of pricing rather than observance of a formula.

Details of price making were also withheld because executives were reluctant to reveal actual cost or revenue totals for specific product areas. They feared such data might prove beneficial to their competitors or possibly be used for antitrust pressure. In some instances, such data were regarded as a private affair of the company. Furthermore, an interviewer seeking maximum company co-operation would be disinclined to press for full details on price if his questions met with resistance or defensive rationalization; occasional retreat was deemed advisable, particularly when a sensitive question could yield only a footnote to antitrust proceedings, and relevant factual evidence was already publicly available. Thus for no product were all cost and price data released for publication.

The pricing materials produced by the interviews are nevertheless believed to be sufficiently important to warrant presenting them to the reader. Precisely such information is not readily available elsewhere, and a consideration of the procedures and their rationalizations provides further insight into the complexity of the pricing process in big business.

The analysis of price policy of corporate giants presents certain initial problems of classification. These stem not only from the reluctance of many managements to think about policy in terms of a formal classification, but also from the inherent difficulties of assigning large multiproduct firms to a single category.

To the extent that the firms interviewed articulated or distinguished between price policies, they did so in terms of broad market situations. These, as the firms saw them, were in part characterized by differences in degree of responsibility assumed by the seller for the economic position of the product.[2] To some extent, therefore, the perspective of

---

[2] Although the corporations interviewed have in common the feature of large size, they are not alike in the position they hold in the market. Some, like U.S. Steel, International Harvester, and Johns-Manville, hold primacy in an industry and occupy the position of price leaders. A few companies face competitors of such various sizes and abilities that in spite of their absolute size they are far from being able to make the price decisions for the market and may not even think of competition in terms of actions of one or a few competitors. Still others fall between these extremes.

the firm seemed to conform to a classification roughly comparable to the conventional textbook market analysis. That is, it would move from what are conventionally called purely competitive to highly rationalized (oligopolistic, monopolistic) market structures. But the market situations as envisaged by the large firms could not be easily limited by a simple classification based on one factor such as relative size of participating firms.

The individuality of a product, which would contribute to creating a "monopolized" market, is not an independent determinant; it is subject to some control by the firm. By maintaining prices, the firm may have made a decision to preserve quality and maintain a long-run market; by keeping prices stable, short-run profits may have been foregone in order to provide the stability that many buyers prefer to temporary and unpredictable bargains. Then again, traditions in the method of marketing the commodity influence company pricing policy. The closeness of substitutes, as has often been pointed out, is partly a question of potential competition. A market can seldom be designated with assurance as "purely competitive" or "monopolistic" unless in connection with some short-time period. One characteristic of the large firm is its habit of looking over a longer-time interval than the small firm; it can afford to do so, since it has greater resources and is usually diversified. Hence, its appraisal of the nature of the market and that of the outside observer, who sees it in terms of current transactions, need not coincide. As would be expected, the managements, even of the firms with patent protection, put a much larger proportion of their products in the competitive or potentially competitive category than would outsiders.

It was apparent, therefore, that pricing policies could not be explored as manifestations of market structures, since the market structures, conventionally defined, were by no means recognized as such by the firms interviewed,[3] nor were the markets situations conceptually distinct from the process of pricing itself.

The fact that the companies in the sample are large, multiproduct concerns raises certain additional problems of classification. Those companies using similar pricing policies and procedures might be

[3] Almost every firm insisted that most of its products faced intense competition.

grouped, but as a rule the large, multiproduct company does not readily fit into one pricing policy classification because of the different production and demand requirements of the different product divisions, which deal with their particular types of customers and markets. Separate treatment has to be given to the company as a corporate unit with general policies capable of co-ordinating the operations in all the product fields in which the company operates. This general policy, however, is not represented by a single objective. A company that is highly conscious of its targets of return may in one case have a bold and promotional approach to price making, while another thinks of target return in terms of a cost-based structure of prices in which price stability has high priority. A company may, on the other hand, give a high degree of autonomy to product groups, which respectively exemplify both approaches, and have its co-ordination almost exclusively at the financial investment level without regard to the differences in price methods, which enroll particular divisions to achieve profitable results.

Because of the diversity of products and the amorphous nature of the markets, the discussion of price policies begins in Part I by describing the method of pricing specific products, selected to represent the market situations differentiated by firms included in the sample. These product studies will serve to introduce the reader to a consideration of the price policy of the company in the context of its position as a multiproduct firm.

Division of the case histories roughly by "product characteristic"— a term that embraces the whole congeries of influences playing on a particular price decision—tends to highlight the impossibility of pigeonholing in any simple way the policies of the big multiproduct corporations. Undeniably there are, in many instances, pricing routines, sometimes expressed as rules; but given the diversity of products that most of the companies sold, it was impossible to equate product policy and company policy in every area. Swift's dog food cannot be priced in the same way or under the same guides as fresh meat. Union Carbide's Prestone antifreeze requires a different type of pricing from its oxygen. Thus, there were few companies in the sample that were in a position to say "Our policy is to price our products according to a uniform procedure and target." If there was a universal rule, it usually was said to function mostly with respect to new products, in that they were required to promise, at projected prices, a minimum return on investment before large-scale output would be attempted.

In a few instances, however, the firms have provided cases in which the products were sufficiently similar so that company policy and product policy were shaped by almost identical forces. This was true of steel, copper, automobiles, and to a lesser degree of tin cans and rubber tires. In some cases, the nature of the product changed over time, but the pattern of maturing was far from invariable.

Against the background of the product studies, the survey of company price policies is next presented. The categories under which the companies are classified are arbitrary, in the sense that a company may fit into more than one of them. The reader may weigh independently the validity of the classifications finally adopted, as some of the managements have already done. The selections were usually based on formulas voiced by management, such as "target return." In some cases, the company policies were not explicit, but could be presented as reasonable deductions from the interviews—where, notwithstanding diversity in products and pricing at the product level, the corporate organization seemed to evolve a minimum and discernible consistency.

Part I also describes the internal organization for price making.

In Part I, no attempt is made to generalize about discrepancies between formal and actual policy. The emphasis at this stage is on conveying objectively the policies and procedures of price making as given by the company management. In Part II, however, we express our own views on the meaning of the interviews. We attempt an interpretation and rationalization of company price policies to bring out group differences and common characteristics for the sample considered as a cross section of big business.

Although the case material presented in Part I is largely based on the interviews, it is supplemented by other data from published sources, which are indicated in footnotes.

1 / *Pricing Selected Products*

THIS CHAPTER PRESENTS a series of product pricing situations, with a view to illustrating the ways in which big business faces the problem of price formation. It seeks to show the various ways in which the product line gets priced in the market. In some instances, especially of new products, pricing is almost exclusively a one-company problem. Similarly, in cases where one company has dominated the picture over the years, pricing will be influenced by the role and actions of that company in the industry setting. In the case of a multi-product producer, a product-by-product analysis may disclose different policies for different products.

For several reasons, this chapter does not include a discussion of the pricing of individual products by every company in the sample. In some cases (Sears and A. & P., for example) because of the multi-product nature of the company's operations, it is not possible to single out a product or product line as representative of company pricing. In others, companies are excluded because they did not disclose sufficient details about their pricing to permit adequate treatment of the pricing of particular products. The available information on the pricing process in both groups of firms is examined in the following chapter in connection with the analysis of general company pricing policy and its implementation.

It should be kept in mind that pricing decisions are resultants of pricing procedures, pricing policies, and company goals. These three levels can be distinguished, though their boundaries are not always sharply demarcated.

1. Pricing procedures are the formulas or rules of thumb on which the company relies in setting the price. One illustration is the use of a conventional margin between tank wagon and tank car gasoline price

in selling to distributors. Another is the various freight equalization devices adopted to meet competitors' prices. Price followership may function as a pricing procedure in so far as a company automatically follows the price announced by the industry leader. A food processor in the case of new products proceeds to calculate margins in accord with a principle of extracting the high mark-up that a specialty can take, although the percentage is not an invariable one. A large petroleum refiner has an elaborate formula for finding what it believes to be the correct price for gasoline, but checks closely on competitors' moves to set price. Here a procedure or formula shades into a policy. These techniques may be characterized as operational decisions usually made at the product department level.

2. Pricing procedures or methods are usually aligned with what the company executives think of as their pricing policy, which is a standard to which prices of the company's range of products are in general expected to conform. While pricing policy is not always explicit, there were a sufficient number of companies in the group that thought, wrote, and talked at length about something they called company pricing policy to warrant using it as an identifiable area of business behavior.

Pricing policy is obviously not wholly insulated from decisions in other areas than prices, or standing rules regarding other matters. It may be contingent upon nonprice variables; the pricing of a refrigerator or an automobile or even a new breakfast cereal may be inseparable from a style decision. The lease, rather than sale, of can manufacturers' closing machines at a nominal figure may be part of an over-all marketing policy designed to assert a company's leadership in the can market. Standard of Indiana's tank wagon price structure is one phase of its larger marketing policy, which obviously involves it in decisions about retail station locations, although it does not have to decide on distribution methods every time it alters the tank wagon price.

Pricing policy for a product line of a large company is sometimes regarded as a feature of a wider spectrum of corporate policy concerning marketing or investment stability or growth. But just as a company's union recognition policy might be isolated from its over-all labor policy or its promotion policy from its personnel policy, so we can speak of its pricing policy without having to treat in detail other features of a broader policy area of which it may be a part, or that may influence it. If pricing policy in some large corporations is part of marketing policy, and decisions about alterations of pricing policy are never reached except in conjunction with decisions on style or methods of distribution, this is important and will be indicated.

When the character of the product shifts virtually each time the price changes, as in the case of automobiles, pricing policy will be more intimately tied to other strategic decisions than it is for a metal ingot or plate. Reactions of direct rivals and possibilities of substitution play a part in determining price policy, as they do also in determining broader marketing policy. They modify procedures correspondingly. Thus, the pricing *procedure* for a district manager of a petroleum marketer may be to follow a particular rival's gasoline price. The pricing *policy* may be to meet competition. Or the pricing procedure may be, as in building materials at Johns-Manville, to use a percentage mark-up over the cost, modified by the policy that where the sales of a rival below Johns-Manville's list price cut too deeply into its position, it will make reductions, but not as far as the lowest competitor's. The policy may differ from that of meeting competition only to the extent of waiting a certain length of time before responding to a rival's price change. A familiar type of price policy is that which requires that the price shall be sufficient to return a given percentage of the related investment. The procedures by which this policy is carried out may involve the use of standard costs or some other kind of pricing formula.

3. These procedures and price policies are in turn often subordinate to what may be designated as the *goal,* or *objective,* in all policy areas, of the company itself. Just as the pricing procedures are used, or modified, to carry out price policies, so the price policies are instruments for achieving long-term goals. It is recognized that some companies have not formulated long-run objectives but appear to live from day to day. However, the large companies are less likely to have such limited horizons since their financial strength permits them to

look ahead and to set an objective other than simply month-to-month survival.

Is there always a three-level stratification of price decisions—the procedures, the policy, and finally the dominant company objective? In many, if not most cases, the stated price policy is perhaps as close as the firm ever gets to articulating the long-run goal. If a large retail distributor is endeavoring to acquire a definite percentage of business in every territory where it has stores, this will determine its pricing policy. The goal of the company, if stated at all, is growth—meaning expansion of sales. The overriding goal of other business organizations may be insurance of continuity of investment return, whether through adherence to stable pricing or attention to maintenance of a market share in established products. Still others may emphasize branching out into new areas of research and development, with greater promise of growth and profitable return than is provided by established products. One area of decision making for achieving these goals is the formulation of pricing methods and policies. Pricing would be measured directly against the desired goals, which could also be called, though not exclusively, price policies.

These three levels of decision will become apparent when the individual product histories are integrated with the analysis of company policies in the following chapter.

Steel

The pricing process in steel reflects the industry's history of price leadership and the influence of vertical integration. Earlier studies of steel pricing have concentrated on such factors as the forward integration of the major steel producers, the method of price quotation, the heavy investment and overhead costs, and the peculiarities of demand.[1] In the present context, however, interest is focused on the determinants

[1] *E.g.* Carroll R. Daugherty, Melvin G. deChazeau, and Samuel S. Stratton, *The Economics of the Iron and Steel Industry* (1937).

of policy as they appear to a leading firm. Hence, little purpose would be served by attempting a detailed summary of factors that may affect steel pricing. Nevertheless, certain aspects of the price history of steel that are directly relevant to an interpretation of the views of management require consideration.

The quoted base price for basic steel and steel products tends to be uniform among firms following the lead of United States Steel. Finished steel is sold mostly by specification—this being true not only of highly fabricated pieces like structural steel, but also of the general run of sheets, plates, bars, rods, etc. Extra charges, which are imposed for variations in alloy and other specifications, are important in the final delivered price. Up to the Second World War, the industry apparently agreed on uniform extras to tie in differences in specifications with a uniform base price; but in recent years, this practice seems to have become less prevalent.[2] Room is left for differentials among companies in the final price, despite the fact that most standard products are quoted at base prices plus extras showing no appreciable spread from the quotations of U.S. Steel. There still remains the freight advantage or disadvantage of location in relation to particular market outlets.

MECHANICS OF PRICING

United States Steel states that it employs a "stable margin" price policy, that is, in general it aims at maintaining margins despite variations in sales volume. In so doing it uses standard costs,[3] computed

[2] Special prices are made for large contracts, and there is evidence that charges for extras are less uniform than they once were. In this connection, there is strong opinion among producers that discrimination and secret price cuts are not characteristic in the industry. The reason offered by one steel executive is that virtually everyone knows everyone else's costs; in effect, that the industry operates in a gold fish bowl. Also "the price cuts of the thirties taught everyone a lesson."

[3] Standard cost may be defined as "predetermined cost for each operation, or each unit of finished product . . . intended to represent the value of direct

on the basis of 80 per cent of capacity as normal, and including an assignment of overhead burden to every product. Although the company continuously watches actual costs, it follows standard cost logic for pricing purposes. Standard costs are revised annually to account for such factors as increased labor costs, rising markets, new machines, new processes, new kinds of coal used, and similar factors affecting actual costs.[4]

Standard costs are determined for each mill, but these individual standards are used primarily for gauging efficiency and for stimulating incentive at the local level. For pricing purposes, the standard cost used is an average, weighted by the volumes at respective mills. This means that in addition to changes in the factors mentioned above, as occasioning revisions in standard cost, allowance is also made for higher capital costs of new facilities. Thus, high capital costs exert an upward push on company-wide weighted standard costs and prices.

The company stresses the distinction it makes between what it calls "price structure" and "price level." Price structure involves "a hard-boiled application of standard costs in pricing individual products"; price level is concerned with the general or average level of prices

---

material, direct labor, and manufacturing burden normally required under efficient conditions at normal capacity to process a unit of product." E. A. Green, National Association of Cost Accountants Bulletin, Vol. 16, cited in *Accountants' Handbook* (1944), p. 225.

One of the main purposes of employing standard costs is to avoid the presumption of significant changes in profits or efficiency when these may be due in a particular instance to a temporary change in the cost or market situation respecting a specific item. To provide for these shifting situations, cost standards are used to make the stated costs of parts, assemblies, and finished products accord more closely with planned objectives. A common objective to which standard costs are frequently geared is a break-even point regarded as normal or optimum—*e.g.*, 70 or 80 per cent of capacity. Another purpose of standard costs is to control plant operations by developing and analyzing variances or differences between standard and actual costs; or by developing cost ratios or trends which use the standard costs as measuring rods.

[4] The market against which U.S. Steel measures adequacy of its capacity and its hoped-for share of sales is the projected total national market (including imports), broken down by individual product groups, by regions and mills. On the basis of these figures and the amount of various products the company feels it can and wishes to sell, the company's "operating plan" for the year is determined.

for the corporation, which in the final determination of prices involves much more than standard costs. The distinction can be seen more clearly by a discussion of the use of standard costs in connection with the mechanics of an actual price change, such as occurred following the wage settlement of 1956.

GENERAL PRICE REVISION,
AUGUST 1956

The average increase of $8.50 per ton in steel prices on August 7, 1956 was determined essentially as follows: With the wage negotiations as a backdrop, the Executive Vice President, Commercial directed his Price Division to recommend price schedules on the basis of hypothetical wage settlements.[5] According to a tradition in the steel industry, each cent-per-hour increase in direct labor costs adds another cent to steelmakers' non-wage costs per ton of steel. This working figure has been derived from experience in earlier wage settlements. With this labor-to-total cost ratio, the anticipated wage settlement is roughly doubled and multiplied by a traditional figure of twenty man-hours (more recently a figure of fifteen has been used to reflect higher efficiency) to yield the expected cost of a new wage package per ton of steel. Since the new contract (July 1956) was estimated to add 24 cents to the company's hourly labor cost per ton, an increase of $9.60 per ton was indicated.[6]

The Price Division bases its recommendations on more than this rule of thumb. It also makes a product-by-product analysis in which

[5] The Price Division consists of four or five price analysts charged with the responsibility of continuing examination of the price problem from many different angles (demand, costs, competition, market strategy, etc.).

[6] The custom of using this crude method of estimating price increases largely explains the expectation of the "trade" generally that prices would go up by at least $9.60 per ton. Some estimates ran as high as $12 per ton on the average, since in 1955 the industry used a 2.5 to 1 basis of estimating the total cost impact of the wage settlement. *Business Week* (Aug. 11, 1956), p. 25.

it considers proposals of the various product departments regarding changes in individual products. Whenever a product section of the company feels a change in base price is needed, it makes such recommendations in writing to the Commercial Department. The form used for this purpose calls for a detailed justification of the recommendation in terms of the pricing history and competitive information on the product and the expected impact of the proposed revision on specific company accounts or industries. The recommendation is accompanied by financial information prepared by the comptroller showing on a per-ton basis the present and proposed cost, together with the present and expected profit or loss.[7]

These recommendations and attached supporting information are presented to the director of the Price Division for his evaluation and in turn are submitted to the Vice President, Commercial for final action. It is important to note the kinds of information before the price makers at this level of management (which actually evaluates proposed price changes and determines the changes to be made, when, and by how much). The changes are considered in terms of profit return on *sales,* not investment.[8] This illustrates, as in the case of other companies in the sample, the way in which pricing officials view their product pricing problems, in contrast to the top level management, which views price policy primarily in terms of return on investment, but which does not actually determine prices.

Although the 1956 general price revision increased the composite average 6.25 per cent ($8.50 per ton), the prices of different products were not raised uniformly. Many products were raised more than 6.25 per cent, some less. The items tabulated on page 18 taken from U.S. Steel quotations announced immediately after the wage settlement illustrate the variations in the price increases.[9]

These differences show, among other considerations, such factors as: holding back on changes during the year, the post-wage settlement being regarded as the most propitious time for a complete revision of prices; the labor cost factor in the given product; the company's

[7] See App. 2.
[8] *Ibid.*
[9] *Iron Age* (Aug. 9, 1956), p. 124.

	Aug. 7, 1956 Price (Per ton)	Previous Price (Per ton)	Per Cent Increase
Alloy steel			
Billets, blooms, slabs..................	$107	$ 96	11.5
Hot rolled strip and sheet..............	155	144	7.6
Wire—Premier spring, high carbon........	168	152	10.5
Wire products			
Nails.............................	167	152	9.9
Barbed wire........................	187	175	6.9
Carbon steel			
Cold finished bars....................	137	125	9.6
Light rails.........................	120	113	6.2
Plates, high strength (Man-Ten S)........	127	120	5.8

leadership position in the product; expectations of the trade (and the potential pressure from congressional committees and the public). With the 1956 three-year contract, management expected to make more selective price changes as it deemed appropriate, rather than follow its earlier practice of general annual changes.[10]

COST-PRICE RELATIONSHIPS

That standard-cost doctrine has not been rigidly followed by the company in pricing is suggested by price changes that do not seem to conform to the usual varieties of standard-cost plus target return pricing. Standard-cost pricing is designed to avoid the necessity for making short-run changes in burden that would result if adjustments were continuously made for temporary changes in volume. Actually, U.S. Steel has not been able to ignore short-term shrinkage of demand. Moreover, it has not been able to carry its "fair return" logic to the point of forcing price increases in depressions to offset higher unit costs at low volume, because its competitors would not follow. Nor has it

[10] This selective policy apparently was not followed in the general price increase of $6 per ton announced by U.S. Steel on July 1, 1957.

cut prices in boom periods, which would be the corollary of price increases in depressions.[11] (See chart on page 20.)

Differences in margins among products were not demonstrated by the corporation in terms of cost and price data on given product lines, but were assumed to be generally recognized in the industry. Mill prices cannot be directly related to costs for U.S. Steel or its competitors, whose prices, with certain exceptions noted below, are generally designed to meet the corporation's prices. United States Steel has the same prices at Pittsburgh and in Ohio, Illinois, Indiana, and Alabama, and apparently averages mill costs to get such equalization.[12]

THE COMPETITIVE IMPACT
ON PRICING

The intensity of competition from other steel companies varies with the effectiveness of U.S. Steel's price leadership. With swings in the business cycle, there has been some modification of the "full-cost stable-margin" pricing philosophy of U.S. Steel and its leading competitors. Competitors of the corporation are more likely to take premiums in periods of prosperity, while U.S. Steel appears to demand no more than its published prices. In recession, however, the company has followed the trend toward concessions initiated by competitors. United States Steel has tended to be the laggard in recognizing the price cuts of its rivals. The ostensible regularity and comparative rigidity in steel prices have been appreciably modified by the policies of steel companies other than U.S. Steel. From 1946 to 1950 the prices

[11] *Investigation of Concentration of Economic Power,* Hearings before the Temporary National Economic Committee, 76 Cong. 2 sess. 1939), Pt. 19, "Iron and Steel Industry: General Price Policies." Statement by Benjamin F. Fairless, pp. 10536-37.

[12] According to one pricing official, "standard costs on most products are much closer among mills than is commonly supposed: the variations run about 5 per cent." The Fairless Works is evidently an exception.

of many steel producers were substantially higher than those of U.S. Steel.[13]

When pricing through the basing point system was in effect, there were apparently fewer exceptions to the leader-follower pattern. Yet, even in 1936 U.S. Steel had to cut its base prices to reflect levels prevailing generally in the industry but not yet "official." With all mills on an f.o.b. basis, when demand is heavy, there is perhaps less of a

Average Prices of Steel Products and
Average Capacity Operated, 1948-55[a]

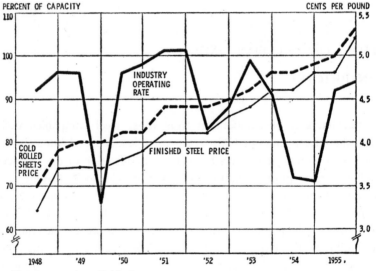

[a] For data see App. Table 1.

disposition on the part of competitors to follow U.S. Steel. The corporation's public announcement of October 1953, reiterated in its *Annual Report* for 1953—that when necessary to get the business, it would meet the lower delivered price of a competitor—suggests that when rivals expect operation will be less than capacity, they are more disposed to undercut U.S. Steel.[14] There is no indication that the

[13] *Study of Monopoly Power,* Hearings before a Subcommittee of the House Committee on the Judiciary, 81 Cong. 2 sess. (1950), Pt. 4-B, pp. 629-36.

[14] "Under the revised policy, U.S. Steel will continue to quote prices f.o.b. its mills, or, if the customer so desires, it will quote delivered prices which

October 1953 policy resulted in U.S. Steel's having to match price reductions that yielded its competitors a lower base price than U. S. Steel had set.

Opportunities to differentiate prices to take advantage of locations within a given natural market may vary with the particular products and sections of the country that are involved. In the East, for example, where Bethlehem Steel has four mills, the mill prices for semifinished steel plates, bars, and sheets are the same at all its mills and identical with Pittsburgh prices. Structural prices are slightly higher than Pittsburgh, but are the same at all its mills, even Johnstown, which is near Pittsburgh. Yet, Sparrows Point prices are higher than Pittsburgh on wire rods, wire, and tin mill products. Some of these are made at the Johnstown mill, but for these products Pittsburgh prices are applied. Similarly, U.S. Steel's Fairless Works enjoys a $3.00 per ton price differential over other mills on standard bars, small shapes, and special quality and concrete reinforcing bars, and a $1.00 differential on hot- and cold-rolled sheets. Farther west, National Steel's Great Lakes plant near Detroit has enjoyed a differential over Pittsburgh of $2.00 (formerly $4.00) per ton on sheets. It is a moot question whether such differentials could be maintained in conditions of slack demand and underutilization of plant capacity by other steel producers, such as prevailed in 1953-54.

It also seems clear that firms will quote outside their natural territory and absorb freight. United States Steel management indicated in interviews that the 1953 announcement regarding its intention to meet the delivered prices of competitors should not be taken to mean that it will shade its base prices to meet individual situations. An officer explained that the company "is committed to a one-price policy; if it

---

reflect full transportation charges from shipping mill to destination. The revised policy, however, permits the meeting of a lower delivered price of a competitor when necessary and commercially desirable in order to participate in the business of an individual customer. This change in policy is consistent with the stand long taken by U.S. Steel—that it has the right to compete in good faith in any market for the business of any consumer. This provision for meeting the lower delivered price of a competitor does not constitute a return to the so-called multiple basing point pricing method which was abandoned by the steel industry in 1948." U.S. Steel Corporation, *Annual Report, 1953,* p. 12.

is deemed desirable to change price, it will be an across-the-board change." The management stated that it will do no more than equalize the freight disadvantage, even in those instances when U.S. Steel's base price is higher than a competitor's.[15] The company's determination to implement this policy strictly has been spelled out in a memorandum to all sales offices, with specific instructions respecting the conditions under which freight absorption cases would be considered by the Commercial Department.

Competitors, meanwhile, complain that prices on many steel products, even after the broad price readjustments carried through in 1956, have not been high enough to stimulate the desirable level of new investment in the industry. Generally, the assertion takes the form of the specific accusation that U.S. Steel is pricing as though new capacity cost $100 instead of the current $300 a ton. United States Steel has joined in complaints of an insufficient return, yet apparently does not intend to relieve the pressure on its competitors.[16] A campaign by steel men to boost prices was dampened when U. S. Steel would not go along with a general price increase in the fall of 1955.[17]

Although steel producers have complained, it is evident that the "art of followership" is still deeply embedded in the philosophy of pricing in the steel industry. National Steel has been a price follower in every line in which it engages, in two of which (tin plate and light sheet steel) it has been an important producer. Despite former President Weir's adoption of the position that steel prices should be based on full cost of the most efficient firm, the company nevertheless has

[15] This would appear to be somewhat inconsistent with the earlier announcement about "meeting the delivered prices of competitors." Also, it is difficult to understand how customers could be gained or held (except in periods of steel shortage) if it meant that U.S. Steel's delivered price (with freight equalized) would still be higher than that of a rival steelmaker. It would appear that U.S. Steel will not *initiate any price shading,* but if threatened with loss of customers will retaliate as necessary to keep them—*e.g.,* by freight absorption.

[16] Since 1940, according to a statement made by Mr. Fairless in 1953, U.S. Steel had not, in ten out of twelve years, recouped "a dime of added profit on the millions of extra tons of steel that [it] produced for the people of this nation," nor earned "one cent of increased return on the billion and a half of additional capital that has been poured into [its] business." *New York Times* (Apr. 26, 1953), p. 5.

[17] "Steel: Prices Can Only Go Up," *Business Week* (Nov. 5, 1955), p. 25.

rested profitably under the umbrella of U.S. Steel prices during a large part of its history.[18] National's price has generally followed the Pittsburgh price, with freight allowed when necessary. While the company unhesitatingly meets price cuts—and does so by reducing the base price rather than the extras—it makes no effort to lead in price reductions.

Thus, U.S. Steel's competitors, except to the extent that they produce specialities or otherwise tailor their services, feel forced to go along with the U.S. Steel base price plus transportation cost in "normal" times when demand is heavy. By concentrating in those areas of steel making, particularly tin plate, where it can operate at low cost and raise technical standards, National appears to have been a successful operator. Indeed, one officer of U.S. Steel who has been with the corporation for many years has expressed the opinion that companies like National and Bethlehem, with more centrally located facilities, have been able to improve those facilities at the same location. United States Steel, by contrast, was disinclined to abandon its original locations and less adaptable steel capacity "because of long-continued obligations to community and to staff." Hence, it has had greater overhead burdens and lower margins in comparison with other steel companies. These disadvantages have been offset in part by the advantages accruing from "a very broad product line and also complete geographic coverage."

Patently U.S. Steel's policies pervade the pricing structure and price levels for all steel products. Even with products numbered in the thousands, and customers exceeding 100,000, the company has sought to apply a uniform, universally applicable pricing policy. Its price policy was characterized by one of the senior officials interviewed as follows: "U.S. Steel has never tried to price to maximum profit not only in the short run but even in the long run." It appears that U.S. Steel holds the philosophy of cost-plus pricing. Nonetheless, even such a company has difficulty in following a formula in pricing steel products—partly because of the differences in costs among plants

[18] Recently the pinch of higher costs has led to industry criticism of prices under U.S. Steel's leadership as being inadequate to provide for depreciation and new capacity. National Steel Corporation, *Annual Report, 1955*, p. 6, and *1956*, p. 5.

and the heavy overhead factor, and partly from the desire to hold customers.

The corporation has given evidence of limiting profits and refraining from exploitation of shortages, which can be viewed as manifestations of awareness of its responsibilities and vulnerability as the largest and dominant firm in the industry. In the past, according to U.S. Steel, it has refrained from cutting off its semi-integrated customer-competitors in periods of shortage when it could make higher profits by sharply raising prices or by finishing the steel products itself—a problem that is not so important today with increased integration of smaller mills. President Fairless testified that the company has checked with its customers before raising prices and has held off in reducing published prices, in the interest of customers with heavy inventories.[19] Moreover, on occasion it has accepted orders for certain items at a loss to keep its regular customers.[20] Competitors, on the other hand, even when they believe that U.S. Steel's prices are not high enough, will not ordinarily go above them. The period following the Second World War was an exception. When U.S. Steel has suffered a decline in volume, as in 1954, its pricing philosophy has predisposed it to resist significant cuts. The relative regularity of steel prices through marked changes in operating levels occurring since 1947 seems to bear out the traditional tendency to resist price revisions in steel until action is unavoidable.

Aluminum

The transition from one-company pricing, through 1946, to pricing under a government-created industry structure of three integrated

[19] TNEC Hearings, 76 Cong. 2 sess., Pt. 19, pp. 10492-93, 10510.
[20] Executives pointed out that often U.S. Steel accepted business at less than normal profit or at a loss in order to keep a customer. According to these sources, the company thought in terms of the customers rather than the items sold, particularly when there was a potential of large volume that might be jeopardized by refusing to meet a competitor's price.

aluminum producers has not as yet produced any dramatic changes by way of direct price competition in primary aluminum. The new position of Alcoa vis-à-vis Reynolds and Kaiser, however, has modified the relative importance of intra-industry and inter-industry considerations for both price and nonprice competition. Aluminum ingot

Index of Aluminum Ingot Prices and
Wholesale Price Index, 1926-56[a]

(1947-49 = 100)

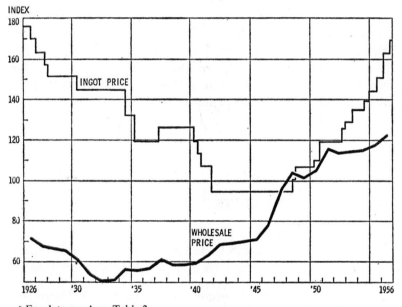

[a] For data see App. Table 3.

prices, designed for penetration of the markets for copper and other substitute products, gradually declined from 35 cents a pound in 1920 to 15 cents a pound in 1941, and that figure was maintained under war price control and until June 1948. Following the Second World War, the price of ingot did not follow the general upward trend of wholesale prices. But since 1948 it has risen faster, as shown in the chart above.

During the years before Alcoa ceased to be the sole American producer of aluminum, its management had developed a general guide for pricing that set as the ideal a level that would enable the company, when operating at 70 per cent of capacity, to realize on the product or product line a return of 20 per cent before taxes on the investment it represented.[21] An officer of Alcoa stressed that although this target is expected to provide a general guide for pricing, the company deliberately establishes prices to return, in some instances, less than its general target. This is because of (1) the desire to get tonnage and expand markets over the long haul and (2) the realization that a higher return, especially in fabricating lines, would tend to shift demand to competitors, or potential competitors, and therefore limit Alcoa's sales. Alcoa has persisted in this limit-pricing or limit-profits policy in the postwar period, even though at times its prices are somewhat lower than those of its competitors. A further complicating factor in Alcoa's pricing is the 1946 mandate of the United States District Court.

PRICE BUILD-UP FOR

ALUMINUM PRODUCTS

Alcoa finds it useful to build a target price for each product manufactured, whether or not that price is obtainable in the current market.

---

[21] This goal was also stated in congressional hearings by I. W. Wilson, president of Alcoa.

"*Mr. Wilson.* We attempted to set our prices—or let me put it this way: In setting our prices we set them so that if, and when, and as we have a normal expected load in our plants, we will make approximately 15 to 20 per cent return on the capital used in connection with the operations for producing that particular aluminum commodity.

"Now, that results after taxes—over the long period of years—that results in a profit to the company of about 10 per cent on the equity capital in the business. That is the history that has been shown and litigated over in the antitrust case, and I think is not disputed at all. But, that is the basis on which we set our prices." *Study of Monopoly Power,* Hearings, 82 Cong. 1 sess., Ser. 1, Pt. 1, Aluminum (1951), pp. 634-35.

For purposes of determining its full costs on a product-by-product basis, the company has explained the procedure and its rationale as follows:

> We use a job order system of gathering costs. Actual direct labor and actual direct material are applied to the job orders. Factory burden is applied by standard machine hour burden rates which are developed for each production center. These standard machine hour rates are designed to apply the actual variable burden to product costs, and to apply fixed burden on a basis of absorption at capacity operations. This is accomplished by developing a capacity budget (exclusive of direct labor and materials) for each production center, and relating this budget to the number of machine hours which would represent plant capacity operations. The resulting machine hour rate will thereby absorb the total fixed burden in product costs only when we are operating at capacity. If we operate at 60 per cent of capacity, then only 60 per cent of the fixed burden is absorbed in product costs. The remaining 40 per cent, representing the fixed cost of idle facilities, is treated as a period charge, and is not charged to job orders or included in inventories.
>
> We think this system provides a sound basis for costing and pricing our products. Since fixed costs are charged to product in direct proportion to *machine utilization,* we can recognize an appropriate share of investment costs in the price of each commodity. . . . Two different alloys of sheet or extrusions, having identical material costs, may vary as much as 10 to 1 in machine utilization, and the burden associated with these machines may be $100 per hour or more. Under these circumstances, proper recognition of investment costs in pricing individual products is vital. Also, we have found that this system of applying fixed burden on a basis of absorption at capacity adequately eliminates the effect of volume change in production costs. . . . If fixed costs were applied on the basis of *anticipated* or *actual* level of operations, we would be faced with increasing fixed costs per unit of production during a prolonged period of abnormally low volume level. Conversely, the fixed cost per unit would decrease when we attained a period of abnormally high volume. Obviously, this is contrary to the trend of sales prices, and costs then become of little use in price making. When volume is low, it is usually a poor time to inform your sales department that prices should be increased.[22]

[22] T. W. Kerry, Aluminum Company of America, in a speech delivered before the South Florida National Association of Cost Accountants, March 1956.

The composition of the target price and a comparison with actual price are presented in the table on page 29 for an unidentified fabricated product. Price is based on "full costs" of production. The ingot or metal value (including other metals than aluminum in many cases) is valued at the market. All aluminum and aluminum products are sold on a uniform delivered price basis anywhere in the United States (a postage stamp system),[23] so a freight factor is added based on average freight costs, included in the "total works cost," for this particular item. General administrative (main office, research, and other overhead) and selling expense are allocated in proportion to "total *works* costs" to derive total (unit) cost at standard rates.

PROFIT TARGETS AND REALIZATIONS

The proposed selling price is determined by adding a margin with a view to earning the general target return. In the review of target price attainment for basic items of a product line, margins are also figured in terms of return on sales. The margins finally decided upon are affected by the market outlook as well as competitors' prices. Thus, in the case of the product for which the table on page 29 was supplied, the target is based on a margin of about 30 per cent on estimated (average) total cost ($.216/$.684), or 24 per cent on selling price ($.216/$.900). Because actual costs were running somewhat in excess of estimated, the actual margin on selling price was about 22 per cent.

[23] This price system was inaugurated in 1921 by Alcoa and has remained intact down to the present. Officials of the company explained that initially this choice of policy was based on several considerations: (1) its obvious simplicity for pricing purposes; (2) the relatively minor importance of freight as a cost element—it averaged about three to four per cent before the Second World War; and (3) the desire of the company to place aluminum fabricators on an even footing pricewise in the use of aluminum irrespective of location. Its perpetuation after the war with all producers is difficult to explain, except as an industry tradition.

Target Price and Performance on a Fabricated Aluminum Product, Aluminum Company of America, 1956[a]

Elements	Target Price (Cost Estimate)		Actual Cost and Price	
	Dollars Per Pound	Per Cent	Dollars Per Pound	Per Cent
Metal value (including commercial metals).............................	.261	29.0	.243	27.0
Prime Cost of Fabrication				
Direct labor.....................	.038	4.2	.040	4.4
Direct material..................	.145	16.1	.167	18.6
Factory burden at standard rates..	.125	13.9	.131	14.6
Total prime cost of fabrication..	.308	34.2	.338	37.6
Transportation allowance...........	.015	1.7	.016	1.8
Allowance for idle facility cost[b]......	.029	3.2	.032	3.6
Allowance for plant administrative expense........................	.032	3.6	.035	3.8
Total works cost..............	.645	71.6	.664	73.8
Allowance for general administrative and selling expense..............	.039	4.3	.040	4.4
Total cost.....................	.684	76.0	.704	78.2
Allowance for profit margin.........	.216	24.0	.196	21.8
Price.........................	.900	100.0	.900	100.0

[a] Figures rounded.
[b] For determining target costs and price, the norm is 70 per cent of full capacity. Since the itemized costs are figured on the basis of full capacity, a general allowance is made to spread the full burden of the facilities over output averaging 70 per cent of full capacity use. (See text referring to this table.)

COURT DIRECTION OF ALCOA PRICING

The general formula used by Alcoa in pricing a fabricated product may be modified in particular instances for such purposes as promotional pricing or meeting special market conditions.[24] There is, however, one additional consideration which, although a matter of general policy concern, should be mentioned in connection with the pricing of a fabricated product—the 1946 antitrust judgment against Alcoa.

The management of Alcoa pointed out that the company is not entirely a free agent in pricing fabricated products. It is extremely sensitive to the judgment of the District Court on April 23, 1946, which states:

> The defendants, Aluminum Company of America, Carolina Aluminum Company and The United States Aluminum Company, and the successors, officers, directors and agents of each of said companies be, and they hereby are, *enjoined and restrained from selling aluminum ingot for the fabrication of aluminum sheet or aluminum alloy sheet at higher than fair prices, if the fabricator of such sheet is thereby prevented from fabricating and selling aluminum sheet or aluminum alloy at a reasonable profit,* provided that such fabricator is efficient, well equipped, and otherwise able to fabricate and sell such sheet on a fully competitive basis; and *further enjoined and restrained from selling aluminum sheet and aluminum alloy sheet, both coiled and flat, at prices below its selling prices for aluminum ingot, plus the cost of manufacturing and selling such sheet.*[25]

In the circumstances, Alcoa's pricing of fabricated products must take into consideration not only its own cost of fabrication but also its estimate of competitors' costs. According to Alcoa, this means that, on some items, the company's pricing initiative is circumscribed by the prices of competitors. If Alcoa wants to reduce the price of sheet, to encourage its wider utilization, it will have to cut the price of ingot too. This added deterrent may have the effect of freezing up the price of sheet.[26]

[24] Variations in the formula for different product lines are discussed in the following chapter.

[25] *United States v. Aluminum Company of America et al.*, U.S. District Court for the Southern District of New York, Judgment on Mandate Against Aluminum Company of America et al., Equity 85-73 (Apr. 23, 1946), p. 18. Italics added.

[26] The company stated that in the case of sales from one subsidiary to another, the product sold is transferred at market price; thus, the cost of the buying

MODIFICATIONS OF TARGET PRICING

In common with most multiproduct companies selling in dissimilar markets, Alcoa modifies its target pricing according to the nature of the product, the character of demand, the severity of competition, and the peculiarities of the market. This is not to say that its target price build-up is by-passed; variations in pricing are explained as modifications of the norm. Broadly speaking, differences may be related to product-line groupings. Run-of-the-mill products that are ordinarily turned out in large volume are usually priced to return the target. Products fabricated to meet rigid buying specifications with respect to physical properties, tolerances, and the like, usually carry an increased profit-margin factor to allow for greater risk in production, greater idle facilities cost, and increased scrap loss. On the other hand, on "jobbing-type" products such as castings, where Alcoa encounters severe competition with some 2,000 sand and permanent mold foundries and over 800 die casters, the company cannot uniformly set prices according to the target formula. New products and those in competition with substitute metals, the company may price promotionally, taking a small margin initially in expectation of building volume and lowering costs; or it may set price enough below that of a substitute metal to achieve penetration, although in some cases the price may yield less than the target margin for a long period. This general picture can be clarified by examining the pricing of specific products in detail.

Ingot and Pig. Within the framework outlined above, the top management of Alcoa stated that its pricing of aluminum ingot, the pivotal price for aluminum products, has been based on promotion of the

---

subsidiary includes the profit of the selling subsidiary as determined by the market price. Transfers from the smelting division to the fabricating division, or from the smelting division to the casting division, are also made at market prices. However, *within* the smelting division, *within* the fabricating division, *within* the castings division, or between the fabricating and castings divisions, transfers are made *at cost* to the originating division, including the appropriate proportion of burden and overhead, which was allocable on the production of the product in the originating plant.

use of aluminum. The company "has consistently refrained from charging all the traffic will bear in order to enhance the prospect of a prosperous, growing business and hence steadier profits in future years." Believing that low prices were the key to broadening markets for aluminum, Alcoa held to a low-price policy from the end of the Second World War until June 28, 1948, during which period aluminum ingot remained at 15 cents per pound. In the same period, the prices of competitive metals rose rapidly. Since 1948, the company officers have emphasized the need for moderation in price increases.

Until recent years, Alcoa was the leader in setting the prices of ingot and pig. The other two producers, like Alcoa, use the greater part of their ingot for their own processing rather than for open-market sale. They have likewise followed Alcoa in selling ingot on a uniform and stabilized price basis, with infrequent changes in quotation. With the skyrocketing postwar demand for aluminum, Alcoa's price leadership weakened, as did that of U.S. Steel in periods of scarcity and high capital-expansion costs. It was forced to give way to the upward price decisions of Reynolds and Kaiser on several occasions.

Ingot Price Changes Among Major Aluminum Producers, 1950-56[a]

Price Per Pound[b]	Alcoa	Reynolds	Kaiser
$.175	May 22, 1950	May 23, 1950	May 25, 1950
.19	Sept. 25, 1950	Sept. 29, 1950	Sept. 28, 1950
.20	Aug. 4, 1952	Aug. 4, 1952	Aug. 4, 1952
.205	Jan. 23, 1953	Jan. 23, 1953	Jan. 22, 1953
.215	July 15, 1953	July 20, 1953	July 20, 1953
.222	Aug. 5, 1954	Aug. 6, 1954	Aug. 6, 1954
.232	Jan. 13, 1955	Jan. 10, 1955	Jan. 12, 1955
.244	Aug. 1, 1955	Aug. 6, 1955	Aug. 2, 1955
.259	Mar. 29, 1956	Mar. 27, 1956	Mar. 26, 1956

[a] *United States* v. *Aluminum Company of America et al,* U. S. District Court for the Southern District of New York, Stipulation Concerning Agreed Facts, Equity 85-73 (May 31, 1956), p. 32.
[b] 99 per cent plus primary aluminum ingot (30 pounds).

As shown in the table on page 32, Kaiser led increases in pig and ingot prices on January 22, 1953 and March 26, 1956. On January 10, 1955, Reynolds took the lead in raising pig and ingot prices one cent per pound, after trade sources had insisted two days before the increase that, if Alcoa did not take the lead, there would be no increase.[27] Alcoa followed on January 13. An earlier example of Reynolds' effort to raise the price of ingot occurred on July 19, 1950. Alcoa refused to go along at the time, presumably because it was making a profit it regarded as satisfactory in view of its desire to stick to a low-price policy and to help hold down the inflationary spiral. Twenty-four hours after Reynolds announced its increase, President Truman issued a general request to industry to do everything possible to hold the line against the threatened inflationary surge of the Korean War. In response to this appeal, Reynolds retracted its increase less than forty-eight hours after it was announced.

Fabricated Products. Alcoa executives stated that almost from the beginning, the company entered into the production of many products as part of the effort to expand the use of aluminum generally, and not for the immediate profit anticipated from the particular line. Such items have not been priced according to the target formula. Cooking utensils, which were taken on by the company to demonstrate the feasibility of fabrication and market acceptability, represent the company's classic example of its promotional philosophy.

Aluminum Wire and Cable Products. Priced promotionally in the first instance, wire and cable products were cited as examples of Alcoa's inability to hit its target consistently. The return on these items has varied over different periods for different reasons. Aluminum cable was introduced by Alcoa in 1897 for power transmission, and in 1909 the company developed an aluminum cable with a steel reinforcing core (ACSR). Prior to the Second World War, Alcoa priced cable with an eye to promoting its use. Competition was primarily with copper and, with copper prices comparatively low, it was not possible for Alcoa to realize a return anywhere near its target.

[27] *Iron Age* (Jan. 13, 1955), p. 118.

Following the Second World War, a different kind of competition emerged in aluminum cable. The rising cost of copper rapidly priced it out of the high-voltage field, and the entire new conductor business began going to aluminum cable. To meet the large demand, cable manufacturers installed new stranding equipment and companies that formerly produced copper cable turned to aluminum. For several years after the war, therefore, Alcoa realized its target return or better on cable. By 1954, however, the capacity of the available aluminum stranding equipment in the United States surpassed the demand for cable, and price cutting broke out in the market. In order to obtain business, Alcoa was forced to bid on contracts at firm prices with no provision for escalation to compensate for increasing costs over the longer term. This situation has persisted since mid-1954, in the face of increased base metal and labor costs, and Alcoa has fallen far short of its target. Company officers stated in 1956 that rigorous price competition on cable prevailed, especially from the eight nonintegrated fabricators. The company has found it difficult to make a recent increase of around 5 per cent stick in the market.[28]

Alcoa indicated, in discussing its promotional pricing policy, that when it had underestimated the market acceptance and sales of a new product, with the result that unit costs were lower than expected, it would reduce prices to be more consistent with the realization of the desired target return. Such reductions, of course, are not automatic or built into the target price calculations, without regard to market conditions, but are governed by the degree of market acceptance and behavior of cost. An example mentioned by Alcoa executives was a strong alloy sheet for aircraft, which was introduced at 44 cents per pound in 1939. With a 530 per cent increase in volume and con-

---

[28] In wire and cable products, demand analysis played a direct part in pricing, not mentioned with regard to Alcoa's other prewar products. The demand of utility companies was said to be related to income, not prices. When wire and cable products moved from the promotional to the published-sheet basis, presumably demand was taken into account in setting prices to yield the target return. Nevertheless, it appears questionable whether variations in utility income would be reflected in the formal cable and wire price sheets, except after increased volume reacted in gradually reducing the price.

comitant cost reductions resulting from standardization of sheet sizes, the price was lowered to 31.7 cents per pound in 1943.

Alcoa officials stated that because of the rising demand and its pressures on capacity following the Second World War, the company has had less immediate incentive to reach out for new markets using price as a weapon for penetration. There are, however, a few new markets that have been tapped despite the heavy demand for standard products.

Indexes of Prices and Volume of Shipments of Fine Gauge Screen Wire, 1948-55[a]

(1948 = 100)

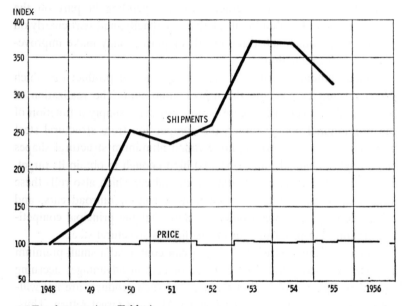

[a] For data see App. Table 4.

Fine gauge screen wiring, introduced in 1948, exemplifies the penetration of a postwar market. The volume has continued to increase materially, making it feasible to hold down the price, in contrast to the general upward trend of prices in aluminum, as well as in the competing product areas.[29] Until a few years ago, fine gauge screen wire represented competition between aluminum and bronze, but the sharp increases in the price of copper have greatly reduced the position of bronze in this market. Galvanized steel is currently a more important factor than bronze, but the non-rusting and non-staining qualities of aluminum and its relatively small differential in price appear to be favoring aluminum in competition for the screen market. As a consequence of the successful penetration by aluminum, Alcoa has been able to achieve more than its target return on this product by retaining part of its wide price advantage over a metal substitute like copper. It represents an area in which Alcoa may in time settle down to its average return, depending in part on the general demand for aluminum relative to capacity, and particularly on the degree to which substitute metals or plastics may make improvements or price reductions.

Rolled aluminum structural shapes are another product for which Alcoa desired to promote the use of aluminum. The realization of less than the target in this case is not, however, simply a function of the promotional policy; rather, the competition from structural steel prevents Alcoa from pricing large rolled aluminum structural shapes (e.g., angles, channels, and I-beams) high enough to obtain its target. There has been some competition from Kaiser, which also rolls these large shapes used in the construction of trucks, railroad cars, and bridge flooring, but Alcoa officials stated that the principal competition limiting the profit margin in this field is structural steel.

Rolled aluminum structural shapes can command a small premium in price over structural steel because of certain advantages accruing from their lighter weight, but the users of such products are not willing to pay the premium required to net Alcoa its target return. Thus, with the price of steel placing a definite ceiling on rolled shapes, Alcoa has failed to hit its target on these products over the past ten years.

---

[29] See accompanying chart.

CHARGES FOR EXTRAS

In keeping with the refinement of specifications on aluminum, the pricing of extras has assumed increasing importance. These extras grew up like Topsy over the years, and Alcoa has taken steps to revise its extra charges so that they more nearly reflect differences in costs. As a result, extras for such products as sheet, extruded shapes, wire, rods, and bars have increased materially. As expected, customer attitude toward the increases in these extra charges has been one of "tolerable resistance." This closer look at the cost of extras on specific products may be explained in large part by the increasing variety of semifinished and fabricated aluminum products made to order. For a time certain anomalies occurred in the case of dimensional extras. This situation has since been corrected. Present-day sheet mills roll material much wider than could the former equipment; therefore, dimensional extras have been revised to give effect to the changed operating conditions. For example, extras now are charged for any width either narrower or broader than the standard sizes being produced on modern equipment.

It should be evident from the foregoing discussion of Alcoa's pricing of various products that despite the devotion to the target formula and the care in compiling cost data on individual items the company did not attempt to offer a rationale embracing all aluminum products. On a large proportion of its 2,500 products, Alcoa is essentially on a job-order basis. Accordingly, it has found that it cannot be guided too strictly in its pricing by costs based on long-term averages. Analysis of monthly margin statements on individual products discloses the need to re-examine constantly the extent to which administrative, unabsorbed burden, and selling expenses may have been underestimated or overestimated, and the effects such action may have produced on net margins. But the care exercised in ensuring that all costs, direct and indirect, are allocated as closely as possible to conform with actual conditions, is often overshadowed by other considerations. Pigment pricing, involving a wide variety of items, perhaps summarizes the picture for many of the semifinished and fabricated product lines. On these items, margins always have varied substantially, with little relation to specific product costs. At least until the Second World War, this was a high-profit area wherein patents and know-how had effectively limited entry.

It seems clear, too, that on certain aluminum sheets Alcoa did not always attempt to realize the projected return—at least the court found that from 1925 to 1932, on certain gauges of hard alloy sheet and on 2S and 3S flat and coiled sheet—14 gauge groups totaling 112 items—Alcoa maintained differentials with its selling prices of virgin aluminum ingot at such levels as to prevent fabricators of those products from manufacturing and selling them at a reasonable profit.[30] In recent years, aluminum sheet prices have been on a published price basis, and they appear to remain unchanged unless there is widespread sniping that forces Alcoa to reduce its prices to large customers, whereupon it cuts its published prices. To the extent that the original price presumably was set according to the formula, such reductions introduce deviations from the cost-plus-a-fair-return into aluminum sheet pricing.

Size and importance of large buyers are another factor affecting the prices of aluminum and aluminum products. In their efforts to contract for aluminum of certain specifications, large buyers have attempted to play one producer off against another in order to realize the lowest possible buying price. Companies like General Motors and General Electric, for example, have been sold on the idea of getting their aluminum from more than one source, at lower average prices. General Motors has located its aluminum castings works for production of Dynaflow and hydramatic transmission parts adjoining Reynolds' smelter in Arkansas, which, of course, assures Reynolds of a continuing outlet for a substantial portion of its output of basic aluminum in excess of its own fabrication requirements. More recently, Reynolds obtained a similar contract from Ford (for 640,000,000 pounds of molten aluminum over ten years) and is

---

[30] See Findings 257-62 and 280-86, as amended, *United States* v. *Aluminum Company of America*, U.S. District Court for the Southern District of New York, Judgments and Orders of the Court (Apr. 23, 1954).

reported to have made arrangements with G.M. for a smelting plant at Massena, New York, near which Chevrolet will construct a casting plant. Trade estimates indicate that this metal is sold at around 10 per cent less than the market, partly as a result of economies accruing in the operations.

This is not to say that Alcoa's position in the industry has eroded across the board. In the exploitation of opportunities for manufacturing aluminum, it is conceded that Alcoa has gained in strength on both price and quality in the field of building materials, whereas Reynolds has retained a prime position in consumer products like aluminum foil (Reynolds Wrap), with Kaiser falling somewhere in between.

The area of common effort by the leading aluminum producers to expand the uses of aluminum is their attempt to invade established markets.[31] The principal producers appear to be in agreement on the desirability of pricing promotionally rather than on the basis of any current target returns. It appears probable that the bids of the aluminum companies for the business of Western Electric and others in aluminum telephone booths and in an expanding line of aluminum electrical equipment are now being made at figures that have no cost-plus basis, except in so far as substantial increases in volume are likely to bring down unit costs to the point at which a satisfactory return may be reached. Likewise aluminum manufacturers, confronted with the supremacy of copper in residential wiring installations, are assertedly prepared to increase pressure on copper if and when the aluminum companies solve the problems of effectively soldering aluminum, and find ways of overcoming the greater space required by aluminum wire and parts as compared with copper in comparable installations.

[31] It should be noted that the pricing of aluminum products is often influenced by the differences in the elasticity and cross-elasticity of consumer demand among different product groups and among locations. Thus, a reduction in the price of aluminum roofing to achieve its replacement of wood shingles and galvanized sheets has been found successful only in those regions where the comparatively rustproof characteristic of aluminum, and its continued presentable appearance, have sufficient appeal to maintain its sales on the strength of savings in regular painting and other upkeep costs.

Meats

Meat pricing at the packer's level is distinguished by a close linkage between the current selling price of the dressed meat and the bidding price for the livestock. This twofold pricing situation involves, in the livestock coming to market, a supply that is not controllable but must be received and processed as it comes; and, in the dressed meat, a consumer product that is mainly perishable and must be priced for immediate disposal.

The effort to balance, through price, the day-to-day demand of the consuming millions with the varying day-to-day availability of livestock moved independently by thousands of growers, has produced a complex structure of markets and operations in a far-flung industry. It includes large and small meat packers and meat buyers with varying degrees of influence on meat prices. The nature of the operations is also conditioned by the locations of producers and buyers (*e.g.,* surplus versus shortage areas), which affect procurement procedures and processing. Moreover, the sources of fresh meat—cattle, hogs, sheep—are differentiated in such features as seasonality, ease of transportation, character of the cuts, wastage, and storage.

Without going into the refinements of pricing among the many varieties of meat and meat markets, the essential influences in the pricing of fresh meat may be observed through the following discussion of the pricing of pork and of beef in a fully integrated packing firm—Swift & Company.

DAILY CUT-OUT TEST

The large packer recognizes the perishability of the product, fluctuating supply of livestock, and seasonality of demand as underlying considerations in the pricing of his main product. Procedure has been devised to minimize risks of miscalculation. Thus, starting from the current wholesale prices for fresh meats, the packer determines the price he will bid for new supplies by assembling the value of the various cuts to a total product value. This is done by Swift and by other packers through the use of a daily "cut-out-test," which represents an evaluation of the worth of the animals cut up and sold "fresh" at current market prices.

The table below shows an abbreviated cut-out test published by *The National Provisioner,* but this test is not the one used by Swift.[32]

Abbreviated Cut-Out Test[a]

	180–220 Pounds Value		220–240 Pounds Value		240–270 Pounds Value	
	Per Cwt. Alive	Per Cwt. Fin. Yield	Per Cwt. Alive	Per Cwt. Fin. Yield	Per Cwt. Alive	Per Cwt. Fin. Yield
Lean cuts............	$14.03	$20.00	$13.20	$18.39	$12.73	$17.74
Fat cuts, lard........	6.02	8.61	5.98	8.42	5.40	7.46
Ribs, trimm., etc......	2.43	3.51	2.27	3.18	2.08	2.91
Cost of hogs.........	20.44		20.69		20.21	
Condemnation loss....	.10		.10		.10	
Handling, overhead....	1.70		1.50		1.30	
Total Cost...........	22.24	31.74	22.29	31.17	21.61	30.01
Total Value..........	22.48	32.12	21.44	29.99	20.21	28.11
Cutting margin.....	+ .24	+ .38	− .85	− 1.18	− 1.40	− 1.90
Margin last week....	+ .56	+ .81	− .45	− .63	− 1.23	− 1.69

[a] *The National Provisioner* (Feb. 15, 1958).

Swift explains the use of the cut-out test as follows: A cut-out test calculation begins with a test cutting of a sample of hogs of a given weight range and quality to determine the expected weight yield by type of cut (loins, hams, shoulders, etc.) when cut a particular way. Such yield figures are used repeatedly over a period of months but are

[32] Swift did not make its cut-out test available because it regards it as confidential.

adjusted periodically to allow for seasonal changes in dressed carcass yields. The weight of each cut is multiplied by the current market price to arrive at the values to be added in determining the "gross cut-out." Direct expenses (labor, supplies, steam, etc.) and allocated overhead are taken into account, together with hog costs for the particular day, in arriving at the "net cut-out" or profit or loss. In Swift & Company each plant is expected to use yield figures for the various cuts that conform to its particular experience.

The cut-out is a basic consideration in instructions to the company's buyers. Assuming the cut-out shows a loss of 50 cents per hundred-weight, for example, instructions would probably be issued to buyers to try to buy lower by 50 cents or more.[33]

If a plant were operating with a cut-out showing a good profit, it would attempt to buy more hogs at steady or even higher prices in the interest of using the plant more fully, lowering costs further, and possibly improving the cut-out margin. If, on the other hand, the plant is operating at no better than a break-even position, an effort would be made to buy lower, as suggested above. At the same time, the attempt might be made to set higher selling prices for various cuts. Since, however, the market price is generally not determined by cost in the short-run period, the major emphasis is placed on securing better buying prices.[34] This matter will be given some additional attention following a discussion of how the buying instructions are implemented in the market.

---

[33] Formerly instructions were sometimes sent by a wire similar to the following: "Hog and product market very erratic. Market will open with uncertainty. Suggest buy hogs 25 cents to 30 cents lower from Friday's. If cannot buy at steady to lower call me [head buyer]."

[34] The week's operations are analyzed in the "Weekly Hog Cutting Report," which contains greater detail with respect to individual types, weights, and grades of different parts of the animal than the daily ("short form") cut-out test. In brief, the weekly report is in the nature of a summary of the week's results of the fresh pork department showing yields, average cost of animals, gross cut-out per hundredweight, killing and cutting expenses, and net cut-out value per hundredweight and profit or loss on total production. The weekly analysis is related to buying and selling price decisions to the extent that it may test the effectiveness of the day-to-day buying strategy or indicate a trend for future action.

LIVESTOCK PRICING

Livestock is marketed through several channels, the principal ones being terminal markets—public stock yards, auction markets, dealers, concentration yards, usually owned by a packer—or direct from farmer to packing plant. In the U.S. Department of Agriculture statistics, all channels other than terminal markets are sometimes lumped together as "direct marketing." Over the past twenty-five to thirty years packing companies have decreased their purchases at the public stock yards and have increased relatively their direct buying of livestock, particularly with respect to hogs, as the following figures show.[35]

Livestock Purchased at Public Stock Yards as
a Percentage of Total Slaughter[a]

Year	Cattle	Calves	Hogs	Sheep and Lambs
1930	88.2	81.8	59.9	84.7
1935	83.6	76.5	56.0	77.5
1940	75.1	60.9	46.7	63.8
1945	76.8	61.5	37.3	61.6
1950	74.9	56.7	39.3	57.4

[a] Under federal inspection. For 1930–45 data, see U.S. Department of Agriculture' *Livestock, Meats and Wool Market Statistics and Related Data* (1946), p. 45; data for 1950 supplied by U.S. Department of Agriculture, Agricultural Marketing Service, Livestock Division.

The sale of animals involves, on the one hand, commission men to whom growers have consigned animals, and on the other, buyers for the large and small meat packers, shippers who buy for reshipment to out-of-town buyers (the buyers for large packers also purchase for reshipment to other plants), dealers and speculators (feeders), who

[35] The terminal markets vary considerably in size and importance. The following discussion refers to the principal or "major" markets: Chicago, Omaha, St. Paul, Fort Worth, Denver, Kansas City, St. Joseph, Sioux City, Oklahoma City, and East St. Louis.

buy and sell on their own account. The buyer-seller relationships in the stock yards appear to consist of the "art of feeling one another out." Actually, beneath these externals lie the calculations of both sides based on their respective appraisals of what is transpiring in the market, coupled with knowledge of the immediate past and general market trends, as well as their own inventory position.[36] In all this, while it is difficult to indicate on which side the balance of "market power" lies, (*i.e.,* in terms of influence on price), it seems clear that the balance of "market intelligence" probably lies in general with the buyers.

The buying of livestock obviously calls for a more consciously selected combination of decisions than is possible in the selling of meat, for which Swift's wholesale prices for the most part are close approximations of a current market level. Both livestock prices and wholesale prices are well publicized, but in purchasing livestock the company buyers take account of a number of additional considerations that are presented to the buyer not as an order but for his information. These include estimates of future livestock deliveries, the current level of dressed meat prices, the profit margin expectancy of the processing plant as disclosed by daily "cut-out tests,"[37] the level of inventories of fresh meats (and cured and canned meats, if hogs are involved), the needs of the sales department to serve regular customers, and the size of the plant's labor force to which a weekly wage guarantee has been made. The company buyers must continually

[36] How the large packer typically relates its livestock bidding to wholesale meat prices was stated by Armour's vice president, John Schmidt, before the Joint Committee on the Economic Report, in late 1948:

"We bid for livestock from day to day based on our judgment of what the meat would sell for when it was ready for market, mindful at all times of the need, from the standpoint of overhead, of keeping our plants running. As to selling prices, we knew our costs, and they were a factor along with our day to day pulsing of the market in arriving at our asking prices. As against our asking price, the retailer decided what he could afford to pay based on his day to day pulsing of what the consumer was willing to pay. The final selling price was traded out with the retailer." *Profits,* Report of a Subcommittee of the Joint Committee on the Economic Report, Joint Committee Print, 80 Cong. 2 sess. (1949).

[37] Generally the figuring is done from a "break-even" basis, *i.e.,* what prices would have to be realized if the plant is to "break even" or better.

be alert to the effects of their actions on those of competing buyers.[38]

Fortified with their knowledge of the immediate situation, the head buyers give instructions to local buyers for the company regarding the prices at which they should attempt to buy (on order-buying for a branch plant the quantity desired is also specified). When the market opens, buyers of various companies enter the pens one at a time, evaluate the animals, and make offers in line with the instructions of the head buyers.[39] The head buyers, meanwhile, follow market returns and prices continually in all markets that are still open and are in frequent telephonic contact with their own buyers in the yards.

Commission men, mindful of much of the same information on how the market tends, attempt to obtain the highest price possible for their livestock. After some shopping around, the buyers find that some sales have been consummated, and from that point the buying usually proceeds rapidly. Company buyers, seeing buyers of other companies buying or not buying animals, attempt to find out from the commission men what prices were paid by other buyers and telephone such information, with their own reactions, to the head buyer who gives them further instructions. Sellers, meanwhile, are confronted with the problem of deciding whether to hold out for a price to packers, order buyers, dealers, and feeders, to sell at the "jelling" price, or—a rare occurrence—to send the animals back to feed lots, all this depending, of course, on such factors as the trend of marketings and prices, the number of animals on hand in the pens, any special reservations transmitted by the shipper, etc.

The packers point out that since the estimates of livestock values are usually made not for a single animal but for the whole lot that happens to be in a given pen, bidding for livestock becomes a matter of judgment on the part of a buyer for the company on how the whole lot is liable to break up into the various components. However,

[38] It would also seem evident that, if one set of buyers gets out of the market prematurely, those remaining may get the benefit of lower prices for the slow-moving supply that is left to be sold. If they buy more heavily than usual, they may be left with meat that is hard to market through their own organization and may also force the price up to an unprofitable level.

[39] Although there is no order of precedence, in the event of "ties," i.e., two buyers arriving together, the order of entry is largely a matter of custom.

the extent of the discretion of individual company buyers lies almost wholly in their appraisal of the quality of the animals, how they will dress out, value differences due to type, etc., rather than in the specific prices to be offered, which come through the plant head buyer or by way of general market information from Chicago.[40]

FLUCTUATING SUPPLIES—

IMPLICATIONS FOR MEAT PRICING

In the process of the market transactions, the major unanswered questions concern the decisions of the packers, through their central buying office and the head buyers at branch plants, on how many animals to purchase on a given day at different markets, what bids shall be offered initially, and at what prices purchases should be consummated. The head buyers, both at the central office and at company branch plants, have a definite figure in mind with respect to the total weekly purchases desired, which is essentially the minimum number needed to keep the work "gang" going for 36 hours of the week—the guarantee given by the packer to workers if told to report for work on Monday. But the factors governing the upper and lower limits of the quantity purchased on a given day are not clear.

Actually, however, the large packers do not ordinarily think in terms of withdrawing completely from the market or of attempting to buy enough animals to utilize their plants to the fullest possible extent. Withdrawing completely on a given day would mean placing the packer in a position whereby he might not be able to satisfy his standing customers, while an attempt to buy more than a certain quantity would probably meet with the resistance of other packers who are confronted with similar obligations. Thus, the more realistic approach of the packers is to attempt to buy a little more or a little

[40] By-product credits are also an important consideration for the company buyer, since they constitute part of the valuation he makes of livestock purchased. This requires careful consideration of such details as the condition of the hides. If they are damaged, he may be criticized.

less than usual, with an occasional probing of the market (in both directions) to get the reaction of other buyers.[41]

The relative constancy of the proportions of livestock purchased by the principal meat packers at some markets is traceable in large part to the desire to keep the plant operating at least up to a minimum level—governed in part by labor commitments—and the ever-present threat that another packer may secure a larger share of the animals and the market for dressed meats. Accordingly, the buyers for the packers ordinarily will continue buying until at least the minimum quantity is acquired at acceptable prices or until the rising price threatens an out-of-pocket loss on its plant operations. The company views the respective percentages of animals purchased by the major packers logically should be fairly constant over periods of weeks or months in given markets.

The combination of fluctuating supplies, perishability of product, seasonality of demand, and judgment values that enter into the bidding for livestock makes it virtually impossible for the meat packer to price on a cost-plus basis. The packer therefore deems it more accurate to say that at least for the short run "prices of meats determine costs."

Swift has attempted to get around the perishability problem by further processing of meats and more recently by moving into pre-packaged meats under its own brands. While greater effort in this direction may improve the position of the company in the market and may lend more stability to profits, such actions can only in part offset the perishability factor in the pricing of fresh meat. Moreover, the meat packer who considers building inventory when buying prices are down must contend with the penalty on price for storage, even if storage facilities present no bottleneck problems. Frozen pork loins, for example, sell at a discount as against fresh.

The large retail food chains have a significant bearing on this

---

[41] The foregoing was alleged by the Department of Justice to suggest at least a recognition by the packers of what constitutes their usual share of the animals sold in the major public stock yard. The implications of parallel action were the subject of the 1948 Complaint of the Department of Justice. See *United States* v. *Armour and Company; Armour & Company; Swift & Company; the Cudahy Packing Company; and Wilson & Co., Inc.,* U.S. District Court for the Northern District of Illinois, Civil Action No. 48 C 1351 (Feb. 25, 1949), Exhibits B-1 through B-22.

problem of uncontrollable supply, because they can adjust their purchases through mass buying power and facilities for storage. During the Second World War, some packing was done by the chains on their own account, but the experience was not very successful. There seems little likelihood that they will re-enter the meatpacking business, although they show a definite trend toward increasing their storage of meats. Their buying is done mainly through central offices, which, while maintaining certain "standing orders" with packers, negotiate on prices for settlement. In the circumstances, the chains become an important factor in the determination of wholesale meat prices, their influence expressing itself in bargaining that attempts to play one packer off against another.

Automobiles

In consumer durables, where a new model appears yearly, the manufacturer sets a price to the dealer that is essentially the suggested consumer price (minus local taxes and handling charges) less the customary dealer's discount. Decisions of this kind bearing on the consumer price are made for refrigerators, washing machines, television sets, phonographs, and other major appliances, but the manufacturer's role in sponsoring the new model and suggesting the consumer price is most notably exemplified in the automobile industry, where projections of cost, price, and model must be made long before the new models are introduced. Price leadership of the kind found in the steel industry is impractical because the producers introduce the new models and prices at about the same time, and the previous model price may not serve as a satisfactory base; more important, the differences between models give rise to varying price differentials.

In General Motors the pricing of an automobile is a process that occupies some thirty months. Preparation for a 1960 model starts in the spring of 1957. The model and the cost figures will be pretty well established by August 1959; but the suggested showroom price to the consumer may not be final until just before the introduction of new car models in the late fall of 1959.

The determination of the price of an automobile begins with a forecast of what the consumer will want in his car and what he will pay in order to get it. Pricing and styling go hand in hand. By a process of elimination, the new model will include those new features that are considered a must for the future buyer, and exclude those deemed less attractive in terms of the consumer's readiness to pay their cost.[42]

Preparation of a new design, and the estimate of what kind of car can be sold at a projected price in the light of the present or foreseeable competitive picture, starts from the current models and prices as a base. The costs of those essential parts and engineering features that will be virtually the same in the new model as in the old are already available. The proposed new features in the design, introduced after a preliminary discussion of the trend in consumer taste and purchasing power, as well as the trend in costs of materials and labor, give the design group a starting point for exercising its imagination within a practicable framework. After a period of fifteen months the new model will have evolved in a form that has received general approval within the company. Probable costs have been estimated, and, after a short but intensive period of review, a total cost figure is "frozen" to the point where orders may be placed within and without the company for the tools, jigs, and dies required by the new model, as well as for the steel and other materials or parts for meeting the specifications laid down.

During the succeeding fifteen months, almost to the time that the new model is introduced, there is a chance to re-consider the selling price and re-examine the estimated return. Though the company has already estimated the standard costs at standard volume, there is always the question whether any significant recent change in the market climate has taken place. Is it to be a year for realizing the full target return sought on the investment employed, or does it appear that price must be shaved in order to meet expected moves by lead-

---

[42] The wrap-around windshield illustrates a sales-getting feature introduced in the expectation that it would attract enough new volume to justify the added costs and any necessary increase in price to the consumer.

ing competitors and attitudes of consumers? Thus forecasts of consumer purchasing power and taste provide the limits to the price range within which the engineers, designers, and top management feel free to manipulate costs over the thirty months of programing.

The policy group begins its deliberations on a new model with a consideration of the kind of car "the public will go for," and the car is visualized as one suitable to the price range within which the consumer group in mind can be persuaded to buy in the volume taken as a target. But a confidence is manifest among the top officers that General Motors' cost is that of the low-cost firm. And on that premise rests the implicit assumption that a price that will yield to GM the target return it seeks on its investment will in fact be a lower price than its competitors can generally attain.

The result may not bear out expectations to the full satisfaction of the management in every year, but it is confidently expected to do so over any period of three to five years. This confidence in its low-cost position is reflected in the degree to which GM makes use of standard costing in developing the base upon which the price is to be superimposed.

What is said to be the General Motors procedure for pricing a new car has been set forth in some detail in published material by GM executives and others. The formula given by the company for arriving at unit cost requires the calculation of standard costs at "normal" sales volume (generally 80 per cent of capacity). Profit per car, based on a target rate of return, is added to obtain the provisional manufacturer's price.

The price obtained from the dealer is the list price (f.o.b. factory) less the conventional dealer discounts—24 per cent on the lower priced makes, 26 per cent on the Cadillac. The dealer's list price differs from the advertised delivered price to the consumer in a particular community—sometimes called the "showroom price"—in that the showroom price also includes the federal and local excise taxes plus the transportation charges and the normal optional accessories. The dealer can manipulate his realized prices and profits therefore, not within a 24 per cent discount on the suggested list price to the consumer, but rather within the 24 per cent discount on the dealer list price. General Motors accepts no formal responsibility for the consumer's price.[43]

This formula for pricing is subject to modifications arising from the nature of the production process and from the peculiarities of the market for automobiles. As a variety of standard-cost pricing, the procedure explicitly attempts to prevent cyclical or shorter-run changes in volume from unduly affecting price, using the technique of averaging fluctuations in both cost and demand. The use of standard costs provides some link between the models of any one year and those immediately preceding or following. The value of a new model, for example, is related to the rapidity of the probable fall in resale value because, let us say, it is too heavily loaded with nonrecurrent costs. A sense of continuity in the business and in the reputation of the product enters into the cost and valuation of any one year's model. The period for standard-cost calculation may vary with the expected life cycle of a development requiring new design and retooling of equipment, or of estimated trends in business conditions, population, consumer income and habits of consumers as to the length of time before trading in, etc.[44]

On the other hand, not only the price of the car, but the qualities that enter into it at the time of a style change must be worked out with regard for prevailing standards of consumer taste and for changes in consumer purchasing power and willingness to go into debt. General Motors also has to take into account the extent to which competitors are creating, catering to, and successfully exploiting new market trends. In other words, standard calculations themselves need continuing re-examination to avoid becoming a deterrent to progressive growth and continuity of profits.

[43] In the light of their efforts to check "bootlegging" the manufacturers can, however, scarcely be said to be indifferent to the retail price "Auto Bootlegging: Factory Dealer Blasts so far Fail to Stem Cut-Rate Car Selling," *Wall Street Journal* (Mar. 2, 1954); "G.M. to Re-Buy Cars to End 'Bootlegging'", *New York Times* (Jan. 17, 1955).

[44] For a summary of the Ford pricing procedure, in most respects identical to GM's (perhaps because Ford's chief operating executive is an alumnus of GM), see A. R. Oxenfeldt, *Industrial Pricing and Market Practices* (1951), p. 135.

PROCEDURE OF PRICE MAKING

As GM procedures are set up, the division manager, before he makes his firm proposal on price to the Operations Policy Committee, has been provided with most of the material that the top management itself will use in passing judgment on the suggested price. In addition to the cost data, he has pertinent information on the sales of competitive models, population and income changes, and other economic factors that can be expected to influence the sale of his product.[45] He has made an effort to discover exactly what features of the current model should be altered to improve sales; also, which of the novelties on the shelf it would be most desirable, in the light of competitors' moves, and consumers' reactions to this year's models, to incorporate in the next year's model.

Coincidentally with the evolution of a new model, the engineering, manufacturing, and procurement departments are continually called into consultation in an effort to find out what can be anticipated in the way of unit cost for the suggested style and other alterations. Pressure is on these departments to devise methods of cutting costs on both new and old constituents of the model, to provide leeway for introduction of new features.

The cost estimates at this point in the price-making procedure—which is at the same time the style-making procedure—are strategic. Management cannot think in one dimension. It has to face the problem of achieving balance between marketability (style acceptance), cost, and price, in the context of a competitive situation. During the period in which a pricing policy is being arrived at, many alternatives are open. A radical style change can be introduced, and price kept constant, on the assumption that new buyers will be attracted. Or the style can be left almost unaltered, and the price reduced. Another alternative could be to leave both automobile and price at current levels, concentrating on improvement of production methods. In

[45] Consideration of changes in the disposable income as a factor in the automobile demand is focused on the "supernumerary income" of consumers. Since the purchase of a new car is postponable, the expansibility of consumer demand is strongly influenced by the increase or decrease of that part of the disposable income (*i.e.,* after taxes) that is available for basic living costs.

reaching a decision about his price proposal, the division manager must make his choice in the light of his estimates of profit realizations. Suppose, for instance, that an increase in national income of substantial proportions leads to a decision to raise the price of Chevrolets; every effort will then be bent upon showing as generous a profit margin as is practicable in producing a car that will attract purchasers at the higher price.

If the limitations on pricing discretion are ignored, it would appear that once the manager has made his choice among the various possibilities, justification for his price is wholly dependent on combining the costs of the hundreds of parts that go into an automobile. Many of these costs represent purchases from outsiders, but the bulk are costs to other GM divisions. The procurement department checks on various substitutes, obtains competing bids, asks for modifications in specifications, gives and takes with engineering, all in order to minimize costs within the framework of assumptions about the extent of change to be made in the model. The production department carries on similar activities with regard to estimates of internal costs. The final cost estimate for the standard model of the next season's car is a composite of all these costs, which, during the period that they have taken final shape, have influenced changes incorporated in the model and in turn been influenced by them.

It is assumed that an average year will see utilization of 80 per cent of capacity, and indirect costs are allocated on this basis. This is the *standard volume* that provides the foundation for standard costing. In the short run, total costs will vary only with changes in direct costs, for example, for raw materials and labor.

LIMITS TO PRICING DISCRETION

General Motors' pricing discretion for the automotive divisions has been limited by the convention of the price ranges, or groups, prevailing for different cars and by the anticipated prices of rivals in these price ranges. Each division head is well acquainted with these factors and takes them into account when he first begins to think about pricing. A Chevrolet is priced in a historical context; it cannot move erratically above or below its normal price class. It has to satisfy first and foremost a normal clientele, accustomed to spend around a certain amount on a new car. The dealer, of course, does not get the full price of the car in cash in most cases; in fixing the price to the public, the GM executives make allowance for the propensity of Chevrolet consumers to use older models as partial payment for a new car.[46]

At the very start of the pricing process the discretion of the price-making executives is bounded by the nature of the market they have carved out for their product over the years. Regardless of what cost system is adopted, the rough outlines of pricing are determined, at least in the short run, by the consumer's habitual appraisal of a price line, like that of Chevrolet or Pontiac.

The discretion of the car division manager is also bounded by the relations between the constituents of the integrated General Motors organization, which sell to each other at market prices. Thus Chevrolet has to give Fisher Body and AC Spark Plug Company a profit on what it buys from them. True, if it finds their prices excessive, it can in principle go outside the GM organization. There have been such instances, though this is scarcely possible for bodies, since the divisions adopt similar patterns and achieve substantial savings thereby. To the extent that Chevrolet does pay other divisions a profit, its freedom to compress its selling margin is limited. Even though the profit on a GM car over all were $230, Chevrolet itself, as the car builder, might have above its costs, including the cost of purchased parts and bodies, only a $50 margin to slash in the interests of higher volume or good will.

A final and serious limit to the discretion of the divisional manager is set by the reluctance of customers to stick with the car if its price gets out of line with competitive makes. Despite the differentiations of quality and style, there have been times when even a small differential could swing prospective purchasers from one line to another.[47]

---

[46] Thus the scope for price reductions is narrowed by the company's responsibility for protecting the value of the inventory of used cars in both dealers' and consumers' hands. Homer B. Vanderblue, "Pricing Policies in the Automobile Industry," *Harvard Business Review* (Summer 1939), p. 26.

[47] This statement seems to reflect the GM experience with one Chevrolet

The information made available by the auto company on their pricing procedures does not provide a full story of the final car pricing. The closest approximation to a definitive series on actual prices to dealers is the compilation of Advertised-Delivered Prices compiled by *Automotive News*.[48] The advertised delivered price includes the retail list price suggested by the factory, provision for federal excise taxes and suggested dealer delivery and handling charges. It does not include transportation costs, state and local taxes, optional equipment or any other charges that may be passed on to the retail buyer. The factory price to the dealer can be expressed as the retail list less 24 per cent dealer's discount. The profits of the corporation do not conform to the theoretical standard cost average. Nothing in the published or interview material gives any clue on how the company balances expected sales of parts, and the return therefrom, against returns from the sale of new cars, or how accessories or the cost of style changes are integrated with the price. On these points, the company representatives take the position that, after all, pricing is not a science but an art, and that statistical or accounting data could never provide the full story of automobile pricing. Just where the art leaves the science behind, and why the executives have spent so much time in publicizing their standard-cost system if it is not determining in fixing prices, remain unanswered questions. It seems probable that like many policies it serves more as an internal discipline than as a dominant technique for arriving at price to the dealer.

Consumer Appliances

There are several stages in the pricing process of a major consumer appliance. During the early period of development of the new piece of equipment—automatic washing machine, refrigerator, TV set— prices differ widely as experience accumulates to determine the most wanted type. After the experimental years, when the consumer has

---

model. However, Ford and Plymouth do generally manage to get customers though priced much more than $25 in excess of Chevrolet (for the standard models in each case).

[48] For the Advertised-Delivered Prices for two representative models of the Chevrolet (1947-55) see App. Table 5.

Automatic Washing Machines Price Lines, 1954[a]

MACHINES SELLING AT ABOUT $300 (LIST PRICE)

$299.95 Bendix WGD	Bendix Home Appliance Division of Avco Mfg. Corp.
299.50 Hamilton 330	Hamilton Mfg. Co.
299.95 Maytag* AMP	Maytag Co.
299.95 ABC-O-Matic 53	Altorfer Bros. Co.
299.95 Kelvinator AW	Nash-Kelvinator Corp.
299.50 Thor 453	Thor Corp.
299.95 GM Frigidaire WO-65-2	Frigidaire Division, General Motors Corp.
299.95 Westinghouse Laundromat LB-6	Westinghouse Electric Corp.
299.95 Crosley Deluxamatic LWF	Crosley Division, Avco. Mfg. Corp.
299.95 Apex Wash-a-matic 6000	Apex Electrical Mfg. Co.
299.95 General Electric WA 450	General Electric Co.
299.95 Speed Queen A11	Speed Queen Corp.
299.95 Universal AWS-30-A	Universal Major Appliance Co.
299.95 Hotpoint 10 LH 1	Hotpoint Co., Division of General Electric
299.00 Norge AW 450	Norge Division, Borg Warner Corp.

* Maytag without drain pump is $294.95.

MACHINES SELLING ABOVE $300

319.95 Apex 6001	Apex Electrical Mfg. Co.
309.95 Kelvinator AWG	Nash Kelvinator
329.95 Whirlpool 501554; 501562, $309.95	Whirlpool Corp.
309.95 Bendix WCG	Bendix Home Appliance Division of Avco Mfg. Corp.
319.95 Crosley Customatic CWF	Crosley Division, Avco Mfg. Corp.
349.95 General Electric 1-WA-650-K	General Electric Co.
329.95 Blackstone 250	Blackstone Corp.
319.95 Speed Queen A10	Speed Queen Corp.
309.95 ABC-O-Matic 53G	Altorfer Bros. Co.

MACHINES SELLING BELOW $300[b]

269.95 Whirlpool 531510; 531520, $249.95	Whirlpool Corp.
279.95 Norge AN 425	Norge Division, Borg Warner Corp.
289.95 Easy ADC	Easy Washing Machine Corp.
249.95 Westinghouse LS-7	Westinghouse Electric Corp.
239.95 Wards Wardamatic 35AC6630	Montgomery Ward
239.95 Sears Kenmore 33530; 33540, $219.95	Sears Roebuck
259.95 Sears Kenmore 33560	Sears Roebuck
239.95 AMC A153AP	AMC Automatic Washer Co.
269.95 Apex 6002	Apex Electrical Mfg. Co.
239.95 Bendix Economat WCH	Bendix Home Appliance Division of Avco Mfg. Co.
239.95 Crosley Supermatic DWF	Crosley Division, Avco Mfg. Corp.

[a] Data compiled from *Consumer Reports* (February 1954), Vol. 19, No. 2, Consumers Union of the U. S., Inc. (38 East First St., N. Y. 3.)

[b] Of the five models retailing at $239.95, one is sold by Montgomery Ward in its retail stores only and one is put out by Sears exclusive of shipping charges. The two models put out by Sears can be had for $20 less without "suds-saver" (*i.e.*, for $219.95 and $239.95, respectively, exclusive of shipping charges).

Cost Breakdown, De luxe Automatic Washer, 1954

	Break-down of Price to Consumer	Whole-saler's Costs as Per Cent of his Selling Price	Man-facturer's Costs as Per Cent of his Selling Price	Per Cent of Price to Consumer
List price to consumer.............	$299.95			100.00
Retail mark-up....................	121.65			40.50
Administrative expenses				
Owners' and managers' salaries....	10.81			3.60
Office salaries...................	6.31			2.10
Salesmen's pay..................	17.13			5.70
Servicemen's wages and expenses..	15.32			5.10
Vehicle expense................	7.20			2.40
Other administrative expense.....	5.10			1.70
Occupancy......................	7.51			2.50
Advertising.....................	7.81			2.60
Bad debt.......................	.60			0.20
All other expenses..............	8.71			2.90
Delivery, installation and post sale-demonstration..................	21.03			7.00
Profit.......................	14.12			4.70
Wholesale selling price..............	178.30			59.50
Wholesale mark-up.................	22.33	12.50		7.40
Salaries, traveling and commissions..	12.74	7.14		4.30
Occupancy......................	1.93	1.08		.70
Office expense...................	1.60	.89		.50
Bad debt.......................	.24	.13		.10
Advertising and promotion.........	.88	.49		.20
Taxes..........................	.75	.42		.20
Profit.......................	4.19	2.35		1.40
Manufacturer's selling price..........	155.97		100.00	52.10
Direct material cost..............	74.87		48.00	25.00
Direct labor cost................	8.27		5.30	2.80
Factory overhead.................	10.61		6.80	3.60
Transportation....................	5.46		3.50	1.50
Taxes..........................	17.62		11.30	5.90
Advertising.....................	9.83		6.30	3.30
Development....................	12.32		7.90	4.20
Field service guarantees...........	2.95		1.90	1.00
Sales and distribution expense.......	3.90		2.50	1.40
Administrative and other..........	6.86		4.40	2.30
Profit.......................	3.28		2.10	1.10

come to know the general character of the product, the result of continuing surveys of dealers' experiences and consumers' reactions is to produce a consensus on what constitutes the "right" price for retail distribution. In the case of 1954 models of automatic washers, there was apparently a general understanding that $300 was the "right" figure to aim at in producing the standard model, for among twenty-four leading manufacturers' brands of automatic washing machines two out of three were priced at $299.95, or within a dollar of that figure.[49] The list price being accepted as the starting point, the problem shifts to a consideration of what the manufacturer can profitably put into the product.

The information on consumer appliances (as with other electrical equipment) has for the most part been supplied by General Electric, the only electrical equipment company in the sample; but in the case of the automatic dishwasher, the cost and price breakdown given below was provided by a large appliance manufacturer not interviewed for this study. It will serve, nevertheless, to illuminate several aspects of pricing policy enunciated by General Electric representatives in respect to consumer appliances.

Starting from the retail list price of $299.95 the manufacturer deducts 40 per cent for the retailer's margin and about 7½ per cent for the wholesale distributors' margin, leaving roughly $156 out of which the manufacturer must get his cost plus profit. With all manufacturers having a similar target to work on, the competition appears to turn mainly on whether one manufacturer can put into the $156 more appeal value than another.

The competition can be shifted to greater emphasis on price by carrying in addition to the standard "de luxe" models more or less stripped models, which eliminate certain automatic controls or trims featured in the former. At this lower level ($239.95 was a common figure), the manufacturers' standard brands encountered the private label brands of the mail order houses and the brands of various manufacturers catering to price-conscious buyers.

General Electric does not follow cost-plus pricing in the sense that it would determine the selling price from a calculation of its own costs.

[49] See table on p. 56.

It prices for the market, actual or estimated. In pricing a new item, it prefers to go directly by market surveys to the consumer buyer where a controlled pricing experiment offers the same product with different prices in different areas and also, where feasible, through different channels of distribution.

In the opinion of a General Electric executive, the firm's experience shows that neither distributors and dealers nor the company's salesmen and executives are fully dependable in their guesses of what the consumer will pay for a product. Direct access to the consumers, confronting them with a real choice in a realistic selling environment, is the way to get answers to questions concerning the price-quantity relationship. Dealers can be more helpful in other aspects of marketing than pricing and determination of the features a product should have. This executive believes that in the future G.E. will pay more and more attention to the housewife in determining price and product features.

General Electric, like the other leading manufacturers, carried a $299.95 model among its 1954 automatic washers. But, unlike its competitors, G.E. featured its $349.95 model and treated its $299.95 as a partially stripped version of its standard model.

General Electric's approach to pricing a new consumer product can be illustrated directly by its development for the market in 1949 of a portable dishwasher. The dishwasher was tested in three markets, and the following three prices were set: $149.50; $169.50; $189.50. Each of these prices represented a different method of distribution, ranging from home demonstration at the top price to orthodox department store distribution without demonstration. (Several hundred dishwashers were made by essentially hand processes for this test). The company thus learned about the relative effectiveness of various distribution methods and what needed to be improved in the product, particularly in styling, to make it more salable. General Electric price policy does not stress; indeed G.E. does not consider desirable, the use of low price in the early stages of development of a product as the means of tapping new markets and expanding uses. For example, when the new dishwasher was sold at $200 instead of $250, no more than 5 per cent of additional sales was believed to result. This was because the "service" idea of an automatic electric dishwasher was not yet so fully accepted as to make a price concession expand sales significantly. When the service idea caught on so that the sales reached about 15 per cent of the market potential, demand became very responsive to price. Similarly, in this early stage the stripped models of dishwashers were not particularly effective. The new portable dishwasher, for example, "looked too cheap." Another $5.00 spent on streamlining and in embellishment made it look like another $30 to the customer.

In its present policy on appliances, G.E. apparently exercises a degree of independence associated with maintenance of quality prestige for its products. Thus G.E. itself adheres to quoted prices. At the end of a year, when a new model is coming out, G.E. gives notices to distributors and dealers and expects them to work off their inventory before the new model comes along.[50]

At the level of distributors, and more importantly at the level of dealers, it is recognized that quoted prices are as a rule not strictly adhered to. General Electric does not fair trade its major appliance lines. Executives explain that the techniques of indirect price concession on "big ticket" items have been so finely developed "that it would take a large staff of lawyers to police fair trading in 40 states." Evasions through trade-ins and wiring charges are hard to detect and harder to prevent. These General Electric products, however, have been fair traded in a few states where distributors make the decision. While G.E. has no right to tell distributors to whom to sell, and at what price, it does believe in maintenance of the margins considered necessary to perform adequate service. It is interested in seeing that service does not deteriorate.

Whether to advertise prices of major appliances nationally has been a moot question at G.E. During the immediate postwar inflation, the policy of advertising prices nationally was abandoned because of un-

---

[50] This was contrasted with the practice of some rivals of making early price cuts on the old model. One manufacturer has been known to make large additional quantities at the end of the model year and to dump the old model at low prices, while simultaneously selling the new. The general impression is given that large companies typically adhere to quoted prices of major appliances and that small companies with less well established brands are less punctilious on this score; but this was not explicitly stated to the interviewer.

settled conditions, in which production of the advertising frequently lagged behind the rising cost level.[51]

The experience with television sets, which in 1948 and 1949 were selling at about a 20 per cent mark-up in New York City rather than the larger margin allowed for in the suggested list price, illustrated the difficulty of preventing price shading at the dealer level. The irregularities were related to the mortality rates of independent dealers in different areas. From the standpoint of General Electric, a fair estimate is that a dealer who carries major appliances and electronic items needs about 2,000 wired homes. This is probably a factor in its selection of dealers. The company likes to see dealers big enough to have at least two outside salesmen.

Although G.E. does not regard itself as operating on a cost-plus basis in the field of consumer appliances, its realizations nevertheless do not change drastically over time, partly due to the tendency noted above for manufacturers to settle through experience on a customary price and then adjust cost to price with a "normal" profit margin in mind. What changes there are would not be mainly attributable to departure of actual prices from quoted prices but rather to variations in the proportions of long and short margin products. This type of variation is not regarded as very important. However, there is a broad secular downward change in percentage of net profit to sales as well as cyclical fluctuation.

Small portable appliances, which are sold by G.E. to a great variety of dealers, were generally fair traded in the interest of maintaining profitable margins for the dealers. The small appliance fair trading unit of General Electric has pointed out that the number of small appliances it is possible to dispose of is largely dependent on ability to attract dealers. Up to a point, sales volume may be determined by consumer elasticity of demand, but as soon as the retail price is reduced to the point at which the dealer's profit margin begins to be undermined, there is a progressive decline in the number of dealers willing to carry the article and in the extent to which they will push its sale. The problem of the manufacturer, therefore, is to set

[51] However, on small appliances under $25, which were fair-traded until 1958, prices have been nationally advertised.

the "optimum" price, which is the one that combines attractiveness to the consumer with a profit margin satisfactory to the dealer, and ensure it through fair trading. Since many of these items are supplied as gifts, their biggest sales occurring before Christmas and on other gift-giving occasions, the company may concentrate on building consumer prestige through attractiveness rather than on an effort to be the lowest priced producer in the line.

General Electric has supplied the following case history of a small specialty item that is not fair traded, as an example of the tests applied to determine the "right price" to be suggested to retailers.

ADJUSTABLE NIGHT LIGHT

The market for night lights has been well established in the American retail economy. Introduced more than twenty years ago, these small lights have increased in sales until today the annual sales volume is several million units. General Electric played a dominant role in introducing the original night lights and has enjoyed a satisfactory market position ever since. Several retail channels handle the sale of these lights. Variety chains were among the first actively to promote the item, but hardware stores, drug stores, and more recently food stores have all successfully merchandised night lights.

Recently General Electric looked for product innovations which would help:

1. Expand the market.
2. Add features to better suit the customer needs.
3. Secure larger share of available market.
4. Improve G.E.'s profit position.
5. Enhance the value of the entire G.E. Wiring Device Consumer Line.

General Electric recognized that if they were to find such a product it would be necessary to employ the "double profit" system, a profit for the manufacturer and a larger profit or benefit for the customer. The question arose as to what additional features, performance, or attractiveness could be added to the present product to increase the appeal to the customer. Actually, performance and attractiveness of the present night lights left little to be desired so it appeared that the solution must involve the matter of product features.

The Marketing Section had long realized that customers' comments concerning the present night lights were centered on two general areas:

1. *Quantity of Light*—some customers complained that there was too much light—others too little. There was no control of the intensity of the light in the present products. Light intensity control was particularly desirable in a sickroom.

2. *Position*—Two forms of night light were available. In one form the light was essentially parallel to the wall where it was out of the way and could not easily be disturbed in passing. However, since some outlets are mounted vertically and the remainder horizontally, some customers would find the night light in a vertical position and others in a horizontal position. Customers generally preferred the light to be vertical. In the second type, the light protruded straight out from the wall. This light was adjustable so that light always shone down but had the disadvantage that it was easily disturbed by persons passing by.

Product Planning Specifications

The Marketing Section decided that if they could have a "de luxe" item with the above two features at the "right price," they would have a product that would satisfy the requirements. But what was the "right price"? The earlier night lights had a retail price of about 59 cents. How much would the customers pay for the additional features? The Marketing Section concluded that since this was largely an impulse item, a top price of 98 cents was desirable. Further, since more and more retail outlets were going to self-service, the package became more important since it must do the selling job to a large extent.

A preliminary investigation indicated that an attractive number of customers were willing to pay this premium for the "de luxe" item. A Product Planning specification was prepared describing the desired features, performance and attractiveness of the product. It was recognized that color was important since the item must attract attention on the counter. Conventional night light colors are brown, ivory, pink, and blue. Ivory was rejected because it was too translucent to achieve desired lighting effect (see below); brown was rejected because it was relatively unattractive; pink and blue were selected for their attractiveness on the counter as well as their nursery appeal. G.E. felt that the higher-priced item would be more attractive as a gift than the conventional 59 cent item. Further, it was hoped that the new item would not only appeal to the new customers but would also be sufficiently attractive to cause persons who had previously purchased night lights to purchase the new, more desirable one.

Engineering Problem

The major engineering problem consisted in finding a suitable means of dimming the light that would not be too costly. Conventional methods of dimming by the use of variable resistors or variable auto transformers were rejected because of cost and size. Finally, an ingenious means of dimming the light by a mechanical shutter was devised and this was designed into a light using the "Moon and Stars" as the motif. For full brightness the shutter was adjusted mechanically to "Full Moon" effect. For lowest brightness the shutter could be adjusted so that only the "Stars" gave off light. This design was found to be patentable.

The cost estimates, based upon this design, were somewhat disappointing. Since a lower than normal return would be realized at the previously considered retail price of 98 cents, the entire price question was re-opened.

Setting Selling Price

In the final determination of price it was necessary to review the objective of the development.

1. The new light was not intended to replace existing lights but rather to up-grade a portion of the market. Even though the total annual volume of night lights was several million units, the sale of anything over 100,000 units would be considered satisfactory for the new product. Costs were essentially constant after this volume was achieved.

2. This new light was originally conceived as a 98 cent item because this is the generally considered top price for "impulse" items. However, with price inflation, customers were conditioned to seeing items of this type move up beyond the dollar figure. Also, because this was conceived as being a gift item, the higher retail price might attract more customers. Since there was no competitive product, the customer had no direct method of establishing value and could only compare it to the then available but less desirable products selling at 59 cents. However, one difficulty with even the 98 cent price was that this item was designed to be sold on the electrical counter of the retail outlets previously mentioned. Since most items on this counter sold for a much lower price, there was the question of customer resistance to a product of this price being sold on this counter.

[It was noted that from the standpoint of the retailer the item must produce a profit compatible with the counter space required to display it. A higher priced item might produce for him more dollars of profit than one selling at a lower price with higher volume. Consequently a lower sales volume (with a higher price) could justify the necessary counter space as against a drive for volume through low margin pricing.]

3. A study was made of volume-selling price relationship required to achieve the same dollar profit to the Department. These data were calculated at 99 cents, $1.09, $1.19, and $1.29 selling prices. The study disclosed that it was necessary to sell twice as many at 99 cents as was necessary at $1.09 to achieve the same dollars of profit for the manufacturer. It was necessary to sell twice as many at $1.09 as at $1.29 to achieve the same dollar profit. Four times the volume was required at 99 cents as was required at $1.29 to produce the same dollar profit. Furthermore, since costs were estimated to vary only slightly with volume above 100,000, the higher selling price provided a better return on investment.

4. Items of this type often require special pricing for special promotions. The selling price was established high enough to allow for this type of promotion on a profitable basis.

5. The final question was the effect of pricing on volume in actual test situations. If the higher price reduced sales much below 100,000, it would not be considered despite the reasons cited above. Tests were conducted in various retail outlets in selected cities to test the effect of price on sales. These tests indicated that price was not a particular factor up to and including $1.29 but that sales fell off above this figure. Consequently, the item was introduced with a suggested retail of $1.29. However, since none of our wiring devices is fair traded and no effort is made to control or establish retail prices, we have no assurance that the price was followed in all instances.

Industrial Electrical Equipment

General Electric products range from small, fair traded items to large items involving individual contracts. If the problem is the installation of a turbine generator or a battery of turbine generators for a large utility operation, the price develops out of months of consultation with the customer, the primary consideration being the latter's requirements on fuel costs and other operational efficiencies. Specifications may be developed in terms of a combination of generators that will make it possible to provide the power at a fuel cost not in excess of a given figure adopted as a target for efficient operation. The resultant price to the customer thus emerges as the figure at which

General Electric believes it can profitably furnish the load required within the limits of operating cost at which the customer is aiming.

MEDIUM AC MOTORS

The medium AC motor is fairly representative of a GE industrial product with regularly quoted prices. While such motors may be included in the estimates of large contract installations, they also enter into wide distribution, serving customers in machine shops and in the manufacture of electrical equipment.

Medium AC motors are mostly used where a heavy piece of equipment is to be driven by alternating current through a motor of the induction or synchronous type or synchronous generators driven by engines or turbines. Those using such motors include electric utility companies, engine manufacturers, paper manufacturers, pipe line operators and oil refineries, steel makers and the mining industry. In motors of these sizes, there is very little "shelf" buying. The high engineering content of each motor and the diversity of customer requirements for application and special features relative to the volume produced require that the majority of transactions be treated on an individual basis. A customer requiring a motor will discuss his needs with apparatus salesmen, who are highly skilled engineering sales representatives prepared to help the potential customer make an intelligent choice from the possibilities open to him. This may involve an engineering study of the driven machine and the possible demands to be placed on the motor.

ESTABLISHED PRODUCTS

A handbook is available to the customer containing a wide variety of electrical, mechanical, and design features that can be incorporated into the product for a specific application. The handbook also contains price information, so that the customer can select the motor and associated equipment that will meet his needs most economically. General Electric stated that the price structure for the different ratings and types was developed over a long period, reflected the relative value or cost differences between the various items and bore a logical, if not always precise, relationship to the cost of basic motor types. Many of the products in this area are well enough standardized so that competitors cannot deviate appreciably from the market price for the industry as a whole.

In the process of selecting a motor, the customer will often be talking to several electrical equipment manufacturers who are in competition with General Electric in the motor business. Many engineering man-hours may be spent with a potential customer before there is any assurance that General Electric will get the order, for it is only after the motor has been completely specified that the price can be established and delivery dates and other details of the sale worked out. If a standard motor currently being produced will do the job, the customer will be able to get price quotations and delivery dates in a very short time and can place the order immediately. In other special cases, a longer period may be necessary in order to design the motor and get a shipment date from the factory. The deciding factor in a particular sale may be the price, but more often it is a question either of delivery promise or the customer's evaluation of the relative merits of the different manufacturers' products.

The price level on motors, according to General Electric, is set in markets operating through the thousands of transactions between motor salesmen and motor customers. "The department's policy is to evaluate and interpret the market forces and reflect as closely as possible the free market price level in its published prices." In order to avoid the speculation that is inherent in anticipating inflationary forces, the products are sold on a policy of "price in effect at time of delivery."

After the "initial" contract price has been agreed, certain adjustments may be made on the price. The usual provision is that adjustments may not exceed 10 per cent if they have to be made within twelve months of the date of order; 20 per cent for twelve to twenty-four months; and 30 per cent for twenty-four to thirty-six months. The prices on any shipments made beyond thirty-six months are subject to adjustment with no ceiling on the amount of any increase. An alternative provision, when the date of shipment is more than twelve months from the date of order, is that the purchaser may at his option take an adjustment to incorporate increases in labor and material costs on the basis of a general formula allotting 55 per cent of the price to labor and 35 per cent to material content.

Published prices are changed only when the market forces a change, sales at off-list prices being definitely discouraged and only made under exceptional circumstances. When any such off-list sale is deemed desirable, it is made simply to meet the actions of a competitor. The policy is to change the published prices rather than to meet extensive price shading.

NEW OR UNUSUAL PRODUCTS

The above discussion on prices refers to motors for which there is a fairly well-established market. In dealing with new or unusual products the same policy of finding the market is not applicable because the market is so limited. There is no market level for the product. An example of this sort of product would be the "canned pump motor" for atomic power installations, a highly engineered product, designed to operate submerged, for pumping radioactive materials from nuclear reactors. The specifications for these motors are so precise that the motors are not comparable to the usual industrial motors. In this particular case, sealed bids are used to select the supplier. The policy of the motor department in such cases is to determine a price based in so far as possible on the value to the customer and then to determine whether it can be produced at an economical cost that will allow a fair return on the necessary investment.

Farm Machinery

The largest manufacturer in the agricultural implement field is the International Harvester Company. It has, however, yielded a substantial fraction of the dominant share it held at the time of the antitrust suit that culminated in the consent decree of 1918. The relative position of International Harvester in the farm implement field has been declining ever since 1904, when its share of harvesting machine production averaged well above 75 per cent. The company's percentage of total domestic sales of farm machinery companies dropped from 44 per cent in 1922 to 23 per cent in 1948, although dollar sales increased more than five-fold.[52]

The 1956 market positions of the company in farm implements are indicated by its percentages in leading product groups, as given in the table on page 70. This information has some bearing on the nature of the market for farm machinery; it does not disclose the variations and unevenness of competition in different products, or its impact on price policy and practices. However, with these data as background, some insight into the determination of prices for farm machinery may be gained through an examination of the general pricing principles of the company and their application to specific product situations.

Basic Price Determinants. In discussing price policy on farm equipment, International Harvester officials tended to stress the company's concern for maintaining its reputation as a quality leader. The ideal price is tied to a traditional company objective of developing machines that, at the prices charged by the dealer, will pay for themselves within a satisfactory pay-out period. The period contemplated may be three to ten years, depending upon the type of product and use involved. At the same time, the company, in pricing farm equipment, is conscious of its role as a full-line producer. This involves keeping the prices on all its models in some proportionate adjustment despite the degree of competition to which they are exposed from the

[52] See App. Table 6.

Estimated Market Shares (in units) of International Harvester and Principal Competitors in Selected Farm Implements, 1956

Implement	Approximate Market Share (Per Cent)	Principal Competitors
Combines	20	Allis-Chalmers, Deere, Massey-Harris
Corn pickers	25–27	Dearborn Motors (Ford), Deere, Allis-Chalmers, Oliver, New Idea
Tractor plows	25	Deere, Oliver, Case
Cultivators	27	Deere, Ford, Case, Allis-Chalmers
Cotton pickers	65	Deere, Rusk, Allis-Chalmers
Mowers	25–30	New Idea, Deere, Case
Farm tractors	28–30	Ford, Deere, Massey-Harris, Allis-Chalmers

short-line companies.[53] The determination of prices requires a careful balancing of adjustments to individual product markets with the desired divisional and company-wide profit performance. Hence, the company, in pricing, starts from established prices as a basis, and works back to its costs to see whether it can afford to offer the product at or below the competitive prices or whether an additional cost can be justified by a product that on comparative performance can command a somewhat higher price than the going market average.

The pricing of individual products by International Harvester involves the use of essentially the same costing practices as were outlined for the Temporary National Economic Committee in the late 1930's. The company calculates three types of costs—normal, season's, and specific costs. For price decisions generally, Harvester uses normal costs; these are full costs covering current material and labor and overhead, based upon an estimated percentage utilization of capacity, or

[53] In addition, one official noted, the company must be careful about the price differentials between farm machines and similar machines sold by other divisions, since implement and machinery buyers purchase largely according to performance specifications regardless of the source. As an example, the company manufactures several crawler type tractors, which with only slight modifications can be used either for farming or industrial purposes. This makes for a definite limit on the differentials the company can maintain between the farm and industrial types.

"normal" operations (*e.g.,* 70 per cent in one division), projected from the experience of past years, both good and bad. Season's costs are the actual unit costs of the individual machines or implements by size and model.[54] Season's costs are reviewed periodically, customarily at the close of the manufacturing season (after October 30). For the initial determination of prices, normal costs are used; and these are followed closely, at least unless and until the season's cost experience has indicated the need to adopt more realistic measurements.

The company has found increasing use for "specific costs" in some significant pricing situations, particularly in service parts, discussed below. Specific costs represent only the actual cost of material, prime labor cost, and the direct overhead incurred for the production of the item in question.

COST-PRICE RELATIONSHIPS

The company, when contemplating the introduction of a product, prices it out on the basis of prices of similar pieces of equipment, competitors' prices, and the estimated performance value to the farmer. It then works toward producing at a cost that fits within this price and makes provision for the target profit. Estimates are first made of a target cost, on which the desired target profit may be realized. The target cost is a theoretical one used for planning purposes, and must be converted into a real cost based on design. Engineering and production personnel work out the estimated cost of the first models to be introduced to conform as closely as possible to the targets. Subsequent experience will reveal how far actual costs prove out of line with the estimates.

[54] Normal and season's costs include these components: (a) material costs (purchase price, if purchased outside the company and normal cost, plus actual freight, in transfers within or between plants); (b) direct labor costs; (c) overhead pro-rated on the basis of direct labor costs; and (d) sales, service, collection, administration, etc. (allocated in proportion to their total sales value). *Industrial Wage Rates, Labor Costs, and Price Policies,* TNEC Monograph No. 5 (1940), pp. 98-191.

Price-Cost Analysis, Representative Farm Impleme

	Product "A"			Product "B"			Product "C"		
	Target	Intro-ductory	Actual	Target	Intro-ductory	Actual	Target	Intro-ductory	A
(1) List Price.......	$592.60	$592.60	$592.60	$455.85	$455.85	$455.85	$687.40	$691.35	$6
(2) Trade discount 23%..........	136.30	136.30	136.30	104.85	104.85	104.85	158.10	159.00	1
(3) Dealer price.....	456.30	456.30	456.30	351.00	351.00	351.00	529.30	532.35	5
(4) Cash discount— 2%..........	9.13	9.13	9.13	7.02	7.02	7.02	10.60	10.65	
(5) Net from dealer..	447.17	447.17	447.17	343.98	343.98	343.98	518.70	521.70	5
(6) Sales and admin-istrative expense[a]	67.08	67.08	67.08	51.60	51.60	51.60	77.81	78.26	
(7) Net...........	380.09	380.09	380.09	292.38	292.38	292.38	440.89	443.44	4
(8) Manufacturing cost[b]..........	270.00	274.97	359.43	214.00	217.42	232.62	380.00	395.33	4
(9) Profit margin (dollars)........	110.09	105.12	20.66	78.38	74.96	59.76	60.89	48.11	—
(10) *Profit margin as per cent of:*									
a) *Manufacturing cost*..........	*40.8*	*38.2*	*5.7*	*36.6*	*34.5*	*25.7*	*16.0*	*12.1*	—
b) *Total unit (6)+(8)*......	*32.6*	*32.5*	*4.8*	*29.1*	*27.9*	*21.0*	*13.3*	*10.2*	—
c) *Net from dealer*	*24.6*	*23.5*	*4.6*	*22.3*	*21.8*	*17.4*	*11.7*	*9.2*	—

[a] Allocated as normal percentage (15%) of net from dealer.
[b] Target and Introductory prices based on normal manufacturing cost, including plant overhead.

The table on pages 72-73 shows the sequence of target cost and price, introductory cost and price, and the cost-price situation after a few months of production, for six farm machinery products introduced in 1956. From the net proceeds on the sale to the dealer— which is the retail price minus the conventional "trade" discount (23 per cent) and "cash" discount (2 per cent), the company deducts a standard allowance for sales and administrative expense, yielding the net to the company at the wholesale level. It is against this net that the company places its estimate of the manufacturing cost to which it must hold if the desired target return is to be realized at normal volume.

Target Pricing. International Harvester has a profit objective of 10 *oduced in 1956, International Harvester Company*

	Product "D"			Product "E"			Product "F"	
rget	Intro- ductory	Actual	Target	Intro- ductory	Actual	Target	Intro- ductory	Actual
2.50	$208.70	$208.70	$354.55	$354.55	$354.55	$4,607.05	$4,609.10	$4,609.10
4.27	48.00	48.00	81.55	81.55	81.55	1,059.61	1,060.10	1,060.10
8.23	160.70	160.70	273.00	273.00	273.00	3,547.44	3,549.00	3,549.00
2.96	3.23	3.23	5.46	5.46	5.46	70.95	70.98	70.98
5.24	157.47	157.47	267.54	267.54	267.54	3,476.49	3,478.02	3,478.02
1.79	23.62	23.62	40.13	40.13	40.13	521.47	521.70	521.70
3.45	133.85	133.85	227.41	227.41	227.41	2,955.02	2,956.32	2,956.32
6.72	108.24	127.19	170.00	176.52	201.95	2,246.00	2,406.00	2,798.46
6.73	25.61	6.66	57.41	50.89	25.46	709.02	550.32	157.86
7.6	23.7	5.2	33.8	28.8	12.6	31.6	22.9	5.6
2.6	19.4	4.4	27.3	23.5	10.5	25.6	18.8	4.7
8.4	16.3	4.2	21.5	19.0	9.5	20.0	15.8	4.5

per cent after taxes (on invested capital) as a general guide in pricing its products. This target is roughly equivalent to 7 per cent on sales, since International Harvester's sales figure has averaged about 40 per cent higher than the invested capital figure. The target profit the company considers a reasonable one for the particular machine under consideration may, as the table shows, be above or below the target return for the division as a whole. The company has various profit objectives for different machines, depending upon such factors as the competitive situation, the intricacy or orginality of design, and the estimate of economic worth to the customer. Weight is also given to full-line advantages in marketing for items that cannot themselves carry the full mark-up. On the other hand, when the product has an edge over competitive brands, it has been practicable to set a price that yields a better return than more competitive items in the product group.

Introductory Pricing. The introductory price is based on the estimated costs of production at normal capacity of the product that has been designed. The attempt to design a product within the target figures is sometimes successful, sometimes unsuccessful. Cost estimates on the developed model may prove so high that a decision will be made not to go into production. But the mere showing that the target profit will not be realized does not necessarily mean that the product will not be manufactured. International Harvester considers it important to maintain a full line of products. If the product is one that will create a substantial demand for the Harvester line generally, the company may decide to produce regardless of estimated profit on the particular item. Thus the target cost and the initial cost of products given in the table do not necessarily coincide; in fact, there are often material differences between the two. In some instances, the estimated cost is higher because the engineering department insists on incorporating certain quality features into the product even though competitive pressure precludes a commensurate increase in the price. In others, the engineering department may be able to design quality into the item and yet bring actual costs below target costs.

Actual Pricing. After a period of production and sales experience, it becomes necessary to examine the cost-price structure in the light of the production and market conditions encountered. Competition may be keener than was anticipated, involving a decision to lower the price; or volume of output may be higher than was expected, with a consequent reduction in costs. On the other hand, costs may have exceeded the estimates in a situation permitting the company to consider raising the price.

In the table on pages 72-73 actual costs during the first season are seen to be substantially higher than the estimates for each product. In the most favorable case (Product "B"), a moderate cost increase and consequent reduction in profit margin may be attributed to the normal difficulties of getting production started in a new product area. In this particular case, management advises that sales have been running close to capacity and that expectations for the product may be substantially realized. At the other extreme (Product "C"), the manufacturing cost of the item has run nearly 20 per cent above the original estimates—enough to change the expected profit margin into a deficit. In this situation, the company, if it is to stay within the competition, may have to redesign its product, drastically reduce costs, or else supply features that will justify a higher price against the competition. Otherwise the product may be abandoned unless it is deemed so essential to the full line that the company will be satisfied to realize only the specific costs instead of full cost and an adequate return. The various intermediate situations can reflect degrees of slowness in building up sales volume to normal capacity or making the most of opportunities for cost reduction and product improvement.

Management has pointed out that the introductory price is set close to the competition and can seldom move upward without a material change in the competitive picture. In any event, a change will normally not be made before the end of a full season's operation. A recent example of a situation in which an upward move was feasible was that of a product for which the retail list price in May 1957 was $218.00 ($175.30 net to dealer), and the manufacturing cost was too high to permit what the company regarded as a satisfactory profit. On July 22, the price was raised to $228.00, which was still in line with the competition. While this improved the profit position, the company still did not consider it satisfactory but hesitated to raise the price further. A recent example of a downward move was that of another product, which cost $264.35 to manufacture and was listed to sell at retail at $525.00 ($396.17 to the dealer). This was a lower price than the price for similar equipment sold by the company's big competitors, but two smaller competitors specializing in this implement were selling more cheaply, and International Harvester was unable to sell its estimated volume. To meet the competition of its smaller rivals, the company (in March 1957) reduced the price to $490.00.

One machine that has been successfully priced to yield what the management regards as a satisfactory profit is the cotton picker. This machine, a Harvester innovation, which became important immediately after the Second World War, is sold in volume large enough to hold costs down to the original estimate. It illustrates the case of a new machine developed with no existing competitors—and having what the company regarded as a high utility or economic value for potential users. The price at which the initial offering was made was designed to be sufficiently attractive to users and at the same time to yield the target return or better. Since the introduction of the cotton picker, a number of competitors have entered the field, but the competitive price has nevertheless enabled the company to obtain substantially the target return.

Pricing of Service Parts. It is in connection with service parts that International Harvester makes the greatest use of a marginal approach to pricing. The pricing of such parts varies according to type of part and whether it is manufactured by the company or purchased on the outside. Three distinct groups of parts are handled by the company: (1) captive parts manufactured only by Harvester; (2) parts manufactured by Harvester for which there are other sources for its dealers; and (3) parts procured by Harvester from independent parts manufacturers.

The captive parts manufactured by Harvester include mainly slow-moving items (*e.g.,* engine blocks and cylinder heads). These parts are priced on a formula basis, *i.e.,* in relation to unit costs (normal) and desired target return on investment. The second group of parts includes items like transmissions, ball bearings, and radiators, which Harvester prices with an eye to the prices of GMC, Mack, Chevrolet, and Ford. Also in this category are the fast-moving, highly competitive service parts for which the company surveys carefully the prices of its competitors, large and small, before establishing its prices— prices that do not necessarily hold for an extended period. The prices of these parts do not bear any uniform relationship either to unit costs or to desired profit return on investment. The third group of parts (valves, piston rings, roller bearings, etc.) constituting the most important by volume, are merely distributed by the company organization, and the prices charged dealers follow closely the pattern of the industry, with International Harvester passing along to its dealers the price changes made by the parts manufacturers.

In the second group of service parts, the market situation frequently precludes the possibility of pricing on a full-cost basis. In this area, competitive manufacturers are occasionally able to capture a large share of the business of International Harvester dealers, due essentially to attractive quantity discounts. Pricing these parts on a "normal" or "season's" cost basis means a steadily declining share of the dealers' business. In such cases, the company meets competitive prices even if it has to price on the basis of covering only the specific costs. This type of pricing has also been used in cases in which the company has not previously manufactured certain parts and is contemplating their production. From the viewpoint of the company, in both cases, so long as price covers the "specific" costs, it regards production as worth while since it not only helps maintain or fill out the line of the company parts, but also helps spread the overhead burden of the company.

LEADERSHIP IN FARM IMPLEMENTS

International Harvester has traditionally been viewed as the industry price leader in farm implements. As a practical matter, its ability to exercise price leadership in this field is anything but uniform, because it depends upon the nature of the particular item involved and the company's market position therein. For illustration, Harvester manufactures not more than 5 per cent of all plows sold (25 per cent of tractor plows); and, because of the large number of companies engaged in manufacturing different types of plows, its leadership is slight. On the other hand, the company has long held a commanding position in tractors, mounted cultivators, and corn pickers and mowers, with sales that are substantial in the national total; and with respect to these, it continues to be in the position of price leader. Management views its price leadership in farm machinery to the extent that it exists as having emerged over the years largely as the result of its efficiency in relation to rival producers.[55]

[55] International Harvester has never seriously been charged with price wars aimed directly at the destruction of rivals, even though prices apparently satisfactory to the company's target objectives were inadequate to support many of

Marketing patterns, of course, also shape the pricing of agricultural implements. Traditionally, Harvester has given the same discount from list prices to all dealers regardless of size. In addition, volume discounts are given ranging from 2¼ per cent to 4 per cent.[56] These discounts assume considerable importance since the retail list price is merely a "suggested" price, and as the farm machinery market has become saturated from time to time, the dealers have sold at much less than the suggested price.

The picture of the farm implement industry presented by International Harvester is, therefore, one in which the pricing method, depending on the product involved, ranges from straight formula type pricing based on normal manufacturing costs to market pricing with only slight emphasis on manufacturing costs, and to straight incremental cost pricing. The experience of management in pricing this line of products is that the demand for agricultural implements in general is relatively inelastic with respect to price.

The level of farm income is considered to be more important than price changes in determining the volume of sales. Company officials believe that when farm income drops there is a tendency to defer new implement purchases and to repair old equipment, and when farm income rises, worn out implements tend to be replaced by new ones. Management reasons that these relationships would not be appreciably altered by adopting different policies for pricing its machinery and equipment—a rationale paralleling that of the automobile manufacturers.

While price is always important in the sense that agricultural implements must be able to pay for themselves over a reasonable period

---

the smaller firms highly susceptible to shrinkages in demand. It has been observed that had prices charged by Harvester in past years been at levels high enough to keep all of its rivals alive, they would have yielded still larger profits to the company. The Attorney General and the Federal Trade Commission agreed in the 1920 inquiry that the dominance of International Harvester Company arose from its advantage in manufacturing costs as compared with its competitors. Arthur R. Burns, *The Decline of Competition* (1936), pp. 114 ff.

[56] The discount is 2¼ per cent on the first $10,000, 2½ per cent on the next $10,000, etc., and reaches 4 per cent on $50,000 and over. Discounts are not retroactive.

of use—the level of prices required being in large part a function of farm income and the savings that the equipment will make possible— the major impact on competition in the implement field is, in the view of International Harvester, quality manufacturing. Aside from price, quality of product is believed to have a market effect as great as design (although it is admittedly difficult to separate the two). The company stresses the point that the farmer must have durability, reliability, and functional economy built into his equipment, with immediate availability of spare parts, and sufficiently simplified design of the machine to permit relatively easy emergency servicing by the operator himself in the field. The compromising of these elements of cost and buyer motivation underlies the approach to the company's problem of how to price farm implements and helps explain why no single or uniform approach to pricing has been feasible.

Gasoline

Some twenty integrated petroleum companies generally referred to as the "majors" share responsibility for the over-all pricing patterns in the petroleum industry. Their leadership is more marked in refining and transportation than in production and marketing. Esso Standard, generally recognized as the leader among the majors in making tank-wagon prices for gasoline on the Atlantic Seaboard, south of New York, provided the Brookings study with a detailed memorandum summarizing its pricing procedures.[57] Thereafter the company's marketing vice president, in a hearing before a congressional committee, testified at length regarding the determinants of price changes made by the company in 1953, and a review of that testimony with Esso representatives has provided further insight on how the company's gasoline prices eventuate. Standard Oil of Indiana also provided some detailed data on the development of its pricing policy over the years.

[57] See pp. 91-96.

ESSO STANDARD OIL COMPANY

(STANDARD OIL COMPANY, NEW JERSEY)

The basic objective of Esso's gasoline pricing policy, as stated in the memorandum, is "to build its prices based on its costs of manufacture, distribution, and selling with the allowance of a reasonable margin of profit at each of the various steps in the process of manufacture and distribution." The Esso formula starts with the market price of crude oil rather than cost of production (although one half of crude comes from affiliated companies). A reason for this is that the company assumes that "the market price of crude oil is established competitively, at a level related to cost of production, which is high enough and no higher than the level required to maintain sufficient exploration and production activity to keep abreast of demand for crude oil." Hence Esso takes this profit margin between cost of production and market price as one that should be included as a cost.

In the transportation of crude to refineries, Esso uses as its cost the regular tariff of tankers or pipe lines (except that for tankers of affiliated companies the figure charged is one between a floor of "cost of operation" and a ceiling of "cost, plus 20 per cent of book value of the fleet.") No profit margins are added to tariffs and charter rates.

Gasoline cost at refinery is derived by adding processing cost to cost of crude at refinery, minus sales realization of fuel oil produced in the process. For intermediate products (*e.g.,* kerosene, diesel, and heating oil), manufacturing costs are calculated on a so-called "replacement" basis, *i.e.,* the additional cost of crude and additional processing required to "replace" gasoline lost by withdrawal of intermediate products, less the realization on fuel oil yield from additional runs. To this synthetic cost for each product at the refinery is added a "reasonable margin of profit" on refinery investment of 10 to 15 per cent.

For the transportation of products from refinery to terminals, Esso uses the same costing basis as described for crude, plus a terminalling charge and a profit margin of one fourth cent to one cent per gallon, which yields the terminal price—the price to jobbers or distributors who buy by tank cars or transport trucks for secondary distribution. Product cost at bulk plant is the terminal price plus freight tariffs paid, or equivalent. To this, Esso adds an over-all distribution charge of two cents per gallon for gasoline and two and three quarters cents per gallon for heating oil, which gives the tank wagon price. Thus, in a market situation in which the formula can be substantially implemented, a tank wagon price of say 15 cents per gallon would build up from crude oil cost, pipeline or tanker transportation to the refinery, refining, transport to the terminal, and finally tank wagon distribution.

According to the company, the formula prices are made available to and are considered by those participating in a pricing decision. This occurs frequently, since even continuation of current prices in the face of changing costs is a type of pricing decision. The relation of these formula prices to price decisions, however, should not be overstressed. In essence, there are two constituents to the formula calculation: average total unit costs and the company's notion of a reasonable profit margin. Management has stated that "the vagaries of demand, and the variety of responses thereto by the various suppliers, are no respecters of one company's notion of a reasonable profit margin nor, for that matter, of average total unit costs." Perhaps the most useful function of the cost-build-up involved in the formula price, therefore, is to provide one piece of evidence on the direction of longer-run forces on the supply side of the market. It would seem that the formula price provides a rough "norm" about which actual prices will oscillate.

The company said that when it comes to actual pricing

. . . A good many years of experience have demonstrated to us that the only practical way to establish a realistic refinery billing price is to follow the market closely and set our refinery billing prices in line with the lower level of current market prices. Through the reports of our salesmen, our buyers, our customers and trade journals we keep in close touch with the current refinery market and establish our refinery billing prices accordingly. Many times these prices will be below our calculated cost and sometimes they will be higher than we would normally expect to set them, i.e., cost plus say 10-15 per cent return on investment. In the former case we simply sell at our refineries below cost until a more normal price structure has returned or curtail refinery operations and buy the products we need from other refiners who currently are willing to sell at prices below our costs. Under these circumstances we usually consider our "out of pocket cash costs" before curtailing operations and continue to operate without recovering our fixed charges. In the latter case (which has been very rare) where refinery prices for too long a time stay too high, we have usually refused to raise our refinery prices as high as the competitive market would permit, and simply sell our products at what we consider a fair price.[58]

Mr. H. G. Burks, Jr., executive vice president of Esso Standard Oil Company, testified on July 13, 1953 regarding the products price increase of Esso Standard that occurred on June 22, 1953.[59] Burks' testimony stressed the company's decline in earnings during the years 1950-52. The dollar total had dropped, although net investment had gone up 18 per cent. Direct costs had also increased. Thus, the company's price analysis group determined in May 1953, after gasoline had advanced in the "primary" markets, that it should recommend to management an increase in Esso's products prices. Local area managers were consulted before this recommendation was made. However, before Esso could put the recommended increases into effect, a competitor (Socony-Vacuum) raised its prices, but by not so much as Esso, presumably following the procedures outlined earlier, would have liked. Nonetheless, it felt obliged to follow the competitor, and it announced the same price on June 11 for New York and New England. On June 15, Esso increased its price in New Jersey, Pennsylvania, Delaware, Maryland, Virginia and the District of Columbia. In these states it was able to adhere more closely to the formula basis for pricing, which Mr. Burks summarized as follows:

The amount of these increases varied to some extent, but all were initially calculated on the basis of taking the value of the product

[58] See "Pricing Formula for Gasoline—Esso Standard," pp. 91-96.
[59] *Petroleum Study*, Hearings before the House Committee on Interstate and Foreign Commerce, 83 Cong. 1 sess. (1953), pp. 381-447.

at the primary gulf market and adding to it transportation cost, terminalling, inland freight, bulk plant throughout, and other factors which we regularly use in determining the price we would like to charge at any given delivery point. The desired price would then have to be considered in the light of known competitive conditions, such as availability of lower-cost product to a competitor, and the like. These are merely some of the considerations which must be taken into account in deciding what price shall be asked for delivery of gasoline at a particular point, and the combined judgment of a number of our people who are responsible for the various aspects of our business is brought to bear on the question. In the last analysis, the price of a commodity, such as gasoline, in an active market is fixed by competition, since any seller can bring the price down by offering products of comparable quality and market acceptance at a lower price.[60]

Mr. Burks went on to show how changes in demand and in inventories of stocks of products were strong influences in determining the timing of price changes. Esso presented, in short, an explanation of its pricing policy in which a cost formula was used as an ideal but in which the final price was inevitably modified by competitive pressure.

At any given time Esso's posted tank-wagon prices may vary widely in different areas after allowance for transport cost differences, depending in large part on whether the company is being subjected to local competition. In certain areas, where there is little or no competition from independent refiners, posted prices may remain unchanged for months at a time; in other markets, posted prices may decrease or increase sharply coincident with the outbreak or ending of price wars.[61]

The accompanying table illustrates the range of variations for certain selected cities at which Esso quotes tank-wagon prices. Sev-

[60] *Ibid.*, p. 383.

[61] The posted tank-wagon prices often are only a point of departure from which actual terms of sale are negotiated. The prices at which gasoline actually moves to service station operators are affected by a variety of concessions granted by sellers in order to get business, including discounts, equipment concessions, improvement allowances, and other special terms. In these circumstances, varying refinery nets, or netbacks, result, depending upon the concessions granted on the posted price.

Dealer Tank Wagon Posted Prices, Housebrand Gasoline, Selected Cities, Esso-Standard Oil Company, Jan. 1, 1946-Jan. 4, 1956[a]

Date	New York, N.Y.		Newark, N.J.		Albany, N.Y.		Charleston, S.C.	
	Price	Change	Price	Change	Price	Change	Price	Change
1946: Jan. 1......	9.9		9.5		9.2		10.25	
23......							10.0	− .2
Feb. 9......	9.7	− .2			9.1	− .1		
13......			9.2	− .3			9.7	− .3
19......	9.5	− .2			8.9	− .2		
Apr. 24......	9.7	.2			9.1	.2		
May 4......	9.9	.2			9.2	.1		
July 27......	10.8	.9			10.1	.9		
Aug. 1......			10.2	1.0			10.4	.7
22......	10.9	.1			10.3	.2		
Nov. 30......			10.5	.3			10.7	.3
Dec 3......	11.1	.2			10.5	.2		
1947: Mar. 1......			10.8	.3			11.1	.4
6......	11.5	.4			10.9	.4		
21......	12.2	.7	11.6	.8	11.6	.7	11.8	.7
Sept. 30......							11.3	− .5
Oct. 30......	12.5	.3	11.9	.3	11.9	.3	11.6	.3
Dec. 22......			12.8	.9			12.6	1.0
23......	13.3	.8			12.7	.8		
1948: Apr. 6......	12.8	− .5						
Sept. 1......			12.3	− .5				
Nov. 22......	13.1	.3	12.6	.3	13.0	.3	12.9	.3
Dec. 23......	13.6	.5	13.1	.5	13.3	.3	13.4	.5
1949: Apr. 6......	14.1	.5	13.7	.6	13.8	.5	13.9	.5
Nov. 17......	14.0	− .1						
25......	13.7	− .3	13.3	− .4			13.6	− .3
Dec. 19......					13.7	− .1		
1950: Apr. 25......	14.2	.5	14.2	.9	14.2	.5	14.2	.6
July 18......	14.7	.5	14.6	.4	14.7	.5	14.6	.4
1951: May 29......	13.7	−1.0			13.7	−1.0		
June 30......	14.7	1.0			14.7	1.0		
Nov. 5......							14.5	− .1
1952: Jan. 16......			10.6	−4.0				
24......			9.6	−1.0				
Feb. 4......			8.6	−1.0				
20......			11.6	3.0				
29......			14.6	3.0				
Nov. 8......							14.6	.1
1953: June 11......	15.4	.7			15.4	.7		
15......			15.1	.5				
22......	16.2	.8	15.9	.8	16.2	.8	15.4	.8
Nov. 10......	15.9	− .3	15.6	− .3	16.0	− .2	15.1	− .3
Dec. 11......	15.7	− .2	15.4	− .2	15.8	− .2	14.9	− .2
1954: Jan. 30......	15.5	− .2	15.2	− .2	15.6	− .2		
July 9......	15.0	− .5	14.7	− .5	15.0	− .6		
10......							14.2	− .7
Aug. 19......	15.8	.8	15.5	.8	15.8	.8	15.1	.9
Dec. 6......			14.9	− .9				
1955: July 14......	15.5	− .3			15.5	− .3		
15......			15.0	.1				
29......			14.0	−1.0				
Sept. 22......	16.0	.5	15.0	1.0	16.0	.5		
Oct. 14......			13.5	−1.5				
Nov. 7......			14.5	1.0				
1956: Jan. 4......			13.5	−1.0				

[a] In cents per gallon.

eral interesting features of tank-wagon prices are disclosed by the table. Posted prices in New York and Albany tended to change simultaneously and by the same amount. Newark and Charleston prices showed less conformity, and lagged behind the other two cities until the end of 1948. Charleston price changes, while typically more in line with Newark, did not show any consistent relationship with the changes in other cities.

In response to questions raised concerning the timing and magnitude of the price changes, an officer of Esso said that "because of its decentralized management and use of the committee system, it is seldom possible to point out a single individual as having made a pricing decision, precisely why it was made when it was made, or precisely why the change was of a particular magnitude." Nevertheless, in the case of the 0.8 cent increase in the Newark tank wagon price of Esso on June 22, 1953, and the 0.5 cent decrease on July 9, 1954, the official said a dominant factor can be isolated:

In the case of the advance, this factor was the increase on June 15, 1953, in the price of crude of about 25 cents per barrel. The subsequent 0.8 cent per gallon rise in the price of gasoline reflected its increased replacement cost resulting from the price advance of its major input. Similar price increases were made on all products at this time, and for the same reason. As for the decrease, this followed a similar cut by Socony. Esso felt unable to maintain a higher price in the face of this competition. In both cases, as is generally true, the product price changes originated as recommendations of Marketing management and were reviewed by other officers of the company. In the case of the increase, the date of June 22nd was the earliest following the crude price increase when all information could be accumulated and discussed by management—action deemed necessary since Esso was initiating the price change. In the case of the decrease, it followed promptly on Socony's, since there was little choice if volume were not to be lost.

While the rationale seems clear, a spokesman for the company has made this qualification: "Ex ante and ex post views seem to diverge, although we have never really succeeded in pinning down the extent of the divergence because we have not been able to pin down the ex ante reasoning in satisfactory detail—or, for that matter, the post hoc explanations."

STANDARD OIL COMPANY (INDIANA)

Standard of Indiana has made available to Brookings a recent survey of its pricing policy for gasoline. Its early experience indicated that attempts to base prices on cost were undermined by actions of competitors. In 1934, it adopted a policy of basing its tank wagon prices on the wholesale tank car quotations for the Oklahoma area plus freight and marketing margin. This shift of emphasis toward a meeting of its principal price competition was revised in 1949, by which time tank car movement from the Tulsa area no longer represented the principal competition in Indiana's marketing territory. Thereafter, tank wagon prices in each local area were to be based upon the competitive situation in that locality, reflecting the various sources of crude and products and types of marketing that characterized the individual local markets. The developments in the pricing of gasoline are given in the company's survey as follows:

Dependence Upon Rigid Price Formula, 1920-34. From April 26, 1920 until September 11, 1934, Standard of Indiana maintained a tank wagon price structure built upon prices established at refineries. Each bulk plant was assigned to a normal or customary refinery supply source. To the base price was added freight to the various distributing points to arrive at the consumer tank wagon price. The service station price was determined by adding a differential of one cent per gallon above the consumer tank wagon price. Under this pricing formula, Standard's share of the market steadily declined. The situation reached crisis proportions in the early 1930's.

Attempts were made to introduce into Standard of Indiana's pricing the flexibility essential to meet competitive conditions in particular areas. Upon receipt from the field sales personnel of proper evidence concerning competitive prices below those given by the refineries of Standard of Indiana, local price reductions were approved when the differential was injurious to Standard Oil sales. Certain disabilities incident to the above plan were mentioned by the company (*e.g.,* the erroneous assumption in its basing point plan that competition originated only in certain basic supply areas, the consequent inadequate consideration given to other competitive sources of supply, and the technological improvements leading to increasing gasoline yields from crude). After prolonged investigation of the causes of and possible solutions for the depressing effects on prices of finished products, the company adopted in September 1934 a price system based on the quotations at the Tulsa basing point. Under this policy, Standard established tank wagon prices of gasoline at its local bulk plants on the basis of the published price quotations for the Group 3 shipping area (Oklahoma) plus rail rate to destination. Standard did not operate a refinery in the Group 3 area.[62] It was, in effect, adoption of a new formula that would permit the company to lower its prices.

Revision of Pricing Practices after the Second World War. The whole question of reviewing the price policy was stimulated by a series of rapid changes that took place after the Second World War. Costs of raw products, labor, and materials spiraled upwards, and the industry was for a while hard pressed to meet total requirements. Purchasers of petroleum for one use bid against consumers for other uses. Prices were correspondingly unstable during this period of bidding for supplies. The margins and profits showed a great deal of diversity, from levels that seemed ruinously low to others that were of the black market variety. The industry seemed during this period

[62] For convenience in handling freight rate problems, the Interstate Commerce Commission characterized the refineries in Oklahoma as the Group 3 shipping area.

An interesting incidental aspect of the Tulsa basing point for pricing adopted in 1934, was the effect upon the company's local managers. It was found that the intensity of competition for the accounts of jobbers tended to vary inversely with respect to the location of the buyer and the nearest terminal source of supply. As one official explained: "The business of the buyer who was located nearest a terminal was more diligently sought after by competitive suppliers than the business of one a considerable distance cost-wise from the terminal." In the same way, the intensity of the competition for different accounts was also found to vary according to the relative costs of servicing the particular accounts. It became clear that one objective of any new pricing policy, therefore, would be to combine general market factors with particular customer-buyer relationships and local advantages or disadvantages. It was equally evident that Standard could not afford to reach out for special situations of a temporary nature; it had to regard its general price policy more in terms of maintaining its volume over the whole territory, of retaining its market position, and of providing for future profit possibilities.

to have no accurate economic guide to competitive pricing practices on which to establish a revised pricing policy that would reflect competition as it was being modified by the changing competitive facilities.

Standard of Indiana, like some of the other large companies, tried to hold the line while making every possible effort to get the maximum quantity of petroleum to midwestern consumers. It did not, however, adopt a rigid hold-the-line policy. To have stuck to strict hold-the-line pricing would have made it profitable to reship gasoline in arbitraging transactions, and many long-distance shipments at high transportation costs would probably not have been made at all. The effort was made to achieve a middle ground where the prices reflected approximately the increased costs. The net effect was for the prices of Standard of Indiana to be substantially below those of a large part of the competition on burning fuels during the winter of 1947-48. During the same period, however, competition did not cut below the gasoline prices of Standard of Indiana to any substantial degree.

When conditions were restored to something resembling the prewar period, it was possible to make a revaluation of pricing policies in an effort to select one that would give the company the "best possible interpretation of competitive conditions." Accordingly, the company inaugurated a number of studies of price movements in specific Standard of Indiana markets in order to arrive at an ideal or norm for a new pricing policy. Since that time, the price policy of the company has continued to be one of meeting competitive conditions on both a broad industry basis and on a local market basis. The price adopted to meet local competitive conditions is not guided by the company's own costs, and is not primarily influenced by the wholesale tank car market (which cannot always be readily evaluated); however, the evaluation that is made of the wholesale tank car market is obviously a significant factor. It can be said that in the postwar period Standard of Indiana has reversed its formula-type pricing policy and has sought to measure local competitive and economic conditions at individual bulk station markets in setting price.[63]

[63] In meeting "the local competitive situation" special situations may call for experimental programs to determine the most workable method of matching the market. The Twin Cities area, for example, has undergone a market change

Under the revised policy, the management stated, "Our costs do not determine an ideal price. Actually when we attempt to determine what it will cost a competitor to serve a given market we are merely making a first approximation of what the competitive price in that community may be. This calculation is not based on Standard's cost but is tied to the prevailing competitive prices at principal supply points." Moreover, "A shift in the price of crude oil, a shift in the refinery costs, a change of freight rates and other similar changes have no automatic effect on new prices, but along with all other economic factors are considered with market trends in determining whether changes are warranted either in the company's over-all price structure or locally."

The considerations brought to bear on a particular modification of prices may vary from those that were considered of primary importance in a prior determination, and any one factor may have a drastically different weighting at one time from that of another. One pricing official stated that the company's pricing decisions are vitally

---

as a result of greater pipeline deliveries and expanded local refinery capacity processing Canadian crude. This has meant a great expansion of local and private brand marketing directly from the pipeline terminal or refinery to retail station. In order to take cognizance of the indicated trend, Standard discontinued posting tank wagon prices in this market and commenced to sell "at suggested competitive retail prices less a discount to the dealer." This pricing experiment was announced by Dwight F. Benton, vice president in charge of sales, in a press release (Jan. 5, 1956) as follows:

"Henceforth Standard will sell gasoline to its Twin Cities dealers at a discount from 'suggested competitive resale prices.' The suggested retail prices will be designed to reflect competitive conditions, including particularly, other retail prices in the Twin Cities, taking into account not only posted prices but rebates of any kind, premiums, trading stamps, and other forms of price concessions by competitors.

"Discounts below the suggested competitive resales prices which Standard will allow to its dealers will fluctuate from time to time. The dealer's discount will be narrowed somewhat when prices are depressed, and it will increase as prices are restored.

"We, of course, can only recommend that our dealers post our suggested retail prices. What each chooses to do is a matter of individual decision. Our prices to our dealers will be computed at a discount from the suggested resale prices, regardless of the prices actually posted by our dealers.

"Under the circumstances, it will no longer be necessary for Standard to post tank wagon prices to dealers in the Twin Cities area. . . ."

affected by the ability of customers to shift patronage. Among other considerations frequently appearing in price-making sessions are: (1) the trend of the company's sales and its marketing position in the community or area involved; (2) the prices being charged by competitive marketers in the community or area; (3) the company's evaluation of the relationship between available supplies and level of demand in the area; (4) the price behavior in the open market quotations in Group 3 and Gulf markets; (5) the competitive transportation rates incurred in reaching the market and any recent changes in such rates; (6) the trends of costs of production and distribution of competitive brands; and (7) the trend of quality and service associated with the distribution of the company' product compared with competitive marketers.

Usually, price changes are considered for some time before they are introduced, especially when upward revisions are contemplated. On occasions, price adjustments in given markets have been considered, deferred for a period of watchful waiting, and later not introduced, because the conditions that led to a consideration of price changed sufficiently during the interim periods, that a price modification was no longer justified. As intimated earlier, all types of competition, branded and unbranded, at both refinery and tank wagon levels are considered in most price changes.

After eight years of experience with new pricing policy (adopted in 1949) the management of Standard of Indiana expressed the opinion that it seems to be working out as "perhaps the soundest approach for insuring an accurate measurement of competition, of the economics of the market, and of the basis for operating in the midwest that the company has yet been able to achieve." It was the opinion of one officer that the company's prices are really competitively determined in each local market and that there is no formula by which a competitor can predetermine prices in any given community and submit bids below such formula price. The company says it does not recognize any price advantage for any particular distributor in any given community but at the same time does not customarily meet the lowest seller, adopting instead prices sufficiently near the low-price marketer to permit it to retain its sales and hold what it regards as its "proper market position." This indicates that the company still exercises independent judgment in making its tank wagon price.[64]

PRICING FORMULA FOR GASOLINE—ESSO STANDARD

The basic objective of our pricing policy is to build our prices based on our costs of manufacture, distribution and selling with the allowance of a reasonable margin of profit at each of the various steps in the process of manufacture and distribution in the final price to the consumer.

Basically there are six steps in the operation of supplying petroleum products to the consumer:

(A) The purchase of the raw material—crude oil.
(B) The transportation of the crude oil to the refinery.
(C) The manufacture of the crude oil into the finished product.
(D) The transportation of the finished product by tanker, pipe line or barge in large quantities to major distribution terminals.
(E) The transportation of the finished product from the major distribution terminals to small secondary distribution terminals (called bulk plants).
(F) The distribution of the finished product from secondary distribution terminals to service stations or direct to the consumer.

Step A

Esso Standard Oil purchases all of its supply of crude oil from producers. We start therefore with the current market price of crude oil. Even when considering the fact that somewhat over half our crude supply is purchased from affiliated companies we start to build up our prices from the market price of crude oil rather than the cost of production of crude oil. The reason for this is that we assume that the market price of crude oil is established competitively at a level related to cost of production, which is high enough and no higher than the level required to maintain sufficient exploration and production activity to keep abreast

---

[64] The fact that, in its price quotations to the trade it includes both "temporary" and "established" prices suggests that the company distinguishes between the meeting of a true market change and what it regards as a sudden and short-lived price feud. In this connection, the management further notes that "when it becomes apparent that conditions initially believed to be only temporary in character, especially if they extend over an area considerably beyond the immediate locality, are likely to persist indefinitely, then the 'temporary' price may be changed to the 'established' price."

of demand for crude oil. If this be so, the profit margin between the cost of production and the market price is necessary and must be included in the cost of product. No profit on the cost of crude oil to us is added by the refiner in his product price calculations.

Step B

The transportation of crude oil to the refineries is accomplished largely by pipe lines and tankers. Pipe lines have established tariffs which must be paid by all shippers under I.C.C. regulations, and this becomes the second item of cost.

Some of these pipe lines are owned by affiliated companies and some are not, but we always use the published tariffs in calculating our product costs.

Some crude oil is transported to refineries by tankers. Some of these tankers are owned by affiliated companies, some are not. In calculating our product costs we use the cost of the tankers to us. In the case of outside charters this represents the current charter market, either spot or long terms, depending on how the charter was made. In the case of charters from an affiliated company the cost to Esso is based on a formula which starts with the current twelve months' charter market rate. A floor of "cost of operation" is established and also a "ceiling of" "cost plus 20% of book value of the fleet." A good many years of experience have shown that this is about as good a formula as we can develop to reflect a fair tanker rate averaged over the years. The cost to Esso of tanker transportation determined in this way is used in building up our product cost in Step B. There is potentially a profit to the pipe line operator of 7% on his allowed valuation in the pipe line operations. In the tanker operations there is potentially a profit of around 10% on the book value of the fleet using our formula for tanker rates. Where the pipe lines or tankers are owned by an affiliated company these potential profits would of course accrue to the affiliate. Where they are owned by outsiders these potential profits would of course accrue to them. In either case, we as refiners use the pipe line tariffs or the tanker charter rates as expense items and add no profit to them in our product price calculations.

Step C

Our manufacturing costs are calculated on the "replacement" basis. This method of costing recognizes the fact that all fractions from a barrel of crude may be converted, by proper processing, into gasoline and fuel oil and gas. By starting with the cost of a barrel of crude oil at the refinery, adding the processing costs and deducting the actual sales realization of the amount of fuel oil produced in processing the barrel of crude oil (gas is valued in terms of fuel oil equivalent) we arrive at the cost of the amount of gasoline which was produced from processing the barrel of crude oil. If it is desired to withdraw, during the processing, any intermediate product between gasoline and fuel oil, such, for example, as kerosene, diesel fuel or heating oil, a certain amount of gasoline and fuel oil will *not* be produced from the barrel of crude. This loss of gasoline can be made up and the original quantity of gasoline balanced by running more crude oil solely for gasoline and fuel oil. The "cost" of the intermediate product withdrawn is then calculated by taking the cost of the additional crude oil and the additional processing (less the realization on the fuel oil from the additional crude run) required to "replace" the gasoline lost by the withdrawal of the intermediate product. Any method of costing a single product in a multi-product manufacturing operation must contain some arbitrary assumptions, but this "replacement cost" method has seemed to us to be the most logical of all we have tried, and is generally used by our company. From Steps A, B, and C we thus arrive at a product cost for each product at our refineries. If possible, we will then establish a "refinery billing price" for each product which will reflect the cost of that product, determined as above-described, plus a reasonable margin of profit on our refinery investment. Considering the rather high degree of functional obsolescence in refining equipment and other inherent hazards in the refining equipment and other inherent hazards in the refining business we generally feel that a profit return of 10-15% on our refining investments would be quite reasonable. As a matter of fact, however, the refining branch of the industry is so competitive that the situation rarely arises where a "refinery billing price" can be set on this theoretical basis. There are so many refineries and the flexibility of the marketer in shifting from one refinery supply source to another is so great that a refiner must always have his refinery billing prices quite closely in line with the current competitive market. Differences in refinery equipment, in efficiency of refining operations, in the desires of some refiners to expand their volume; differences in crude supply and in the proportionate yields of various products; and in the current financial needs and price ideas of various refiners, all combine to establish a fluctuating and rather sensitive refinery product market. A good many years of experience have demonstrated to us that the only practical way to establish a realistic refinery billing price is to follow the market closely and set our refinery billing prices in line with the lower level of current market prices. Through the reports of our salesmen, our buyers, our customers and trade journals we keep in close touch with the current refinery market and establish our refinery billing prices accordingly. Many times these prices will be below our calculated costs and some times they will be higher than we would normally expect to set them, i.e., cost plus say 10-15% return on investment. In the former case we simply sell at our refineries below cost until a more normal price structure has returned or curtail refinery operations and buy the products we need from other refiners who currently are willing to sell at prices below our costs. Under these circumstances we usually consider our "out of pocket cash costs" before curtailing operations and continue to operate without recovering our fixed charges. In the latter case (which has been very rare) where refinery prices for too long a time stay too high, we have usually refused to raise our refinery prices as high as the competitive market would permit, and simply sell our products at what we consider a fair price. This, of course, leads to an abnormally wide spread between low and high prices in the refinery market, and except under very unusual conditions of supply and demand such a condition will not prevail for very long.

It is obvious that to weather the periods when the refinery market is below a normal level or even below cost of production and operate continuously a refiner must be a low-cost operator and our efforts and investments are continuously in that direction. In times of below normal refinery prices, high cost or marginal refiners reduce or discontinue operations and in times of abnormally high refinery prices these marginal operations come back into the picture. This tends to keep refining operations in approximate balance with product demands, but since there is considerable lag or inertia in the marginal operations coming into or going out of the picture the refinery market tends to go well above or below what might be considered a normal price level related to current crude prices and product demands, quite frequently.

It will be seen, therefore, that at the refinery level our product price structure becomes based on a competitive market price level and loses all except an indirect relationship to the actual cost of the product. The refinery billing price which then forms the basis for all our further price structure build-up may or may not contain a profit margin in it.

Step D

In the transportation of products from refineries to major terminals we use the same costing basis for pipe lines and tankers as was described under Step B. Where barges are used the current competitive market rate is figured where we use our own barges and the actual charter cost where outside equipment is chartered.

A terminalling charge is built into the price structure at this point. This terminalling charge approximates our cost of conducting the terminalling operation. In addition to the refinery billing price of the product plus the transportation cost to the major terminal plus the terminalling charge we here add a profit margin for the marketer. This profit margin may vary from ¼¢ to 1¢ per gallon and is the profit which is available to the large marketer who buys wholesale from refineries, provides the investment for large seaboard or pipe line terminals and sells to secondary distributors. This price is the "terminal price" and is the price which applies to jobbers or distributors who buy by tank cars or transport trucks for movement to secondary distribution terminals. In connection with our own operations, where the secondary distribution is done by us, this profit margin represents a return on our investment in major terminals and allied facilities. Competition at times reduces or even eliminates this profit margin in the "terminal price," since it is at this point that much of the "give and take" of competitive marketing activity occurs. The actual cost of operating a major terminal probably varies from .10¢ to .25¢ per gallon and in times of intensive competitive activity terminalling allowances in price formula will go this low, but a fair estimate of the normal allowance for terminalling and profit at this point in the distribution chain might be from ½¢ to 1¢ per gallon.

Step E

In the distribution of the product from the major terminal to the secondary bulk plants, tank cars and transport trucks are principally used. In the case of tank cars and outside transport trucks the actual tariffs we pay are added to the "terminal price" at major terminal. Where our own transport trucks are used a charge comparable to competitive transportation costs is used. We thus arrive at a product cost delivered to the bulk plant for final distribution. No profit element is added in this step, except where we use our own transportation facilities and our operating costs are less than the current competitive cost of similar transportation, which latter cost is used in the price build-up.

Step F

From the bulk plants distribution is accomplished by tank wagons. At this point an overall distribution charge is added to the build-up product cost delivered to the bulk plant. This charge is designed to cover the cost of operating the bulk plant, the cost of operating the tank wagons, the cost of the salesmen operating out of that bulk plant, clerical costs, advertising, and administrative costs allocated from the central office and to provide a marketing profit. This overall charge may average about 2¢ per gallon for gasoline and 2¾¢ for heating oil, for example. This charge is quite generally referred to as the jobber or distributor margin. When it is added to the laid down product cost at the bulk plant we have the final price to the service station operator or to the consumer, as the case may be. This final price is called the "tank wagon" price. The profit element contained in this so-called "jobber margin" varies depending on the efficiency of the distributor. It probably runs on the average somewhere around ⅜ ¢ per gallon, but will vary from ⅛ ¢ to ¾ ¢, possibly. In any given area these distribution margins are generally about the same for all distributors of competitive products since "terminal prices" and transportation costs to the area usually are the same and if they are not the terminal suppliers will equalize delivered prices to the given area to be competitive. Thus there is a real incentive for a distributor in any area to reduce his distribution costs below those of his competitor and improve his profit margin.

Of course in most areas there are one or more distributors who operate less efficiently than the others and these are the cases which continually raise the hue and cry for "wider margins." The play of competition is ever present at this level of distribution and generally takes the form of what is called "under cover" discounts and concessions. When these become sufficiently prevalent they are usually recognized by a change in the "posted" or scheduled price structure.

This general outline gives the way in which we attempt to build our product price structure, and for each point and level of distribution we have a price determined which we would consider as "normal." It should be apparent, however, that a normal price structure rarely obtains and the actual price structure existing at any time in each area of distribution is in reality simply an evaluation of the price which will be competitive at that place at that time.

Cellophane and Nylon

The price histories of two products, cellophane and nylon, have been selected to bring out contrasting influences that, in a large and influential corporation, can shape the pricing policies for new products. These patented items were both initially produced in the United States by du Pont.

CELLOPHANE

The du Pont Cellophane Company was organized in June 1923, and by an agreement of December 1923, it received a license from the French company having exclusive rights to the secret process for the manufacture of cellophane.

Pricing policy for this product has been the subject of intensive investigation and explanation in connection with the antitrust trial involving du Pont. As du Pont views its own decisions, it has been motivated by an effort to expand the use of cellophane quite rapidly and to exploit new uses for the material as they are developed.

Price History of Cellophane. The introductory prices on cellophane (up to $3.25 per pound) averaged out at $2.51 for the first year of operation. The price reductions during the next three years brought down the average to $1.43 for 1927. This was for the *plain* cellophane as distinguished from moistureproof.[65]

The development by du Pont of a patented process for moisture-proofing cellophane sharply increased the market potential, beginning with 1928. [66] This was demonstrated in the data presented in the Cellophane Case.[67] Although the price of the moistureproof product was about one third higher than that of the plain cellophane, it gave new dimensions to the scale of operation. Volume increased rapidly, and the profit rate was maintained while prices were continuously reduced—from $2.508 in 1924 to $.38 in 1940.

The average revenue per pound from cellophane sales and the dollar receipts for plain and moistureproof cellophane, from 1924 through 1950, indicate successive price reductions and volume increases into the Second World War. The average prices, however, mask very important changes in, and variations among, cellophane

---

[65] The moistureproof feature involves a coating of the cellophane sheet which is compatible with the cellophane in respect to pliability, the effects of changes in temperature, humidity, etc.

[66] See App. Table 9.

[67] *United States* v. *E. I. du Pont de Nemours & Co.,* 118 Fed.Supp.41, pp. 82, 123.

prices. Since about 1940, cellophane has been produced in a number of different forms and combinations. It is available as plain transparent, plain colored, moistureproof transparent, moistureproof sealed colored, moistureproof heat sealable transparent, moistureproof heat sealable, adhesive transparent, and so on. These varieties in turn have different gauges. In 1940 du Pont's quotations per pound of cellophane ranged from $.33 for 300 gauge plain transparent, to $1.011 for 450 gauge moistureproof heat sealable colored tango. For major representative types, the range was from $.33 to $.62 per pound in 1945 and from $.59 to $.81 in 1955. All varieties of cellophane were put under government price control at an average of 41 cents per pound during the Second World War, when most of the production was diverted to military purposes.

Since 1946, du Pont has raised the price of cellophane to cover increasing labor and raw material costs.[68] The change in average price over a range of 15 cents per pound between 1945 and 1955 is a composite of varying degrees of change among the different types of cellophane catering to a variety of customers.[69] Plain transparent is almost twice as expensive as it was in 1945; moistureproof has risen from $.41 to $.59 per pound, and there have been substantial increases in prices of other varieties of cellophane. The costs of labor and material components of cellophane have risen faster than the average price of cellophane.[70]

The apparent drop of 1½ cents in the Bureau of Labor Statistics weighted average price of cellophane in 1946 was not the result of a real price change, but represented a change in the relative volume sold among the various types—for instance, the drop in sales of special cellophane for gas capes, the output of which was substantial during the war, and for which the price was 50 cents per pound as

[68] The raw materials include glycerin, sulphur, and lacquer. Until quite recently the supply of glycerin was dependent upon imports from Argentina and the price was made a source of increasing revenue to the Peron government. The Argentinian product priced itself out of the American market with the development in the United States of a chemical process for the production of glycerin in which Shell Oil was a prime factor.

[69] See table, p. 102.

[70] See chart, p. 99. This chart does not indicate the degree to which labor productivity may have changed during the years 1946-55.

Selling Price, Material Prices, and Labor Rates of Cellophane
(1945 = 100)

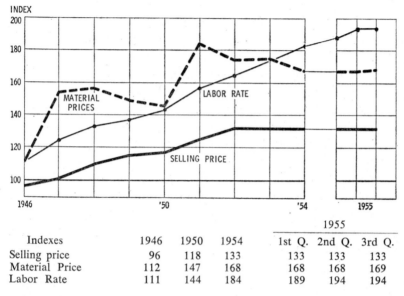

Indexes	1946	1950	1954	1955		
				1st Q.	2nd Q.	3rd Q.
Selling price	96	118	133	133	133	133
Material Price	112	147	168	168	168	169
Labor Rate	111	144	184	189	194	194

Source: E. I. du Pont de Nemours & Co.

compared with 41 cents for the standard moistureproof and 33 cents for the standard plain cellophane. Cellophane prices rose after decontrols, the rise following a similar pattern for the types of cellophane shown in Appendix Table 9. Here, too, however, there are some differences between the average price and the component prices of the various grades, in keeping with differences in their respective markets and costs.

The price increases in recent years were accompanied by material improvements in product and by better tailoring of the product to meet special requirements, as for fresh foods and other perishable items, special conditions of humidity or temperature, and high tensile strength or durability. The prices also reflect service costs, which are regarded as having increased the value of the product for consumers. Among the services to customers is counseling in package design, concerned with both utility and attractiveness of the cellophane container.

The pricing program in cellophane, combined with the promotion of the product into additional fields, has resulted in an increase in volume of du Pont's output from 11.1 million pounds in 1930, when the moistureproof output first exceeded that of the plain form, to 125 million pounds in 1954, of which nine tenths was moistureproof. The pricing program is also intended to be consistent with the maintenance of a rate of return on investment which, after a period of spectacular earnings, remains above the average for the products of the company as a whole.[71] It was noted by the trial court that the net return on the cellophane investment after taxes during the period 1937-49 varied between a high of 28.7 per cent in 1939 and a low of 8.4 per cent in 1942.[72]

Market Penetration Through Price Reduction. Du Pont, in progressively reducing the price of cellophane, did not attempt to make its price coincide with that of substitutes such as glassine and waxed paper. Cellophane was always more expensive than these competitive products. In reducing its price, du Pont had in mind the fact that "each price reduction was intended to open up new uses for cellophane, and to attract new customers who had not used cellophane because of its price."[73] The primary considerations, other than the target rate of return, were its manufacturing cost and the possibility of moving into new markets. The price was reduced year after year during the 1929-46 period, when the prices of its closest substitutes remained relatively fixed.[74]

Comparison of price action with du Pont's competitor, American

---

[71] The profit record on du Pont's total chemical operations for the decade following the Second World War indicates an average not far from 10 per cent after taxes on "average operating investment." Du Pont includes as operating investment the value of the company's current assets plus plants and properties (before deduction of depreciation). On this basis, the most profitable postwar year for du Pont was 1955, when its net operating income of $292.4 million was equivalent to 13.8 per cent of its average operating investment of $2,112.4 million. For du Pont's return on invested capital on a basis comparable with that used for the other companies, *i.e.,* invested capital = capital stock, long-term debt, and surplus, see App. Table 11.

[72] *United States v E. I. du Pont de Nemours & Co.,* 118 Fed.Supp.,41,Finding 714, p. 179.

[73] *Ibid.,* Finding 135, p. 84.

[74] *Ibid.,* Findings 124, 136.

Viscose, during the postwar decade indicates that in general neither company has stood out as the leader or follower in price changes, although the number of changes appears to have been slightly higher for Avisco.[75] It will be seen from the table, however, that while the initiative on price increases seesawed between the two companies, on decreases the initiative was almost exclusively du Pont's. There was no apparent consistency in respect to the readiness of either company to follow the lead of its competitor. The lag in followership ranged from less than a month to more than a year.

The table shows that leadership differs with a particular product. Avisco is clearly the leader on product 450 MST, while du Pont is the leader on 600 PT. The movement of prices is upward with lags by the other seller.[76]

On products in the 300 group (PT, MT, LSAT, and MST), the leadership is exchanged in a leapfrog fashion many times over the ten-year period. The pattern has followed a course in which Avisco raises price, du Pont makes no change for six months or more then increases to a level above Avisco's. With some delay, the latter more than matches du Pont's increase, after which the cycle is repeated. This clearly seems to have been the pattern up to 1951, with Avisco making more changes than du Pont.

The most typical relationship appears to be Avisco leading with du Pont following imperfectly, *i.e.,* not increasing as much, and with some delay, causing Avisco to retract some of its increase—in short a case of Avisco frequently pushing for a higher price than du Pont. A more detailed examination and interpretation of these data might reveal cases in which effective transaction prices came before or after publication of quotations. It might shed more light on whether Avisco was able to make some of its prices, which often were substantially higher than du Pont's, stick. The quotations on their face support only in part du Pont's emphasis of the point that it was pricing

---

[75] See table, p. 102, which combines price lists provided for the study separately and at different times by du Pont and Avisco.

[76] No information was offered on the relative importance of the sales of each company for the different subproducts, but presumably a substantial share of the market would ordinarily have to be enjoyed to make a price change effective.

Price History du Pont and Avisco Cellophane, 1945-55[a]

Date	300 PT Du Pont	300 PT Avisco	300 MT Du Pont	300 MT Avisco	300 LSAT Du Pont	300 LSAT Avisco	300 MST Du Pont	300 MST Avisco	300 MSAT Du Pont	300 MSAT Avisco	300 PC Du Pont	300 PC Avisco	300 MSC Du Pont	300 MSC Avisco	450 MST Du Pont	450 MST Avisco	450 MSAT Du Pont	450 MSAT Avisco	600 Du Pont	600 Avisco	600 PT Du Pont	600 PT Avisco	600 MST Du Pont	600 MST Avisco
1945: Jan.	.33	.33	.41	.41	.56	—	.41	.41	.57	—	.45	.49	.55	—	.46	.46	.62	—	.45	.45	.45	.45	.54	—
1947: Jan. 22	—	.38	—	—	—	.57	—	—	—	.57	—	.54	—	.59	—	—	—	.62	—	—	—	—	—	.54
June 1	.42	—	.44	.44	.54	.60	.44	.44	.54	.60	.54	—	.57	.62	.45	.49	.55	.65	.48	.48	.48	.48	.50	.57
Oct.	—	.43	—	—	—	.54	—	—	—	.54	—	—	—	.58	—	—	—	.55	—	—	—	—	—	.49
Nov. 1	—	—	—	—	—	—	—	—	—	—	—	—	—	—	—	—	—	—	—	.52	—	—	—	—
1948: Feb. 1	.45	—	.48	.48	.56	.49	.48	.49	.56	.59	.57	—	.60	.63	.48	.50	.56	.60	.50	.50	.50	.48	.52	.54
Aug.	—	—	.47	.47	—	—	—	—	—	—	—	—	—	—	—	—	—	—	—	—	—	—	—	—
1949: Jan. 1	—	.46	—	—	—	.56	—	—	—	.56	—	.57	—	.60	—	—	—	.56	.60	—	.60	—	.60	—
May 26	—	.45	—	—	—	—	—	.48	—	—	—	—	—	—	—	.48	—	—	—	—	—	—	—	—
1950: Sept. 1	.49	.49	.51	.51	.59	.60	.51	.52	.59	.60	.61	.61	.64	.64	.51	.52	.59	.60	.63	.63	.63	.54	.63	.60
Oct.	.49	—	.51	.55	.59	.64	.51	.56	.59	.64	.61	.65	.64	.68	.51	.56	.59	.64	—	—	.69	.65	.63	.65
Dec.	—	.53	—	—	—	—	—	—	—	—	—	—	—	—	—	—	—	—	—	—	—	—	—	—
1951: Sept.	.52	—	.55	—	.63	.63	.55	.55	.63	.63	.65	—	.68	—	.55	.55	.63	.63	.67	.67	.67	—	.67	—
1952: Mar. 24	—	.52	—	—	—	—	—	—	—	—	—	—	—	—	—	—	—	—	—	—	—	—	—	—
Apr.	—	—	—	—	—	—	—	—	—	—	—	—	—	—	—	—	—	—	—	—	—	—	—	—
1953: Apr. 17	.57	—	.57	—	—	—	.57	—	—	—	.71	—	.71	—	.57	—	—	—	.70	.70	.70	—	.70	—
June	—	—	.56	—	—	—	.56	—	—	—	.70	—	.70	—	.56	—	—	—	.69	.69	.69	—	.69	—
Sept.[b]	.56	—	—	.56	—	—	—	.56	—	—	—	—	—	—	—	.56	—	—	—	—	—	.69	—	.69
Nov. 1[b]	—	.56	—	—	—	—	—	—	—	—	—	.70	—	.70	—	—	—	—	—	—	—	—	—	—
1955: Sept. 6	—	.64	.59	—	.66	—	.59	—	.66	—	.76	.78	.73	.73	.59	.59	.66	—	.75	.75	.75	.77	.72	.72
Oct.	.62	—	.59	.59	.66	.66	.59	.59	.66	.66	.76	—	.73	—	.59	.59	.66	.66	.75	.75	.75	—	.72	—

[a] Roll prices, dollars per pound, for first grade, major representative types, before deducting discounts and commissions. Dashes indicate no change in price. P=plain; T=transparent; M=moistureproof; L=laminated; S=sealed; A=adhesive; C=colored.

[b] Prices prior to September 21, 1953 for du Pont and November 1, 1953 for Avisco were f.o.b. plants. Prices shown beginning with those dates are f.o.b. destination and apply to shipments into all states except Arizona, California, Idaho, Montana, Nevada, Oregon, Utah and Washington. Prices applying to shipments into these states are 1½ cents a pound higher than the prices shown above.

cellophane to develop new opportunities for use as a wrapping material. Despite such reservations, however, the foregoing data effectively illustrate the kind of price leadership du Pont offered and the extent to which Avisco was willing to accept it or attempt to strike out on its own course.

NYLON

Nylon, like cellophane, presented du Pont with the problem of devising a price policy for a unique product. The initial price could not be set simply by relying on "meeting competition" or following a cost-plus formula. Research in developing this synthetic fiber cost the company $6 million; $21 million was spent on manufacturing facilities before commercial operations and sales began. Cellophane had not absorbed anything like the research and preparatory expenditure that went into nylon; it was acquired as a functioning process, and du Pont made certain improvements entailing large annual expenditures as time went on, which could be paid for out of current receipts.[77] Hence, there was relatively little in the cellophane experience that appeared immediately useful in pricing nylon.

Du Pont, at the time its nylon experiments succeeded, was producing another synthetic fiber—rayon. But it was not the exclusive producer of rayon, and it never had the autonomy in pricing rayon that it was able to enjoy with its patented nylon. That is, as a product nylon was, at the time of its introduction, far from representative of du Pont's line. Unlike the other synthetic fibers du Pont produced, it did not in nylon face direct competition, and thus its pricing policy could be much more autonomous.

Commercial production of nylon began in 1939, but it was practically unavailable for general consumer use until after the Second World War; by 1953, however, production had expanded beyond

[77] While du Pont's total expenditures for "technical activities" in cellophane, 1924-50, were $24,361,065, they were, for example, only $471,374 against sales of $16 million in 1931, when the company was laying the groundwork for a strategic patent. 118 Fed.Supp.41,Finding 83.

Price History, du Pont Rayon and Nylon, 1945-55,
First Grade, Representative Deniers, and Packages

Date	RAYON						NYLON					
	75	100	150	300	1650	Staple	15	40	70	210	840	Staple
September 1, 1945	$ .88	$ .75	$ .55	$ .49	$ .43	$ .25	$6.50	$2.25	$1.75	$1.60	$ —	$1.50
November 12, 1946	.92	.80	.62	.54	.49	.30	—	—	—	—	—	—
February 4, 1947	.97	.85	.67	.55	.52	.34	—	—	—	—	—	—[a]
February 17, 1947	—	—	—	—	—	—	5.50	2.15	—	1.55	—	—
December 8, 1947	1.12	.95	.75	.60	.54	.37	—	—	—	—	—	—
September 10, 1948	1.12	.97	.77	—	—	—	6.00	2.25	1.90	1.65	—	1.60[b]
May 20, 1949	1.02	.89	.71	.57	—	.35	—	—	—	—	—	—
December 1, 1949	1.06	.93	.74	.59	—	—	—	—	—	—	—	—
February 3, 1950	—	—	—	—	—	—	—	—	—	—	—	1.70[b]
May 8, 1950	—	—	.76	.61	—	—	—	—	—	—	—	—
May 19, 1950	—	—	—	—	—	—	—	—	—	—	1.65	—
July 10, 1950	—	—	—	.63	—	—	—	—	—	—	—	—
July 29, 1950	—	—	—	—	.57	—	—	—	—	—	—	—
August 14, 1950	1.11	.97	.78	—	—	.38	—	—	—	—	—	—
September 27, 1950	—	—	—	—	.62	—	—	—	—	—	—	—
December 11, 1950	—	—	—	—	.61	.41	—	—	—	—	—	—
July 7, 1952	—	—	—	—	—	—	—	—	—	—	—	—
November 24, 1952	—	—	—	—	—	.37	—	—	—	—	—	—
May 11, 1953	1.09	.96	.78	.63	—	.34	—	—	—	—	—	—
February 1, 1954	—	—	—	—	—	—	—	—	—	—	1.48	1.50[c]
February 26, 1955	—	—	—	.68	—	—	—	—	—	—	—	—
March 7, 1955	—	—	.83	—	.64	—	—	—	—	—	—	—

[a] Nylon price reduction based on assumption of stability in labor and materials costs, which did not materialize.
[b] Price increase in recognition of higher labor and materials costs, with additional price raise for staple in February 1950; before development of a less costly process.
[c] Price decrease on 840 denier to pass on economies of improved production; on staple, to take account of economies in processing and to improve competitive position versus wool.

160 million pounds annually, representing an annual increase of about 10 million pounds.[78]

The schedule of list prices in the table on page 104 is for representative descriptions of rayon and nylon from the immediate postwar months to 1955. Each of these types goes into a number of uses, with quite different degrees of specialization. For example, a large percentage of rayon 1650 denier and nylon 840 denier goes into tires, nylon 15 denier goes into hosiery in major part but also significantly into tricot knitting and warp yarns, while nylon 70 denier is so widely used as to make difficult the selection of one representative application. Typical uses for the various types are as follows:

Rayon		Nylon	
75 Denier[79]	—Underwear fabrics	15 Denier	—Hosiery
100 Denier	—Dress fabrics	40 Denier	—Tricot underwear
150 Denier	—Linings	70 Denier	—Dress fabrics
300 Denier	—Upholstery and	210 Denier	—Industrial fabrics
	drapery	840 Denier	—Tires
1650 Denier	—Tires	Staple	—Sweaters, men's hose,
Staple	—Sports shirts		carpets, etc.

Denier is obviously a factor in cost per pound. The higher the denier the lower the manufacturing cost of synthetic yarns, due to the fact that both labor and investment per pound are sharply reduced as the output in pounds per machine is increased. Thus, a spinning machine running on 840 denier produces six times the poundage that the same machine produces when spinning 15 denier.

Following is a summary of an account provided by du Pont of the factors influencing nylon price policy over the period 1945-55:

1. This was a period of generally rising manufacturing costs. For example, there were no less than 17 general wage rate adjust-

---

[78] Rayon shipments were 1.9 million pounds per month in 1922 and 25.8 in 1936. (*Economic Almanac 1953-54,* pp. 410-11.) Rayon output in 1955 was almost ten times as large as nylon; during its first years, the rayon industry grew at an average rate of 14 to 15 million pounds annually.

[79] "Denier" is a measure of weight per unit length. It follows that the cross section measure of fiber size is related to denier only in terms of specific gravities of different fibers, *i.e.,* the "heavier" the fiber, the higher is the weight per unit length. A chart prepared for the trade shows denier versus diameter of the filament, for several fibers. Thus nylon 15 denier monofil becomes .00175 inches; 840 denier is .1325 inches.

ments at du Pont's Seaford nylon plant beginning September 1945; average hourly wage rate increased from $.94 to $2.00. Although the rise in wage rates at rayon plants was approximately parallel to the rise at the nylon plants rayon list prices, despite marked weaknesses in textiles after 1950, averaged at least 25 per cent higher than in 1945, while nylon prices remained steady or (as in the case of the 840 tire cord and staple), were undergoing an actual price decline.

2. To meet the market requirements of nylon customers after World War II, corresponding improvements were required in the quality of nylon, "with economic consequences for our customers analogous to price reductions because this improvement [has] permitted lower processing costs and higher yields of first-grade cloth." One example cited by the company was its effort to supply yarn of better quality for tricot knitting, which between 1947 and 1954 resulted in six successive simplifications of the knitting operation. Du Pont estimated "a total effect equivalent to about $.95 per pound of yarn processed."

3. The nylon yarn prices set prior to World War II necessarily involved an estimate of probable demand but they were not high enough in view of the general rise in prices that occurred after the war. Until 1953 there was a substantial market in resale of yarn initially purchased from du Pont. Volumes and prices can be cited only generally, but the company refers to multi-millions of pounds per year at premiums usually $1.00 per pound or more. The gray market was particularly high in 15 denier nylon which the company sold at $6.00 per pound but which was re-sold in large volume during this period at levels reaching $20 to $24 per pound. Particularly during the war scare in the 1950-51 market, any nylon quotation that attempted to reflect yarn price levels at resale would have meant a very sharp rise above the price quoted by the company.

4. With nylon supplies increasing over the years, nylon was appearing in volume-priced merchandise for many uses, even against competition from other fibers on which the list price was considerably lower. One principal reason for this is the fact that fiber price is only a small proportion of consumer price for garments or other items containing nylon, almost always less than 20 per cent and quite often less than 10 per cent. Another principal reason is that the performance characteristics of nylon often are so outstanding that consumers are willing to pay marginally higher prices for items containing nylon.

5. In the company's view there is little to suggest that the market

for nylon could be greatly broadened via price without reductions of severe and unrealistic magnitudes. Important exceptions to this rule occurred in particular instances, of which a significant example was 840 denier nylon for tire cord—a large market dominated by rayon but losing ground to nylon. Nylon 840 denier for this market was first made by combining four "ends" of 210 denier yarns and was sold at the same price as 210 denier, $1.65 per pound. Sufficient business developed to justify the development and installation of equipment to make 840 denier yarn. This equipment and the increased volume that resulted permitted cost reductions, which were reflected in a price decrease in 1954, aimed at further penetration of this market at the expense of rayon.

These factors explain the view of the company that the price history of nylon has been one of continuous decline in *real price*. Presumably, if the first ten years of nylon production had occurred in the 1920's and 1930's, as was the case with cellophane, similar price declines would have been shown for nylon; whereas a steady price with improvement in quality during a period of rising costs of equipment, materials, and wages, was the way in which the real price reductions in nylon were expressed.

In the last decade, the frequent changes in rayon prices are in contrast to the stability of du Pont prices for nylon.[80] This is to be expected from the fact that rayon, unlike nylon, which is still patented, had already attained the maturity of an established market in which a substantial number of firms directly participate and du Pont has a minor share.

Looking to the future in nylon pricing, it is assumed that there will be new entrants in the field of nylon production, following the expiration of basic patents in 1957, in addition to those that had been licensed under the patents.[81] The investment for economical produc-

---

[80] See table, p. 104.

[81] In a decree of the U.S. District Court for the Southern District of New York, July 30, 1952, du Pont was ordered to license its patents on nylon to all interested companies at reasonable royalty rates, and to make available the technical information required in making use of the patents. *United States v. Imperial Chemical Industries, du Pont et al.,* 100 Fed.Supp.504 (S.D.N.Y. 1951); decree in 105 Fed.Supp.215 (S.D.N.Y. 1952).

Between the issuance of the decree in 1952 and the end of the year 1956, ten companies entered the production of nylon under du Pont licenses, as follows:

tion of nylon makes it a capital-intensive venture. Moreover, the presence of other textiles above, below, and at the nylon price, makes it uncertain how far and how rapidly nylon will push forward to create new markets and expand at the expense of substitutes. It is not believed that many companies will enter the field in the near future. Du Pont will probably continue its leadership role in the development of nylon and in pricing it in accord with its appraisal of market potentials. In doing so it will face not only the continuing and progressively smarter competition of cotton and other natural fiber producers but also competition with producers of other synthetic fibers, including du Pont itself.[82]

Organic Chemicals

The products dealt with in the following discussion include certain organic chemicals, oxygen and other atmospheric gases, and various kinds of equipment and apparatus for utilizing the gases in the cutting, shaping, conditioning, heat-treating, and welding of metals. These are products of the Union Carbide Corporation (until recently the Union Carbide and Carbon Corporation) and of its Chemicals and Industrial Gases divisions.[83] The production processes of many of the products under discussion are closely interrelated; the technologies and markets of others are quite different. These differing characteristics are indicated in the different methods of pricing the products.

Allied Chemical & Dye Corporation, 1955; American Enka Corporation, 1954; Chemstrand Corporation (American Viscose and Monsanto), 1955; Dawbarn Brothers, Inc., 1954; Firestone Plastics Company, 1955; Industrial Rayon Corporation, 1954; National Plastic Products Company, 1955; North American Rayon Corporation (Beaunit Mills, Inc.), 1954; Poliafil, Inc., 1954; Polymers, Inc., 1954. *Chemical Week* (Apr. 20, 1957), pp. 126-28.

[82] For a comment on the relation of cellophane and nylon pricing to company policy in du Pont, see pp. 149 ff.

[83] The Chemicals Division is now the Union Carbide Chemicals Company; the Industrial Gas and Apparatus Division is the Linde Company.

The products under consideration include some four hundred synthetic organic chemicals produced by Union Carbide. Like all major chemical firms, Union Carbide produces most of its heavy chemical raw materials. The variety of products obtained from the chemical reactions involved may serve in turn as intermediates in any number of subsequent successive operations. For pricing purposes, account is taken of recovery of these joint products and by-products of chemical technology, the recovery of which is feasible only when large-scale operations make available at a single plant or facility sufficiently large quantities to justify recovery expense.

As a consequence of the high degree of mechanization of operations, the difficulty of assigning expenditures for research and development to individual products, and the unpredictable rate of physical deterioration and technological obsolescence of plant and equipment, no clear-cut basis for price setting is to be found in production costs. The many joint products emerging from any given process, piece of equipment, or research laboratory tend to make allocation of fixed costs a difficult procedure.

The chemical flow charts shown on pages 110-11 suggest the complexity of the problem of costing various products manufactured simultaneously in a single process or series of processes. These charts belong to a series prepared for costing the various components of ethylene production and the manufacture therefrom of such important derivatives as polyethylene (the versatile "squeeze bottle" plastic), ethylene glycol (antifreeze base and a raw material for low-freezing dynamites and synthetic resins), acetaldehyde (an intermediate in the production of DDT), and vinyl resin (for a variety of bonding, calendering, extruding, packaging, laminating, and molding materials). They indicate the various cost items involved in chemicals production (fuel, utilities, direct labor, raw and miscellaneous materials, auxiliary expense, and departmental overhead), and are used by the accounting and engineering departments in allocating costs. The chart summarizes the elements that enter into the costing of ethylene, one of the major olefins in the production of Union Carbide's organic chemicals.[84]

[84] Olefin is a term denoting the chemically reactive compounds ethylene and propylene, which are derived from natural gas by removing methane, cracking

Production of Ethylene, Polyethylene, Ethylene Oxide, Ethylene Glycol, and Vinyl Resin

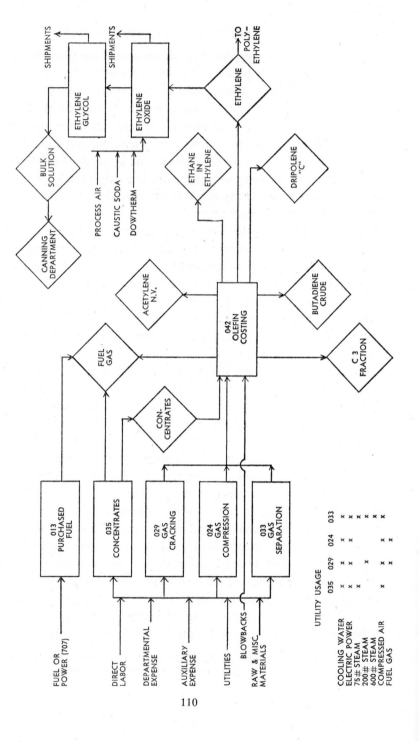

110

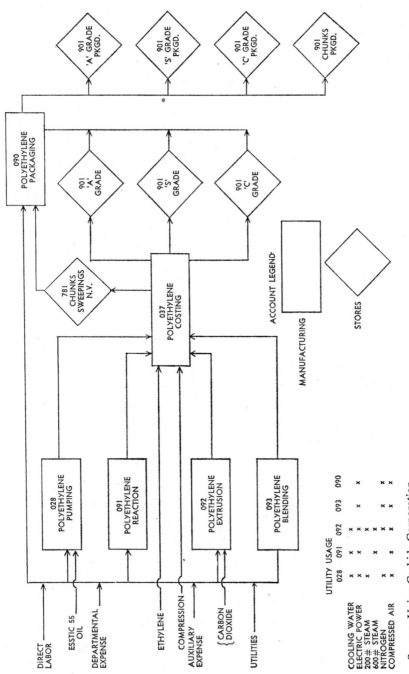

UTILITY USAGE

	028	091	092	093	090
COOLING WATER	x	x	x		
ELECTRIC POWER	x	x	x	x	x
200 # STEAM		x	x		
600 # STEAM	x		x		
NITROGEN	x	x	x	x	x
COMPRESSED AIR			x	x	x

Source: Union Carbide Corporation.

The point in the flow chart at which olefin costing (account 042) is shown represents an accounting "way station" at which the costs of the process up to that point are gathered for allocation to subsequent chemical processing.

Among the olefins used in further processing, ethylene appears to be the most important for Union Carbide. Ethylene is not only the basis of polyethylene (from which many plastics are derived) but, among other products, is also the basis for the production of ethylene oxide and ethylene glycol. Ethylene glycol is the essential ingredient of "Prestone" antifreeze, the most important end product in terms of sales of the Chemicals Division.[85]

The transfer cost within Union Carbide always includes, in addition to direct material and labor costs, a proportion of capital investment.[86] In cases involving common material and labor costs (as well as overhead and other non-separable costs) for several products, all such costs are generally allocated to each product according to its proportion of total physical volume.

It is apparent from the flow charts that there can be no precise basis for pricing these chemical products. The rule of thumb, markups, and margins used by Union Carbide vary with the product, depending upon such factors as newness of the product; prices of substitute materials; whether the item is a by-product or a principal product, an intermediate or an end product; and the nature of the competition on the item.

The problems of costing and pricing are somewhat eased by the

---

the residues, and separating the cracked products into refined materials. The main components found in natural gas are: methane (which accounts for more than 80 per cent of the ordinary natural petroleum gas), ethane, and propane. Methane is, for all practical purposes, the "natural gas" shipped through pipe lines to public utility companies. Ethane and propane are the raw materials from which the olefins, ethylene and propylene, are manufactured.

[85] Ethylene glycol represents the introduction (via ethylene oxide) of two hydroxyl groups to form $HOCH_2CH_2OH$. "Prestone" antifreeze contains some additives that improve the efficiency but do not change the basic antifreeze properties of ethylene glycol.

[86] With integrated companies like Union Carbide, transfer of material costs may also have to include a margin to conform with the price at which an intermediate product is sold to independent manufacturers downstream.

prevalence of one-year contracts to users of chemical products.[87] The presence of these contracts helps to simplify production scheduling and price setting by enabling the company to estimate its operating costs over the contract period. As a result, it is quite common for the company to hold prices steady—prices are guaranteed for ninety days by contract terms—unless competitors' actions interfere.[88]

The interplay of costing and market potentials in pricing chemical products can be seen in the following discussion of new products, and mature products.

NEW PRODUCTS

In pricing new chemical products, Union Carbide uses engineering estimates of expected costs at different volumes of production. With this information as a guide, the company frequently approaches potential customers to ascertain the volume of the new product that might be taken at various prices. The final determination of the introductory price may be guided by the desire to cover "full costs" at actual output rates, or a desire to stimulate sales. There is no general rule that can be applied to these situations: the prices of some products have been lowered to elicit volume sales, while on other products the company has waited for volume to increase substantially before lowering prices. The determination of a margin over cost is probably influenced in the first instance by the experience of the division with similar chemicals. The actual price may fall short of the ideal profit target if direct competition has to be met; if the product is unique, a price acceptable to the market may yield a return higher than the division's average.

[87] "Prestone" antifreeze, which is marketed by another division of the corporation through wholesale distributors, is the important exception.

[88] The chemical industry may be classed with those already noted in which leading customers are capable of manufacturing certain products themselves if they can do so at a cost appreciably below the prices they pay to suppliers—an element of potential competition that may affect the level of prices.

There have been numerous examples of new chemical products, or familiar products developed from synthetic processes, the prices of which have been reduced drastically, opening new areas of demand and making possible expanded output at progressively lower unit costs of production. Two examples cited by Union Carbide are propylene glycol, a solvent for food flavors, dentifrices, sulfa drugs, and Vitamin D, and triethanolamine, used today as an emulsifying agent for cosmetics and floor waxes, and a number of pharmaceutical products.

Triethanolamine was first introduced in 1926 at a price of $3.00 per pound to an interested drug firm—a test tube price. Within the year, the price was reduced to $2.00, on the strength of some improvements in production methods. Over the next two years, as production expanded with the tapping of new markets, the price was stepped down to 90 cents and later to 75 cents. By 1929, when mass production really got under way, the carload price was lowered to 55 cents. With an increase in production from 0.8 million pounds in 1930 to 4.4 millions in 1939, the price was further reduced to 17 cents per pound. Following wartime control at 20 cents, the price of triethanolamine rose to a high of 27 cents per pound (1950-52), from which it has since receded.[89] (See the chart on page 115.)

The price history of propylene glycol shows a similar pattern. Union Carbide explained that its policy was to reduce the price of the product in order to increase its market, and between 1936 and 1940 the price dropped from 28 cents to 12 cents a pound. The entry of Dow Chemical into the field by the time Union Carbide had established a market provided a competitive incentive to a further reduction in price by the latter company. There appear to have been two distinct periods of price reduction for this product. In the first period, 1936-41, the reduction was effected as a Union Carbide promotion, but in the 1952-54 period, a drop in price resulted from increased production by the industry generally. Union Carbide classifies this product as one that has reached the "milk business" stage of maturity—that is, with relatively settled volume and prices. (See the chart on page 116.)

[89] The price quoted as of May 1957 was 22 cents.

Prices and United States Production of Triethanolamine

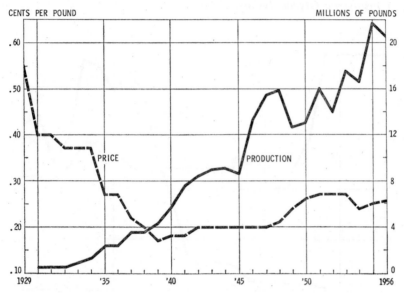

Source: Union Carbide Chemicals Company, Market Research Dept.

Union Carbide's experience with a chemical[90] first placed on the market in 1945 affords illustration of successive reductions in price as volume expanded and former customers entered into the production. The product was introduced at 55 cents a pound and had three customers, the largest of which took the bulk of the first year's output of 100,000 pounds. By 1947, industry sales amounted to 1.3 million pounds, and the price was lowered to 50 cents when competitive producers, including a former customer of Union Carbide, entered the market. In 1948, total production increased to 2.5 million pounds, and the price fell to 40 cents—close to the break-even point for Union Carbide, which was then utilizing only 20 per cent of its plant. The price held until the end of 1950, when it rose to 46 cents—a figure estimated by the company to be the break-even point at the current operating rates. In December 1951, a uniform delivered price of 47

[90] Identification withheld.

Prices and United States Production
of Propylene Glycol, Industrial Grade

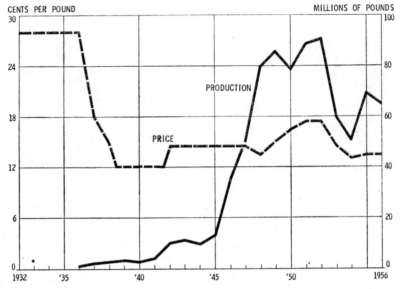

Source: Union Carbide Chemicals Company, Market Research Dept.

cents was adopted by Union Carbide. Increased production, greater realizations from by-products, and more efficient conversion processes brought the price down successively to 44 cents in 1953 and 40 cents in 1957, when production was at an annual rate of 15 million pounds.

MATURE PRODUCTS

The general stability of chemical product prices after the product has reached the mature stage of its life cycle is exemplified in the price curves of five products shown in the chart on page 117. These products were initially priced at introductory levels before settling down to the tank car prices shown in the chart. For example, ethylene glycol was priced at $1.00 per pound in 1922, which was higher than the

Tank Car Prices of Selected Chemicals, 1940-56[a]

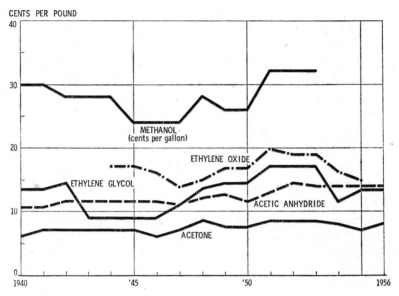

CENTS PER POUND

METHANOL
(cents per gallon)

ETHYLENE OXIDE

ETHYLENE GLYCOL

ACETIC ANHYDRIDE

ACETONE

1940   '45   '50   1956

[a] For data see App. Table 8.

price of glycerin with which it competed. Even though ethylene glycol had properties superior to glycerin, when it reached the commercial production stage, it had to be priced below cost in order to stimulate demand; the price was dropped to 27 cents a few years after introduction (to compete with glycerin at 20 cents) when cost was 35 cents. Within two years, sales increased sufficiently to lower costs to 25 cents, and at that point the price was also reduced to 25 cents. In 1941, with the entry of more and more producers into the field, the price was 12 cents per pound. Since the end of wartime controls, the price has fluctuated between 11½ cents and 18 cents.[91]

[91] The price career of ethylene glycol is not to be confused with that of Union Carbide's branded end product "Prestone" antifreeze, which has been sold over the past 25 years at the following prices per gallon:

May 1, 1933	$2.95	Jan. 31, 1948	$3.50
May 1, 1935	2.70	Jan. 15, 1951	3.75
April 17, 1937	2.95	April 1, 1954	2.95
April 1, 1939	2.65	Feb. 11, 1955	3.25

The prices of individual products, such as those given in the chart, reflect significant differences in margins over estimated cost, depending in part on the ability of other chemical companies to supply equivalents or near substitutes. In determining a "satisfactory return on investment" in the organic chemicals field, the management is conscious of the risks associated with rapid obsolescence and unpredictable deterioration of the plant.

As a raw material supplier with no control over end-product markets, the chemical producer, it was explained, must provide for the possibility that at any time some new product offering or process improvement may upset established positions in the market, thus making obsolete the plant facilities and equipment involved in their production.

A recent example of effects in this technological competition is acetone. Long a stable earner for the company, acetone dropped in price a half cent per pound (from 8½ cents to 8 cents) in April 1954, reflecting in part the impact of the slump of 1954, and portending the decline to follow. In November, the price broke to 7½ cents as a result of the disposal of a surplus of 50 million pounds of acetone (total annual industry production was about 477 million pounds), by three new producers of phenol by a process which yielded acetone as a by-product. The price reached 7 cents in February 1955 and in March 1956 recovered to 8 cents, the price in effect today. At this price, acetone yields a return that management regards as falling substantially below a reasonable return on chemicals.

As the foregoing examples have indicated, there is an identifiable "life cycle" associated with the pricing of chemical products. Union Carbide noted that most of its chemicals have gone through a "test tube price to tank carload price" period. In the case of triethanolamine, the period was about five years, but one year has been more typical among recent cases. Having probed the farthest reaches of demand, chemical products (*e.g.,* methanol, ethylene oxide, ethylene glycol, acetone, and acetic anhydride) tend to fall into a pattern of cost-plus pricing, some providing quite ample margins above average cost while others, exposed to aggressive competition, may have to be carried by the more profitable lines. Some of the oldest products, however, still rank among the most important in terms of profits as well as dollar volume.

Industrial Gases and Related Apparatus

The main products of the Linde Company—another principal division of Union Carbide—relate to the extraction of various gases from the air: oxygen, nitrogen, argon, and the rare gases helium, krypton, neon, and xenon, all of which have a great variety of industrial uses. The largest consumer is the metal industry (especially steel), which uses many of the gases for cutting, shaping, conditioning, heat-treating, and welding. In addition, Linde supplies numerous types of manual and automatic equipment for these operations.

OXYGEN

Linde's production of gas products, and of oxygen in particular, is essentially an extractive processing operation. Prices are based on standard costs determined from engineering estimates and experience cost curves at different rates of utilization. Generally speaking, the pricing of these products represents a range from low volume with relatively high margin (the rare gases) to the large volume and relatively low margin of the more widely used gases like nitrogen and oxygen.

Oxygen production has passed through several stages of technological development, and in the process costs, prices, and margins have been reduced as volume increased. Gaseous oxygen was first produced by Linde in one large plant and shipped to users in heavy containers

Oxygen Prices and Sales, Union Carbide Corporation, 1914-54

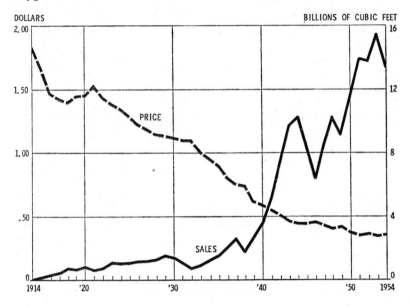

under pressure—twenty pounds of product in a 133-pound container.[92] While both the product and the art of using it effectively were new, the company found it necessary to sell "service" with the product. At this early stage, oxygen in gaseous form was sold in small quantities at a relatively high price. To stimulate volume, the company turned to a policy of relatively low margin and constructed small plants near points of heaviest use. By 1929 about one hundred were in operation, most of them with an annual capacity in the range of 1½ to 5 million cubic feet, with a few of around 10 million cubic feet. The price was lowered from around $1.80 per 100 cubic feet in 1914 to $1.13 in 1929. But transport and handling costs still constituted a large proportion of the final delivered price to users. (See accompanying chart.)

Heavy users of oxygen, especially the metal industries, pipeline

[92] The discussion of oxygen pricing refers to high purity oxygen, which is a product of bulk use. The company's oxygen, meeting U.S. pharmacopoeia standards, must have a purity of at least 99.5 per cent.

contractors, shipbuilders and railroads, found it inconvenient and costly to use the cylinder product. In 1932, after five years of experimental work, Linde met the problem of high transport and handling costs by developing a liquid oxygen distribution system. Linde produced liquid oxygen in large plants and later gasified it at the various sites near points of use. (Linde's Kittanning, Pennsylvania plant currently has a capacity of over 450 million cubic feet per month.) Industry found this liquid oxygen system much easier to handle and less costly; as a result some important new uses were developed (*e.g.*, conditioning of steel), and consumption generally increased. Reductions in price continued through the 1930's into the Second World War. After four decades (1914-54), during which several important technological changes occurred, the price of oxygen was steadily lowered to 35 cents per 100 cubic feet, down 81 per cent from the 1914 figure.

The major volume of Union Carbide's (Linde) oxygen sales is direct to large users, although the sale of oxygen in cylinders by Linde distributors is of prime importance for small user accounts.[93]

In preparing an industrial gas product price schedule such as that for oxygen, the company considers the following items which go into standard costs:

Plant Cost. Normally, plant cost is determined from previous operating experience modified by engineering estimates.

[93] A leading factor in the postwar continuation of price reduction has been the increasing scale of oxygen use, particularly by steel companies seeking to increase with oxygen the steel output of their furnaces. The economies of scale are notable when supplying oxygen—particularly so when cylinder oxygen (in containers 8 times the weight of the compressed gas) is supplanted by oxygen piped into the consumer's plant.

Quite recently Union Carbide has moved to a new development in oxygen sales, relying on a combination of gaseous oxygen generated on the consumer's grounds for basic supply, with liquid oxygen supplied for supplementary requirements.

The pricing of oxygen is thus intimately associated with the types of facilities for generating and distributing oxygen which can be set up for a given type of consumer. This is an area in which a new competition of processes and corresponding unit costs has developed. An example of the fluidity of the situation is the offering by other companies of relatively mobile oxygen generating equipment, which is purchased by consumers who then proceed to make rather than to buy.

Distribution Expense. Distribution costs are of major importance when a product is sold on a delivered-price basis.

Experimental and Research Costs. These costs are generally relatively high with a new product and are given consideration on a forecast basis rather than at the high initial costs. In the case of established products, the research laboratory program is usually fairly well stabilized, and costs thus can be considered on a current or historical basis.

Selling Expense. The company charges selling costs in one of two ways, depending on conditions of sale. In cases where specialists are selling one product, actual expense is readily determined; where salesmen are selling a variety of products, the allocation is made on the basis of time studies.

On established products, the company finds it relatively easy to estimate selling expense by either of the two methods indicated. On new products, however, initial marketing costs are much like initial research: the company makes its estimate or projection of such costs as of the time when the product is established in the market rather than the high initial costs.

Depreciation. Depreciation allowances are determined from engineering estimates of equipment and installation costs using established depreciation rates.

General Overhead. Auxiliary, Administrative, and General Expense is usually assigned by taking a flat percentage of all other costs.

Profit Margin. The margin added to the above costs is estimated on the basis of expected return on *total utilized investment.* The determination of the desired return is commonly related to the age of products: in an old established market which is highly competitive the margin is largely governed by the competition, whereas in relatively new products, the initial return is normally higher than the average for established products.

GAS APPARATUS

In conjunction with the sale of industrial gases, Linde also sells various kinds of apparatus (and supplies), including oxy-acetylene equipment (welding and cutting machines), blowpipes, regulators, acetylene generators, welding rods, fluxes, etc., for use in welding, cutting, metal conditioning and flame-treating. These products constitute about 10 per cent of Linde's annual sales volume. The number of competitors in this trade ranges from one or two in some lines to around fifty in others. In marketing these products, Linde must rely to a large extent on direct personal selling, backed by the company's long record of technological leadership in this field.

In several important respects the manufacture and sale of apparatus items present a definite contrast to the chemical and industrial gas products discussed earlier: (1) apparatus sales include few items selling in large volume;[94] (2) many different production set-ups and breakdowns are involved; (3) prices of items sold run from a low of $.05 to a high of $15,000; and (4) extensive use is made of resale outlets.

In building prices for apparatus products, Linde normally begins with standard costs at an assumed rate of plant utilization of 90 per cent, i.e., "Unit Factory Cost" including material, direct labor, and other direct factory costs. On new products, engineering cost estimates are used as a base until standards have been established. All other costs are added using an allocation formula based upon certain fixed percentages of "Unit Factory Cost." (See table on page 124.) Thus, each product carries a proportionate share of all indirect costs, which added to direct costs yield total, or full, costs. A provisional or target price is then derived by adding a standard percentage markup to the total costs, called the total breakeven cost.

At sales levels such as to utilize factory capacity efficiently—about 90 per cent—the average turnover (sales per dollar of investment) in the gas apparatus lines is fairly constant at slightly below 100 per cent. Thus, for product pricing purposes per cent return on sales can be taken as almost equal to return on investment.

Following the usual standard-cost logic, prices are normally maintained at the formula levels, subject to modifications imposed by the market for a particular product. Variances from standard cost are examined monthly and are taken up with production and engineering only when they exceed 10 per cent of standard. Standard costs are revised whenever there are consistent variances of 10 per cent or more

[94] On the larger pieces of equipment (e.g., an automatic plate-welding machine), sales volume is in the range of 200 to 5,000 units per year.

Price-Cost Analysis, Representative Apparatus Products, Linde Company (Union Carbide Corporation)[a]

Cost Item	Product "X"		Product "Y"	
	Dollars	Per Cent	Dollars	Per Cent
Unit factory cost (material, direct labor and factory expense)...............	$6.11	100.0	$9.50	100.0
Allocated share of factory tooling costs.	.336	*5.5	.523	5.5
Allocated share of cost variance, idle plant capacity and instruction literature.........................	.208	3.4	.323	3.4
Total plant cost................	6.654	108.9	10.346	108.9
Life adjustment allowance............	.104	1.7	.161	1.7
Experimental cost allocated..........	.297	4.9	.465	4.9
Research cost allocated..............	.033	.5	.047	.5
Distribution expense allocated........	.733	12.0	1.140	12.0
Selling expense allocated.............	2.030	33.2	3.150	33.2
Auxiliary expense (accounting and credit) allocated...................	.214	3.5	.332	3.5
Administration and general expense....	.324	5.3	.504	5.3
Standard depreciation..............	.269	4.4	.418	4.4
Total cost and expense (breakeven)	10.658	174.4	16.563	174.4
Markup........................	b	b	b	b
Target price...................	—	—	—	—

[a] While standard markup and target price were not given, actual base price in effect February 1, 1957 was:

Product "X," $12.50 (in lots of 50 units, $11.25)
Product "Y," $22.50 (in lots of 50 units, $20.25)

[b] Not available from Union Carbide.

from actual costs and whenever labor, material, and other direct costs change.

The foregoing discussion of price formation in two of Union Carbide's principal operating divisions can only suggest the variety of pricing situations found in the many segments of the corporation. Chemicals, on the one hand, evidenced no clear-cut cost bases for pricing primarily because of the complex joint- and by-product production processes. In pricing new chemicals, the company has sometimes selected an introductory price entailing initial losses as a means of stimulating consumption to the point of profitable operation, while in other cases the company has relied on a standard cost base from the beginning, allowing for subsequent successive reductions consistent with lowering of unit costs and realization of the company's estimate of reasonable return. Mature product pricing takes over at the other end of the life cycle—a pattern of fairly stable pricing in which competition can be met at a market figure that makes the investment productive enough to justify continuance of expansion.

On the other hand, industrial gases—where costs are more easily determined—have tended toward low-unit profit and high-volume sales in pricing to achieve the division's "normal" return. Gas apparatus pricing appears to lend itself readily to the standard-cost approach.

In the preceding discussion, we have examined specific situations in which products were priced, giving only the background on company behavior that appeared absolutely necessary to understand the pricing of the given product. These product case studies constitute no more than an introduction to company behavior in the field of pricing—an attempt to set forth what has been done in pricing a representative group of products among those sold by the companies under consideration. These surveys were, as closely as possible, reproductions of company statements of the decisions and the influences bearing on them, yet circumscribed narrowly to the particular product and price. To a degree, this concentration excluded consideration of other influences that bear on pricing, which will receive heavier emphasis in the next chapter on company policies.

The justification for the approach followed, apart from the fact that everything cannot be examined at once, is that some awareness of the pricing of particular products seems indispensable to an understanding of the broader areas of company attitudes, habits, rules, folklore, and principles bearing on and influencing pricing. Our interest in the products and their pricing stems from the fact that they are marketed by these corporations, and the center of our attention is inevitably with the company, the product-price behavior being merely one illustration of the behavior of the large company. In the following chapter, the perspective widens; we focus on our primary concern with price as an instrument of company policy, and deal with the nature of the products as an influence in the making of the policy.

2 / *Company Pricing Policy*

IN THE FOLLOWING DISCUSSION, emphasis is not on description of product pricing in given market situations but on pricing attitudes and habits of the large corporations included in this study. An attempt will be made to generalize with regard to the companies on which material has been made available. In many cases, generalizations must be made on the basis of statements on price policy by company officers, on other less specific price information, or on information not available for a sufficient time span to justify separate treatment. The policy summaries are intended to provide such insight as the material can yield into the way in which the product and market characteristics, combined with attendant characteristics of the company,[1] can affect company thinking about pricing. The discussion attempts, in effect, to view the corporate personality as reflected in its pricing.[2]

The analysis recognizes that a company statement of policy is not necessarily an accurate representation of how the policy works in practice. In some cases, there is an almost complete absence of anything that could be cited as the price policy of the company, other than that of following a market. Nevertheless, a classification is attempted that takes account of company characteristics beyond their common feature as leading companies in their fields. The classification is admittedly imprecise, and in some cases it serves mainly to demonstrate the inadequacy of monolithic classification. Yet, these large companies, by virtue of the fact that they are organizations with a

[1] Investment policies, size of firm, actual or desired position in the industry, diversity or concentration of products, etc.

[2] The administrative organization of the companies, with respect to pricing, is discussed in the following chapter.

past and a future and a line of authority, in which decisions are made against a background of precedent, and which are subject to review by designated individuals or committees, tend to fall into identifiable categories. Cost behavior (though, of course, this also is subjective in part), relationships with rivals, and the general marketing pattern, with its techniques of distribution and varying possibilities of using substitute products, also exert pressure on the company organization and thus have both direct and indirect influence on price behavior.

There are distinctions to be made between companies with a single product, or a dominant product, and those with a wide variety of products; between those selling to customers of the same general type, as Johns-Manville sells to building supply dealers, or Sears to the ultimate consumer, and those which, like du Pont and General Electric, sell to producers and to distributors in many markets.

To reduce these diversities to manageable proportions and to bring out the similarities that inevitably appear in corporate policy, the following classifications will be used to identify the most frequently encountered company policies: (1) pricing to achieve a target return on investment; (2) stabilization of price and margin; (3) pricing to maintain or improve market position; (4) pricing to meet or follow competition; and (5) pricing subordinated to product differentiation. At the risk of repetition, it should be stressed that these policies were the ones mentioned most frequently by company officials in discussing pricing along with production, investment, and other aspects of company policy. Though each of the companies is assigned primarily to one of the classifications, it would be absurd to pretend that all price making by any one company was ruled by a single policy. Even so, the predominance of one of the five is quite marked in most of the organizations surveyed, and discussion along these lines helps not only to bring out major policy goals but also to provide a benchmark for appraising the deviations.

An obvious alternative to using the foregoing classification would be to take profit maximization as the overriding goal of corporate pricing and follow the familiar view that other long-run objectives and their variation from firm to firm simply reflect the fact that different companies, in dissimilar industries, cannot use identical means to achieve the same ultimate objective. But, in order to be operationally useful, the concept of profit maximization needs to be so broadened, in the context of company practices, that it becomes more a concept of optimum satisfaction. This is largely subjective. For instance, management may deliberately subordinate the spread between costs and selling price to a wide variety of more definite and immediate goals to which pricing policies are related.

In the case of a new product to which the public must be educated, and on which there is a seventeen-year span of patent protection, maximization of profits may be represented by a pricing program that attempts to recoup development costs and to educate the public to the use of the new item. Such a program could provide within a company a basis for either a continuing and even spectacular growth to which the limits are not visible (*e.g.*, cellophane), or a build-up to what is seen as the probable maximum volume that can be maintained with continuing confidence at what is deemed an acceptable profit level (*e.g.* nylon). In the case of some of the consumer appliances, the price may be one that the company sets with a heavy weighting of development costs, if it is the pioneer, or a due regard for improvement costs, if it is seeking greater differentiation in a fluid competitive area. In this situation, however, the problem of dealerships and distributor margins may become so important that the maintenance of active reliable outlets to move the product becomes crucial in determining the price level as well as the product requirements.

In the case of an integrated firm, moreover, there may be a price policy that puts less stress on the rate of profit at the primary production stage, regarding that only as a base from which to move into more profitable fields of further processing. The maximization of profits in this situation may be considered in terms of the total target return for the company against its total investment. This approach makes for an emphasis on covering cost, plus what might be the equivalent of a service charge on value added, at the primary material stage, with varying emphasis on maximization for products at successive stages of fabrication. There may also be the kind of price averaging found in meatpacking, in which the packer must determine the best possible adjustment to the conditions of uncertainty that exist in livestock purchase. Here, the return on investment may serve as a goal, the profit being an average of various rates depending on the product and the vagaries of consumer demand.

In attempting to achieve the maximum satisfaction of the company's community of interests, one company will aim at stability, another will seek to expand its market share, or to engage in continuous discovery and pre-emption of new fields, while others will be content to meet competition, to satisfy a set target, or to aim at combinations and variations of these objectives, to the realization of which the pricing policies are designed to contribute.

For the most part, the companies doubted that by changing their pricing policies they could raise their profits in the long run. In any event, the possibility of change is limited by their broader objectives. For pricing must conform to a company policy that represents an order of priorities among a number of objectives rather than to any simple concept of profit maximization. With so many variables influencing business behavior, however, no single price policy is likely to hold good for all market situations. Differing market situations give rise to a variety of goals that serve to determine price action. But it is axiomatic that, whatever the failure to maximize profits in the conventional sense, profit-making is the guiding principle among all the companies in the sample.

Pricing to Achieve a Target Return on Investment

Target return on investment was probably the most commonly stressed of company pricing goals. The role of the target return in companies producing a wide variety of products for a wide variety of markets is notably different from its function in shaping the price structure of companies that concentrate their efforts on producing a dominant product. Differences also appear between the companies having a staple line supplemented by sharply distinguished new products appearing from time to time and those that place no particular emphasis on bringing forth new products.

GENERAL MOTORS CORPORATION

The pricing pattern of the dominant product of General Motors has been duplicated in practically all the end products coming off its assembly lines. The automobile, the diesel locomotive, the major appliance are not subject to continuous price fluctuation. The products are engineered and styled by the company. Several of them undergo, as does the automobile, periodic style change; hence it is practicable for GM to enunciate and follow a standard-cost-plus pricing system. Yet there is much more to the company's price decisions than mere reliance on standard cost. Among the factors that exert a powerful influence on the price decisions for a given model are: (1) last year's price; (2) new features, and the extent to which they have been built into the car, and are therefore not "extra" in a real sense, and their relative profitability; (3) price of the closest rival (presumably outside the corporation);[3] (4) unit cost (not including profit) at the volume it is estimated can be marketed. This volume must be estimated before the price is selected.

The new model price is of great importance to the corporation, for upon it largely depends the realization of the hoped for sales volume. But it is impossible to arrive at it by a mathematical formula, or even by

[3] It must also be assumed that prices for the GM automotive line are built up from a series of price layers for the respective car divisions—Oldsmobiles cannot be out of line with Buicks, nor Buicks with Cadillacs, nor Cadillacs with Pontiacs—though it is not known whether the company makes any systematic attempt to find out what income strata each particular model may be expected to appeal to nor the impact of prices or price changes on these buyers; it is apparently content to rely on general statements by a sample of consumers about their car-buying intentions.

reliance on the firm's standard-cost doctrine. Pressed to explain the price of a model in any particular year, the corporation officers fall back on the assertion that pricing—particularly of a model for which the market has yet to be proved—is, after all, an art, not a science. On the other hand, characteristic of firms with a dominant product and a standard cost system, is the crucial importance, prior to selection of the price, of estimating standard-costs for alternative designs. Thus, in spite of the company's point that there is no certainty in the final price determination, there is, reportedly, a vast amount of estimating the cost of proposed changes before arriving at a decision on the model change. Moreover, suggestions of engineers for improvements, sometimes of a minute kind, are frequently rejected because of the limits to maneuver, at least once the cost-price projection has been decided. This rigidity of costing discipline prevails even though the corporation has been realizing over the past decade a profit above its target for return on investment.

The record is especially worth noting in connection with the point that GM management regards price in the low-price field as a major element of competition, and that here it has been enjoying a price advantage over its principal rivals. It would appear that GM pricing, kept at hold-the-line levels into 1948, thereafter became in effect a kind of umbrella pricing. The situation suggested that if the total automobile market dropped substantially below the current level of sales, General Motors, pricing independently, stood in a position to increase its market share up to the limit of its capacity. When these assumptions were put to several officials of the company, they had difficulty in understanding the problem, and when they did, were inclined to treat it as something most improbable. What GM would do in these circumstances can only be guessed.[4]

---

[4] The kind of dilemma in which GM finds itself in pricing its automobiles is suggested by a recent testimony of President Curtice before the Senate Banking and Currency Committee:

"The Chairman: . . . The sole question here is, that here was an opportunity to expand your market if you so desired. You had $192 million, you might say, to play with. But you choose to carry all of that in the net profit and to

General Motors' pricing is also affected by its relationships with its dealers. Since it is able to offer what is clearly for them, over the long run, a profitable relationship, it has an advantageous bargaining position with its distributors. They can be induced to take and sell a larger number of vehicles than many of them might have ordered on their own initiative. For long-run policy reasons GM has decided to limit the number of dealerships it awards, thus conveying to the dealers an unknown but nonetheless sizable increment of market advantage.[5] The company in turn is in a position to withdraw part of the fruits of this advantage from time to time—*e.g.,* by putting more dealers into rapidly expanding territories.

---

devote none of it to obtaining a wider market to increase your sales. You will admit that the normal procedure is, if you lower prices you will sell more of nearly any article in a competitive market. Is that not true?

"Mr. Curtice: The lower the price the more you sell, if the product you are offering at a lower price has a field.

"Mr. Chairman: That is granted. But you did not choose to lower prices.

"Mr. Curtice: Yes. In effect we lowered prices because we did not increase the prices with the greatly enhanced value that was built into the cars.

"The Chairman: . . . Do you really desire to have 60 per cent of the market?

"Mr. Curtice: As I pointed out in my brief, we have to keep aggressively competitive in all areas in order to make sure of maintaining even our position.

"The Chairman: That is not what I asked you. I asked if you would like to have 60 per cent of the motor car market or not?

"Mr. Curtice: We have no control over the public's approval of the products we offer.

"The Chairman: No, but you can tell me whether or not you would like it, regardless of what it has to do with the public. There is nothing to prevent you from saying yes or no. It is a simple question. Would you like 60 per cent?

"Mr. Curtice: I would answer this way: We would hope to continue to be a successful corporation.

"The Chairman: Would you like 55 per cent of total sales?

"Mr. Curtice: We might very well get 55 per cent, but it will be very difficult to achieve.

"The Chairman: But it will be against your will and better judgment?

"Mr. Curtice: No." *Stock Market Study,* Hearings before the Senate Banking and Currency Committee on Factors Affecting the Buying and Selling of Equity Securities, 84 Cong. 1 sess. (1955), pp. 830-31.

[5] The value this franchise can have is indicated by the 87.2 per cent return on net worth that the dealers attained in 1946, or 98.5 in 1947.

The control of the dealer organization, which provides the company with an assured market that is ordinarily not in a position to question the given prices, simplifies the company's pricing problem. It is essential to the planning of General Motors, under present procedures, that it be able to count on receiving the price for the current season; otherwise the careful cost calculations that determine the changes in the model would be wasted. If the company itself owned the retail outlets the same result might be reached; but this would require heavy investment and, given the flexibility required at the retail level to maintain a high level of volume, would put an almost impossible burden on GM's management.

Although General Motors uses its standard cost standard volume system to determine an allowable cost for each year's model, the connection between this cost and the final price is tenuous. For instance, the management has since 1945 realized returns in excess of its avowed range of 15-20 per cent on invested capital. It speaks of this as an over-absorption of burden but shows no disposition currently to cut it by reducing the price of the car to the dealer.[6] The target return goal did, however, in 1946-48, have sufficient weight to prevent the company from raising its prices to levels that would have given it instead of the dealers the extraordinary windfall profits of those years.

While there is much to show that the views General Motors developed in its automobile business were carried over to its other lines, each has characteristics of its own, particularly on the importance of the periodic style change. Appliances do not have such a notable style change as the passenger automobiles. The diesel locomotives have in fact resisted style changes, putting the primary emphasis on engineering efficiency.[7]

The role of the company return in the pricing of parts and accessories is obscured in part by the fact that the dealer's discount from the suggested retail prices of accessories and parts is much larger than from

---

[6] Since the dealers enjoy some degree of monopoly advantage as General Motors agencies, such a move might, of course, simply swell dealer profits.

[7] Having developed what it believed to be a product that could be mass produced, the company is said to have refused to make alterations in the introductory model, even to clinch a prospective first sale to the Santa Fe.

the suggested price of the automobile itself. This may be because there is keen price competition from independent parts manufacturers; it may be because GM has set a higher retail price, in terms of return on the investment, and is prepared to give the dealers a larger discount.

In general, it may be concluded that the nature of the product, purchased from what the company calls "supernumerary income," plays a decisive role in the pricing of the principal product of General Motors. The nature of the public's demand for new cars—as the abandonment of the Ford Model T demonstrated—is such that an automobile can be regarded as too cheap, and fail to find customers. Thus, the range of possible prices is not wide; and this, in turn, limits the cost. In a broad sense, the public may be said to be indicating what it wants as to content, quality, and cost. The combination of the company's techniques, the fading of several competitive makes, the size of postwar supernumerary income, and consumer concentration on automobiles as a way of life, has enabled GM to achieve and at times exceed its "target" return. The "target" develops out of the characteristics of the firm, its dominant product, and the market. A noteworthy aspect of the marketing relates to the substantial share of the suggested consumer price allocated to the dealer—a margin he can manipulate as the retail trading requires. Apparently General Motors believes that this arrangement—with the dealers responsible for holding inventory and the company, through GMAC, assured of a continuous flow of safe income from retailing of automobiles—is preferable to a full sharing of the problems of direct marketing.

INTERNATIONAL HARVESTER COMPANY

International Harvester has been referred to in this study as a farm implements manufacturer, although it might more accurately be designated as a general farm and construction machinery, motor truck, and equipment producer. Agricultural equipment sales still constitute a heavy proportion of total company sales, although other lines have become increasingly important in the company's product mix.[8] The company points out that it originally entered into the production of the machinery and equipment lines (including trucks and construction equipment) to serve the needs of the farm market; it branched out as new markets developed. In reaching out to these product markets, the company has learned that price policies that have been very effective for many years in farm implements may be neither appropriate nor effective in other product lines.

Policy Objectives and Degree of Price Authority. International Harvester's general approach to pricing is found in a combination of several major objectives not all of which may be fully compatible. The company's price policy is designed to realize a target return on investment of around 10 per cent, after taxes; it strives to maintain the reputation of manufacturing high quality products incorporating advanced engineering features; and, while the company is growth-minded, it "would prefer not to have so large a share that it would control price without regard to competition."

As in the case of General Motors, International Harvester uses a standard cost technique, to provide a foundation for realizing its target return over the years. It was able to realize its target during the first half of the postwar decade (1947-56) but has been substantially under the target rate in each of the last five years. Sales per dollar of investment have increased, as compared with the prewar period. This may be seen from the relative position of return on sales and on invested capital shown in the table below. The reduced ratio of net profits to sales would therefore suggest that the lower profit margins are a result of increasing competition.

The nature of International Harvester's products, sold under condi-

---

[8] In 1956, total sales were distributed as follows:

1. Motor trucks, service parts and service .... 45.8 per cent
2. Farm tractors and service parts 14.4
3. Farm implements and service parts 14.6
4. Industrial power equipment and parts 16.6
5. Refrigeration products and parts 6
6. Steel, pig iron, and coke by products 4.8
7. Baler and binder twine 8
8. Special defense products 2.4

Net Profits after Federal Income Taxes,
International Harvester Company, 1903-56

Year	Net Profits as Percentage of	
	Sales	Capital Investment
1903–1911..........................	13.3	7.4
1912–1921..........................	8.4	6.2
1922–1931..........................	8.8	7.2
1932–1941..........................	7.8	5.0
1942–1945..........................	4.9	5.8
Average 43 years................	7.9	6.1
1947...............................	6.54	10.63
1948...............................	5.89	11.37
1949...............................	6.74	11.85
1950...............................	7.08	10.86
1951...............................	4.93	9.66
1952...............................	4.62	6.15
1953...............................	4.14	6.48
1954...............................	3.65	4.45
1955...............................	4.76	6.58
1956...............................	3.96	5.76

tions very different from those of General Motors, perhaps explains the company's relative lack of price authority, which in turn is shown in the low target return. It has agency dealers and company stores, but they face a greater number of competing dealers than do those of General Motors, for example. In purchases of trucks—the largest single source of income to the company—farm tractors, and equipment and machinery, consumers are motivated largely by considerations of profitable use, not emulation, so that shifts among makes from year to year and variations in the total amount of purchases from one firm appear to be potentially greater than those in the passenger car field. The continuous pressure to improve efficiency, under which International Harvester labors, is very different from the style race in automobiles. The latter market permits greater latitude in introducing changes; it also allows the manufacturer to devise a greater range of appealing variations in color, horsepower, etc., none of which is limited solely by the sober calculations of a business buyer in the product area of International Harvester.

It might be argued that, despite the limited opportunity for product differentiation to support price differentials, International Harvester should have been able to exercise more pricing authority at least in farm equipment, in which it has marked seniority. The company is quite conscious of its tradition of leadership. It led the effort in 1947 to help prevent inflation of farm equipment prices by lowering prices in the face of impending cost increases; more often, it has been followed by the industry in price increases. At the same time, it is aware of the continuous pressure of competitors (including short-line companies like New Idea and New Holland) not only in copying International Harvester, but even in introducing improved engineering features that it must duplicate.[9] Thus, International Harvester is pricing certain products in which the opportunity to achieve a marked differential on the basis of superior mechanical features is limited by the readiness of competitors to match the company's offerings, in part or all of the line. It is particularly limited in the differential it can charge over lines with fewer refinements, because of the farmer's primary interest in cost and basic utility.

In other products, such as light trucks, earthmoving equipment, and refrigeration products (produced until late 1955), the company has not attained acknowledged leadership in price or in setting standards of style and quality. In the truck field, its proportion of the business varies substantially with the gross weight of trucks.[10] Competition in light trucks finds the company at a substantial cost disadvantage vis-à-vis

---

[9] The stress on leadership in the continuous improvement of quality and performance through advanced engineering at times has forced the company to absorb losses lest its leadership be lost. For example, in the case of the utility tractor it was said that International Harvester, to maintain its prestige, was under pressure to match or better the product of a competitor.

[10] The company estimate of output for 1950 was as follows:

Class of Vehicle	Market Share (Per cent)
Heavy-heavy (26,000 lbs. and over)	12
Heavy (19,501—25,999 lbs.)	30
Medium-Heavy (16,001—19,500 lbs.)	27
Light-heavy (14,401—16,000 lbs.)	18
Light (5,000 lbs. or less)	5

the automobile companies, which can use on trucks—especially light trucks—many components (frames and other collaterals) of their passenger lines.

It seems quite clear that in light trucks International Harvester has not gained enough volume to permit it to compete on a cost basis with the automobile manufacturers. The company has been following along as best it could with the product and price policies of the larger producers, accepting a comparatively low return and a small share of the markets involved. Since 1955, however, it has apparently embarked on a new and bolder penetration of the small truck market with a number of advanced models (the S- and A-lines) using both gasoline and liquid petroleum fuels.[11]

In the field of heavy trucks, however, International Harvester has been very successful. It has enjoyed a broad market for heavy-duty trucks far beyond farming needs—in industrial, transport, mining, construction, and other earthmoving uses. Thus, the company has been acquiring a leadership position in the heavy truck market comparable with that which it has enjoyed in farm equipment.[12]

Withdrawal from Refrigeration Equipment Field. The experience with refrigeration equipment illustrates the difficulties International Harvester encountered in attempting to integrate the pricing practices of the appliance industry with policies that it had successfully employed over many years in its principal product lines—in effect, the

[11] For confirmation of this new line of attack, see International Harvester Company, *Annual Report, 1955,* p. 9 and *1956,* pp. 13, 14.

[12] Some divisional heads acknowledged price leadership in certain products (*e.g.,* fiber and twine—though foreign producers evidently have not recognized the company's leadership); others regarded such leadership as a myth. Between the extremes were those who believed it highly doubtful, by and large, that competitors would follow International Harvester in a price increase in present circumstances, although, in the same circumstances they would undoubtedly follow it in a decrease.

It was also acknowledged that the company's price announcements on certain items are among the first. It was emphasized, however, that the "unseen leadership" of certain specialty short-line companies cannot be ignored.

It is probably not incorrect to observe that International Harvester is the leader in farm equipment and heavy duty trucks, but that in light trucks it follows the automobile manufacturers, and in construction equipment, it follows Caterpillar.

problem of a producers' goods specialist adjusting to production for a consumers' goods market. The company had entered into the production of freezers, and later refrigerators, as an outgrowth of its manufacture of milk coolers. At one time, it enjoyed approximately half of the national home freezer market. However, on home refrigerators, International Harvester never attained the volume that, given its cost structure, would have made that end of the refrigeration business profitable. It is clear that the company was not able to price refrigerators in terms of its general target, but found it necessary to accept the industry price structure and concentrate on production costs.[13]

As it became more difficult to reconcile International Harvester's insistence on a certain quality-durability approach with the industry price structure for refrigerators, it was evident that the profits on freezers could not carry the refrigerator business indefinitely. Accordingly, in December 1955, the Company discontinued refrigerator production after consummating the sale of its Evansville, Indiana plant to the Whirlpool-Seager Corporation. The annual report of the company explained:

> Studies which the Company had made pointed clearly to the conclusions that it was advisable either to invest large sums of capital to develop a line of other appliances or to get out of the [refrigeration] business. The Company's management and its Board of Directors decided, therefore, to quit the refrigeration business after these studies had convinced them that the capital therein employed could be more profitably used in other lines of our business.[14]

The withdrawal of International Harvester from the refrigeration field may have resulted in part from the inflexibility of its standard cost pricing in a market where products are priced at a conventional figure, and cost is tailored accordingly. The reasons may also go back to the traditional philosophy of the Company of manufacturing prod-

---

[12] For example, International Harvester attempted to sell refrigerators on a mill-base price, but finding itself unable to meet the competition, it was forced to follow the trade custom of a uniform national price with metropolitan distributors, and with special discounts and allowances for advertising and promotional purposes.

[14] *Annual Report, 1955*, p. 13.

ucts for the farm and the farmer with durability as a primary consideration. The refrigerator was originally regarded by the company as a piece of farm equipment rather than a stylized piece of kitchen furniture. The company realized that, in order to remain in the refrigeration field on a profitable basis, it would be necessary to reach out to the mass consumer market by developing other lines of appliances. This, in turn, would mean the adoption of a different kind of pricing and distributing system and the production of a product differing from what it wanted to make and was accustomed to making. The company, therefore, decided the price was too high in terms of capital and management resources.

International Harvester has developed a pricing policy adaptable to the progressive diversification of its lines. In the discussion of farm machine pricing in the previous chapter, it was noted that the company's target return approach was modified for special competitive situations, particularly those encountered in service parts, with acceptance of incremental returns rather than profits based on full costs. On government orders, also, the company has modified its full-cost targets to take account of the elimination of selling and administrative costs on large volume. The renewed efforts to carry light and medium trucks may likewise tend to shade the company's prices below target levels, at least until a full line has been firmly established, with the company emerging as a low-cost producer. In the process of readjusting its total product mix and meeting strong competitors in a price-conscious market, the policy of maintaining a company-wide target return has been subjected to significant modifications.

In many ways, like other companies studied, International Harvester pays the price of bigness and leadership. The fact that the company's earnings have declined in recent years in consonance with the decline in farm income, reflects among other things the high income elasticity (as against low price elasticity) of the farm equipment demand. It also reflects the narrow area within which the company can maneuver in setting prices. On the one hand, it is no longer a big enough factor in all lines of farm implements to ensure the regular realization of its profit target, and only in certain special types and sizes of trucks can it duplicate the profit performance of the automotive giants like

Ford and General Motors. In those cases in which it can exercise leeway in pricing, as a full-line producer, it must be careful to maintain some sort of proportionate relationship among the prices of related products. And while it is naturally anxious to make the most of any advantages that size might permit, such as in material procurement, it is company policy to lean over backward in its interpretation of the law—partly "because the company is keenly aware that the presumption against size in this country means it must operate in a goldfish bowl."

ALUMINUM COMPANY OF AMERICA

Alcoa enjoyed a protected market for its products over an extended span of years, and it was thus in a strategic position to pursue target-return pricing as general company policy. The build-up and implementation of the company pricing goal of 20 per cent on investment (before taxes) based on 70 per cent of capacity, was discussed in detail in the previous chapter. Company officers emphasized that as a result of the court mandate on pricing and the entry of new producers at both the primary and fabricating levels, however, Alcoa has not found it practicable or feasible to pursue this target in all product markets or segments of such markets.

Impact of Court Mandate on Price Policy. Marked disturbance of Alcoa's conventional pricing formula has resulted from the mandate of the District Court and the action of the government in promoting new entries into the aluminum industry since 1940. The combination of these two influences has introduced the competition of integrated firms into the aluminum industry and has forced Alcoa to consider the effects of its price policy on these new producers. The mandate was directed specifically to Alcoa's pricing of certain gauges of aluminum sheet and aluminum alloy sheet (with some references also to cable) but was equivalent to stating a principle that Alcoa must price to allow a fabricator "a reasonable profit" and at prices not below "its selling prices for aluminum ingot plus the cost of manufacturing and selling such sheet."[15] Consequently, since the principle is equally applicable to any fabricated product and an identical ruling probably would have been made by the court had a squeeze been alleged in any fabricated product other than sheet, Alcoa gives the principle enunciated in the court order a general application and expects to do so even after the court order terminates.

According to a prepared statement furnished by the company:

> While the order of the Court was thus directed only to the relationship between the prices of ingot and certain gauges of aluminum sheet and aluminum alloy sheet, Alcoa has felt that the principle involved in this order was one which should be observed in all the price relationships between products which it made and sold in competition with others who bought the raw material for such products in a market in which Alcoa was selling such raw material. The principle would appear to have less application as Alcoa becomes less dominant in either the field of the finished product or the field of the raw material from which it is made, but regardless of the dominance of Alcoa in either of those fields the principle of law could not be wholly disregarded in the determination of Alcoa's pricing policies.

It is impossible to generalize on the total effects of the antitrust decree on Alcoa's price policies, but the impact on pricing semifabricated and finished products is quite clear. Company officers are now sensitive to the practical fact that both Alcoa's ingot and fabricated product prices must be subject to a consideration of competitors' costs. On ingot pricing, this was undoubtedly more important when Reynolds and Kaiser were getting started in the industry and were confronted with relatively high-cost production.[16] In addition, following the Second World War, independent fabricators, like extruders

---

[15] Whose cost is to be controlling is not clear, although a proviso stated: "Provided that such fabricator is efficient, well equipped, and otherwise able to fabricate and sell such sheet on a fully competitive basis." *United States v. Aluminum Company of America et al.,* U.S. District Court for the Southern District of New York, Judgment on Mandate Against Aluminum Company of America et al., Equity 85-73 (Apr. 23, 1946), p. 18.

[16] Particularly since the Korean War, the gap in costs appears to have narrowed, and it is doubtful that any of the three regard primary aluminum as other than a stabilized, relatively low-margin product, which it produces mainly in order to carry on the later stages of production.

of window frames and related products, have raised complaints of a "squeeze" on extrusion prices in relation to ingot prices. But the exact differential between current prices and those representing the "ideal" or desired levels was not directly brought out—in fact, the discussion of these pressures to raise prices exerted on Alcoa by its competitors was largely in terms of alteration of the going price.

Competitive Relationships: Upstream and Downstream. Sensitivity to competition in aluminum is not visible in direct price competition in the primary lines. It is felt mainly downstream in semifabricated products as a backwash of the competition in which both integrated and nonintegrated fabricators are involved. On the one hand, there is the rivalry the majors display through their dealings with the non-integrated companies.[17] On the other hand, the pressures emerging from the court order and congressional hearings regarding relationships with competitors are reflected in decisions to price some products, such as extrusions at levels that were clearly inconsistent with the avowed target return policy of the company.[18]

[17] Since not all aluminum producers have the same degree of integration and product mix, the majors have engaged in a kind of "arbitraging" through the nonintegrated fabricators. Reynolds, for example, has embraced opportunities to sell some of its semifinished aluminum forms (*e.g.,* circles, rods, bars, forgings, etc.) to fabricators who compete with Alcoa on such products as cooking utensils and construction items (electrical equipment, castings, and machine parts). Contrariwise, Alcoa has supplied sheets to nonintegrated rollers and foil stock to converters under terms that enable them to compete with Reynolds on foil products. Evidently there are enough differences in the degree of penetration of the majors in particular lines that any one of them may feel it wise policy to secure its share of an end product by feeding semifinished aluminum to fabricators who complete with another integrated producer.

The extent to which this kind of strategy may prove a double-edged sword for the aluminum producers is a matter of speculation. In its later efforts to increase its penetration of the foil market more directly with its own foil, Alcoa no doubt hesitated because of the long-run implications of its earlier policy of competing with Reynolds foils through independent foil manufacturers.

[18] The company explained that, during the earlier 1950's, it was confronted with the problem whether to retain its adequate profit on extrusions for window frames. In fact, the profit was sufficiently high for many window manufacturers to see an advantage in installing presses to produce their own window frames. Alcoa said it was inclined to cut the price in line with its desire to stabilize prices at levels consistent with its target and the market forces, but it felt that, if it had done so, serious complaints of squeezing would have been made by the nonintegrated fabricators.

In addition, there has been such continuing pressure (at least until mid-1956) of demand on existing capacity that Alcoa and the other aluminum companies have not been required to depress aluminum prices in order to gain or to hold customers. On the contrary, the situation is such that, if Alcoa were to lower the price of any important product below that charged by its competitors, the immediate result might be that price-conscious customers would rush to Alcoa to supply them with the product they had been securing from other fabricators. Company officers explained that Alcoa would be unable to meet all such requests and might have to defend itself against charges that it was tightening the market by refusing to sell to all comers,[19] and against the possible accusation of squeezing nonintegrated rivals. Moreover, a top executive mentioned that some of Alcoa's customers, anxious to be assured of a continuing supply at a stable, even if high, price, have pressured Alcoa to increase the price of certain products in order to separate those customers "who must have the aluminum and are willing to pay for it, from those that are riding in on the relative cheapness of aluminum as against substitute products like copper."

When the manufactured product is uniform, as in the case of sheets, quoted prices are usually the same for the three companies, and the general tendency is for prices of such items to stabilize until there is a change in direct costs. This policy is tied in with Alcoa's concern for ensuring the dependability of the general price structure for aluminum products. Company officers justify the tendency toward price stability on the ground that not only aluminum producers but also the users of aluminum have a direct interest in protecting the value of the aluminum that goes into the fabricated product. In keeping with this company philosophy, the significant price changes in aluminum since the end of the Second World War have resulted primarily from wage increases and to a lesser extent from higher capital costs of new capacity and rising power costs.

Cross Currents in Pricing Objective. The chart on page 146 shows the price history of seven company products, including pig, ingot, and

---

[19] *Aluminum Industry,* Hearings before a Subcommittee of the House Select Committee on Small Business, Pt. I, Testimony Concerning Shortages and Related Matters, 84 Cong. 1 sess. (1955), pp. 256-58.

Prices of Aluminum Ingot, Pig, and
Selected Fabricated Products, 1939-56[a]

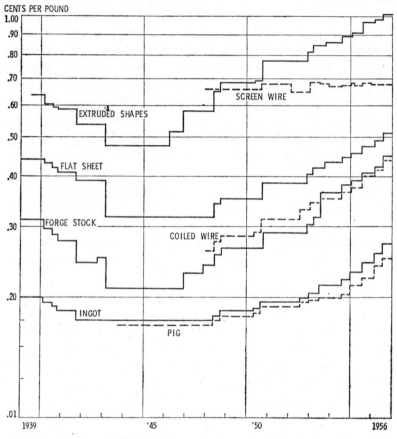

CENTS PER POUND

SCREEN WIRE

EXTRUDED SHAPES

FLAT SHEET

FORGE STOCK

COILED WIRE

INGOT

PIG

1939   '45   '50   1956

[a] For data see App. Tables 13-19.

fabricated items. The company offered several price series that may
serve to demonstrate the cross currents affecting the pricing of aluminum products—*e.g.,* the desire to maintain stability of the price
structure and at the same time to price promotionally, to compete
with other integrated producers after restructuring of the industry,
to meet competition of substitute products and to comply with court

mandates designed in part to prevent a squeeze on nonintegrated fabricators.

It will be observed that ingot prices were reduced just before the Second World War, when Alcoa was the only integrated producer selling ingot on the open market, but have risen steadily since the war, though not quite to the extent of the general price level. As a rule, the fabricated products have followed approximately the ingot price trend. The exceptions are 5056 screen wire and 2024-T4 extruded solid shapes. Screen wire, a postwar product, has been priced promotionally, remaining steady in the face of generally rising costs and prices. The price of extruded solid shapes was higher in 1948 than in 1939, in contrast to the price of ingot, but the reason for this is not apparent. The price continued to rise after 1948 but at no greater pace than that of some other products. The differential between the price of ingot and the price of fabricated products for 1939, 1948, and 1956 is shown in the table below. For forge stock,

Price Differentials Between Ingot and Selected Fabricated Products 1939, 1948, and 1956[a]

Product	1939			1948			1956		
	Price per Pound	Differential Over Ingot		Price per Pound	Differential Over Ingot		Price per Pound	Differential Over Ingot	
		Dollars	Per Cent		Dollars	Per Cent		Dollars	Per Cent
2024-T4 Extruded Solid Shapes (Factors 18–19, .2–.5 lbs./ft.)....	$.635	$.435	218	$.685	$.515	303	$1.040	$.769	284
ALC5056 Screen Wire..	—	—		.660	.490	288	.677	.406	150
2024-T3 Flat Sheet (Mill Finish, .064″ by 45″ by 144″)........	.440	.240	120	.352	.182	107	.514	.243	90
2017 or 2014 Class 1 Forge Stock........	.310	.110	55	.265	.095	56	.450	.179	66
1100F Coiled Wire.....	—	—		.285	.115	68	.438	.167	62
Ingot (99 per cent)....	.200	—		.17	—		.271	—	

[a] See App. Tables 13–19.

the table shows a widening of the spread (percentagewise) between ingot price and that of the finished product since 1948. For
this product, independent fabricators have given active competition to
the integrated aluminum producers; its price behavior is therefore of
interest in connection with the court mandate designed to prevent the
price squeeze between the integrated producer and its fabricator
customer.

Target and Realized Returns. Alcoa's management stated that the
return on investment after taxes has averaged approximately 9.7 per
cent over the years. The officers emphasized, however, that because
of a variety of forces—including rising power costs, the pressure of
metallic and nonmetallic substitutes with which aluminum has exchanged markets, the leaning over backward to avoid antitrust difficulties, and the entry of new competition—the return on investment
has varied considerably by plants and individual product lines. In
the case of products priced promotionally, of course, the company
has consciously accepted temporary low profits in expectation of
realizing its goal on the long haul; cooking utensils, certain wires, and
electrical metallic tubing represent products for which the return on allocable investment has met or exceeded the target after passing
through a period of low and erratic returns. On the other hand, in
foundry operations, structural shapes, cigarette and household foil,
sand and permanent mold castings and die castings, the return has
generally averaged below the target.

In addition to the favorable performance of the products mentioned
above, the generally satisfactory return on a company-wide basis
evidently is traceable to the above-target return on run-of-the-mill
products and custom items, resulting from the operations of the company at above the 70 per cent of capacity norm with consequent
lowering of unit costs.

It appears, in reviewing the Alcoa story, that the nature of the
competition that Alcoa faces from its rivals who are able to produce
items identical to its own, the threat of substitution of other products
such as copper and other light metals for aluminum, and the complications introduced by the antitrust decree have combined to reduce the

emphasis on target return as a primary company objective, if indeed it was ever determining. The introduction of rivals has made it impossible for Alcoa to maintain its position as the controlling factor in the production of virgin ingot, an objective that before the Second World War may have held priority over target return. After allowing for the influence of the antitrust suit, it seems fair to conclude that Alcoa prices as much with a view to meeting competition as to realizing an ideal return. Within the limits of competition it supports stable prices generally; at the same time, it does not hesitate to price promotionally when the opportunity arises.

E. I. DU PONT DE NEMOURS
AND COMPANY

As it expanded rapidly from the explosives line, du Pont was confronted with the problem of devising pricing techniques for a widely diverse and far-reaching product line.[20] This is in contrast with U.S. Steel, which has always priced for much the same group of similar commodities. Like Alcoa, although du Pont's range of products is much broader, du Pont faces the competition of substitutes to which the price response must be adjusted on a case-by-case basis.

Furthermore, du Pont not only acquired heavy chemical and paint companies as going concerns with fully developed pricing systems; it was also active in perfecting inventions originating outside the firm (ethyl and freon); and it created, at great cost, such novelties as duco, nylon, and its successor artificial fibers. Moreover, it entered into agreements with Imperial Chemical Industries and La Cellophane to use their patents and processes in this country and, in so doing, sub-

[20] Du Pont carries a variety of products in each of the following departments: electrochemicals, explosives, fabrics and finishes, film, Grasselli Chemicals (heavy chemicals), organic chemicals, photo products, pigments, polychemicals, textile fibers.

stantially improved some of their original products. The mature products, acquired by the score, and the newly created or improved products could not be forced into the same pricing mold.

In a compilation of pricing methods employed in various du Pont divisions, the company brought to light the indifference that evidently had attended the pricing of many products. While subordinates were familiar with the basis for pricing products they sold, it appeared unnecessary for top management to review the pricing of items that were profitably produced and presented no problems to the sales force. Only when strategic decisions had to be made—such as the way in which price must change to satisfy the requirements of the cement decision, or whether a general movement of prices was necessary—would the higher du Pont officials be likely to concern themselves with the pricing of such things as formaldehyde or paints. Sometimes the origin of prices was lost in the unrecorded history prior to the acquisition of the producing unit by du Pont. Guides based on margin of profit, if they were used at all, were employed in such cases for the purpose of internal control of efficiency, not for setting prices.

Some indication of the diversity of pricing problems facing this company is evident from an examination of the geographic pricing systems used by the company. The variations range from strictly f.o.b. pricing through various stages of freight-equalization to strict "postage stamp" pricing.[21]

Policy Goal. Du Pont has stated that: "Our objective is to build for the long term solid markets which will stick to our ribs through periods of adversity as well as prosperity. We are not interested in temporarily exploiting our customers, who are our most precious earnings asset."

As to its general formula for pricing, the element of cost-based pricing must enter into the price for both new and established products.

> Our price is based upon the obvious elements of conducting a business. The probable factory cost of manufacture is calculated. Expected sales and distribution charges are added. We then con-

[21] See App. 3 for a listing of product groups by types of geographic pricing.

sider what return on investment is desirable, appropriate and consistent with our own long-term risk and tax exposure, and, finally, we make an appraisal of the use value of the product to the consumer, as well as of its worth in relation to competitive counterpart or alternate materials. The end result is usually a compromise of these various factors. On occasion, I have even relied upon my feminine intuition to establish a price for a new article.[22]

Implicit in du Pont's over-all pricing policy is an assumption that its product mix is in continuing flux, as the most profitable use of its investment is sought.[23] In keeping with this policy, the company seeks to retain operations only in those mature and established products for which, under competitive conditions, the firm is a low-cost producer and can enjoy a satisfactory return. Ideally, an established product for which the price must fall below the level of a reasonable target return, stability considered, will be dropped and give way to expansion in more promising directions.[24] A case in point is du Pont's changing objectives in certain areas of rayon production—where prevailing prices have brought profits down to a level which, from the company's standpoint, does not merit continuing production. In 1955, it began converting its Tennessee rayon plants by replacing the rayon equipment with equipment for production of nylon cord and other fibers that hold greater promise of satisfactory returns.

The corporation's Executive Committee, while having a corporate target return in mind, does not expect the same rate of return from all departments. It recognizes differences in earnings potential by product groups; but it expects each to approximate an optimum rate in the light of such facts as the age and degree of stabilization of the product line, the elasticity of the demand, whether the product is mainly for

[22] From a prepared statement to a visiting group by Mr. Kinsman of the du Pont Executive Committee.

[23] "Profitability" embraces the durability of profits as well as the rate.

[24] Many of du Pont's products are required as raw materials for other branches of the company and are retained when for reasons of convenience or economy the company's own production is a better alternative than the purchase of the product from others. On the other hand, the company purchases calcium carbide and facilities connected with its further processing from its chief competitor, Union Carbide, although obviously du Pont could produce its own calcium carbide if that appeared preferable.

use by other departments in du Pont, or whether it is a by-product of another du Pont product.[25]

Approval is sought from the Executive Committee on *general* upward or downward movements of prices, indicating that the initiation of the change comes from the department concerned; furthermore, department managers stated that, in reaching a desired average return, they had discretion in allocating the returns on individual products. It would be difficult to say precisely who sees to it that the standards are enforced, but it is evident that the *esprit de corps* is relied on to work out that problem more effectively than would a formal fiat.[26]

Price Policy on New Products. The declared price policy of du Pont in respect to its patented and other new products is "to endeavor to increase consumption . . . by aiming at a low profit per unit on a large volume of sales rather than a high margin on a small volume." Patent protection is recognized as an aid in carrying out this policy, since the company thereby "can absorb initial losses from low selling prices with greater assurance that volume thereby created will flow to it." Patented items not excepted, the ability of the company to implement its general pricing policy is felt to be dependent upon market factors entering into the determination of selling prices, "including the fact that every chemical product is competitive with natural or synthetic substitutes." The corollary of the company's innovating policy is that "the industrial departments shall not permit the existence of patent protection to influence higher selling prices than can be economically justified on the basis of the other factors involved."

In respect to the target return that the profit margin should provide, the company has stated that its policy takes account of the "character of the contribution" that the product makes:

[25] There was a suggestion that overhead is allocated to different departments on a "handicap basis," according to the ability of a product group to carry the load.

[26] Discussion with the head of one department having a preponderance of mature products indicated that no one at the department level could say with authority how investment was measured—which would leave the rate of return, in the area of heavy chemicals at least, a rather nebulous part of the pricing formula.

If our contribution of an improved or new product is an exceptional achievement because of long and expensive research and development and a high permanent investment hazard, and if it affords profitable opportunities to consumers or converters, we feel we are entitled to an exceptionally good return and we ask a corresponding price for it. If our contribution has been only a moderate one, then we determine upon a price that will give us a profit consistent with our work, effort, and risk.

Price Policy on Mature Products. Price-making in basic chemicals and paint illustrates du Pont's policy in dealing with mature products. In established lines of heavy chemicals, like those inherited by du Pont through its acquisition of Grasselli, a substantial portion of the output supplies other sections of the du Pont operation for further processing. The portion that du Pont sells to outsiders is usually marketed at prevailing prices. The company shows little concern for an increase in its market share or an expansion of the sort that it has enjoyed in exploiting its own pioneer efforts in cellophane or neoprene. It is not as a rule expected that these mature products will benefit to any large degree from research or new markets; sulphuric acid and formaldehyde offer little prospect for revolutionary development.

The basic paint business and its price structure were inherited by du Pont when it acquired Harrison Bros. & Co., Inc., in 1917 in order to capture a supply of heavy chemicals required for making munitions for the Allies in the First World War.[27] There is no evidence of du Pont price leadership in respect to standard paints. To all outward appearances, du Pont has concentrated on merchandising techniques, improvement of equipment and maintenance of the department's position as the maker of a quality line of paints, in conformance with the standard for other products made by the company. The paint division seems to have accomplished the task of growing

[27] The continuance of the paint business was probably due in the first instance to the company's reluctance to leave as an orphan of the war the original labor force of Harrison Brothers and the community area in which it supplied the chief means of employment. Yet, Harrison Brothers might well have been re-sold after the war if a suitable buyer had been available. In any event, du Pont chose to retain the paint company, and with the years it has apparently remade it into the image of a du Pont department.

under these conditions, perhaps finding itself under a profitable price umbrella furnished by the industry as a whole. A question regarding the logic of retaining the paint business as part of the du Pont product mix brought the response of a company executive that he regards the paint business as one of the more satisfactory of the company's lines, having in mind the relative ease and stability of returns against the company's invested capital therein. Nevertheless, in the special sub-area of automotive finishes, the attitude toward prices is less passive; the company has a policy of pushing for product improvement and volume increase, usually accomplished however, with relatively stable pricing tactics.[28]

Active, therefore, in many lines and many industries, with a corresponding variety of methods of price-setting, du Pont sells a number of standardized products having little prospect of being dressed up, either through innovation or improvement of service facilities, and others somewhat more differentiated (but not originated by du Pont), the prices of which apparently are beyond its control. Because of this the company regards its price policy on these standard products as simply that of "meeting competition," in contrast to new products which are expected to meet a rigorous return and pay-out test. Yet the foregoing explanation undoubtedly over-simplifies the target return as it is actually applied. Du Pont spends millions each year on research, constituting an overhead that must somehow be recovered from all of its products. Assessing each "new" product with its fair share of the research that has been done in all areas is not easy and necessarily involves some arbitrary judgment.

There is no question that the Executive Committee makes careful estimates regarding possible return before it engages in the large-scale investment necessary to put a new product into commercial production. Widespread testimony to this effect was found among those interviewed at du Pont. Moreover, the company has stated that in fixing

---

[28] Price indexes for representative paint items disclose the frequent price adjustments in this particular field. The upward drift of prices can be attributed in large part to changes in direct costs, *e.g.,* titanium oxide, leaded zinc oxide, glycerin, containers, and labor.

prices on a new product it attempts, roughly, to adjust the rate of return to the riskiness of the investment in the discovery. The company's idea of a reasonable return cannot be compared with that of GM or International Harvester. We do not know what du Pont regarded as a proper rate of return or what it has obtained in the past—on specific products other than cellophane—and therefore it is not known whether the realized returns were also the target.

The company's tendency to take for granted its old and mature products is a counterpart of its intense concern with the fate of its newly developed products. One is to a limited extent dependent on the other. The company can simultaneously develop only a limited number of products. But there are gradations between the products whose prices are virtually forgotten, those which have to be reviewed from time to time by a minor official to make sure that they are in line with competitors, those facing substitutes, which can reach a profitable market only by moving into it through price reduction (like cellophane), and those which (like nylon) have expanded output into many areas because of their unique qualities, without price concessions.

How does this multiplicity of procedures crystallize into a price policy? It is hard to characterize du Pont's policy in a single phrase; obviously, though it does try to achieve a target return on the investment in some products, this target is a variable one—much higher for new and riskier items than for old products—and in fact it hardly seems to receive consideration for a multiude of items. The company is geared to growth and research; the latter influences price policy only in so far as there is exploitation of those pilot products that pay off commercially. In effect, the company comes close to charging, over the long run, what the traffic will bear; a target return is something that is achieved only on an over-all basis, by mixing the high-return with the low-return products.

It is necessary to avoid oversimplification in pigeonholing even the new products. It is possible to compute the total net earnings on the cellophane investment, yet these reflect pricing of cellophane in different markets where different standards rule. The same observation applies to nylon, which with different deniers can be used for different purposes, and which accordingly carries different prices. They may or may not embody the same target return policy; they reflect a policy of meeting competition where necessary, as in the tire market, and taking advantage of definitely established superior quality, as in hosiery.

ESSO STANDARD OIL COMPANY

(STANDARD OIL COMPANY, NEW JERSEY)

Esso Standard, the domestic subsidiary of Standard of New Jersey, has a relatively small direct production of crude oil but a large interest in Humble Oil, which is primarily a crude producer. Esso, as a refiner and marketer, realizes most of its direct income from the sale of refined products, of which gasoline, though only one of many, accounts for more than half of the company's revenue. Generalizations about gasoline pricing do not apply across the board to greases, kerosene, liquified gases, fuel oil, home heating oil, petroleum coke, or lubricating oils. Each has its own market, demand, distribution system, and consequently, pricing policy.

Information made available centered on gasoline pricing and has dealt in detailed form mostly with ideal formulas for pricing at refinery terminal and tank wagon levels. Although Esso did not disclose what it regarded as a fair rate of return, this standard was an integral part of each step in its pricing procedure. It therefore seems justifiable to speak of Esso as a company that tries to price to yield a target return on the investment—even if it does not succeed in doing so. Also influencing Esso's pricing is its position as the largest refiner in the United States, with surplus gasoline to dispose of, since it does not market through its own channels all that it refines. It is, however, the leading marketer in several states along the eastern seaboard, and its quotations are followed—or at least closely watched—by other marketers in that territory. This affects Esso's decisions. It has, like other marketers with responsibility—United States Steel, International Harvester—tried to dampen down price increases, with equal lack of success, in inflationary periods.

The company is frank to say that it scarcely ever is able to realize the return on investment that its pricing formula would accord it. Competition is usually too strong—deriving from lower open-market quotations at competing refineries, or competing tank wagon prices. The price leader, can, of course, often convince competitors that they should go along with an upward movement, but leadership is far from dictatorship.

Gasoline is marketed not only by tank wagon at posted prices to more or less captive dealers; it is also sold to large consumers on competitive bid and on an unbranded basis at the refinery. Esso, like other refiners, has these diverse methods of marketing open to it, and adopts appropriate pricing procedures and follows different pricing policies for each. The refinery price for unbranded gasoline is more likely to be influenced by spot prices at the Texas gulf coast, while the tank wagon price is less subject to fluctuation. Prices to large consumers are determined by considerations prevailing at the time of the sale, and are often far below tank wagon prices.

Thus, in large measure, Esso follows the pricing policy of "meeting competition"—within the limits that the cost procedures of the industry, with its inflexible raw material price, enforce on its multiple products. The peculiarities of the gasoline distribution system lead to periodic price wars in which the tank-wagon price can slip far below the level that formula computations, based on open-market costs of crude and refinery gasoline, would show to be profitable. But a supplier cannot abandon his dealers.

A rigid target return policy is ordinarily incompatible with a market share policy; if a company wants to expand its share of the market, it will be likely to place less emphasis on realizing a target return. Until a few years ago, Esso appeared passive as to its market share. There have been recent indications that it is trying to expand and even to invade new markets. Carter Oil has begun to expand in Texas and Esso has purchased a marketer in Wisconsin, giving it entrance into the territory of Standard of Indiana. Evidently, the rather static objectives associated with a target return have been displaced by a new spirit.

Although Esso feels that its power is extremely limited in setting domestic prices, and that time and again it has had to adjust its ideal price to a lower level imposed by competitive forces, its outstanding position in the industry, combined with scarcity of supplies of gasoline other than those of major oil companies, sets limits to the competitive pressures. Other large refiners, using much the same criteria, will resist reductions and push for increases under similar conditions. The notable feature of gasoline price changes in Esso's marketing area— other than tank wagon variations in response to local price wars—is that they occur only after prolonged consideration and review of the market situation. A gasoline price is not an automatic adjustment made by a marketer; it involves the application of a price policy.

If anything, Esso appears to minimize both its resort to policy, and its ability to mold that policy to long-run objectives. The 1947-48 episode, in which New Jersey Standard led the effort to hold the line against price inflation in gasoline, demonstrates the willingness of the management, at periods of crisis, not only to sacrifice its avowed target return policy, but also to assume the thankless burdens that are the lot of an industry leader. These burdens are lightened to the extent that others in the industry come close, as they do, to matching Esso's importance.

JOHNS-MANVILLE CORPORATION

This company realizes a substantial part of its revenues from the sale of its principal raw material, asbestos, the price of which can substantially affect its own finished product prices. Its price policy fits into a general goal of maintaining a full line of insulating products and providing extensive engineering services in connection with them. A detailed picture is not available, however, of how the company's stated policies are carried out in pricing specific products.

The price policies of Johns-Manville for fabricated products are complex, but the company has been assigned to the target return section because new products are required to show promise of earning more than the company's last fifteen-year average before they are put into production. However, the conditions in which price of even a new product can be set to realize a fixed target return are not commonly found. The asbestos shingle was first developed for a limited number of buyers who were indifferent to price, but the price was pushed down rapidly as the company explored the expansion possibilities until it was competitive with wood or asphalt shingles for almost any construction job. But when there are no close substitutes for a new product, the company does not claim that it aggressively reduces the price.

Johns-Manville is quite clear in stating that different price policies apply to different categories of products. Generally, in the insulating field, in which it has pioneered and has the dominant share of the market, it is the price leader and the quality leader. In some areas of its full line, on the other hand, it is not the leader and does little more than meet prices of its competitors. The diversity of its products has made it necessary to delegate authority far down the line, in a manner reminiscent of du Pont, through division managers to merchandising managers, each of whom handles many products and may delegate authority to meet local price cuts to the district manager. The divisions within which the merchandise managers function are organized (with the exception of the Canadian division) on a product basis: industrial products, building products, Celite, asbestos fiber, rubber products.

The company relates pricing to the objective of at least maintaining its past level of earnings, which is taken as a base. It tries to protect its mature products from price wars, which apparently are dangerous threats in the building materials business. First, it strives to maintain price stability by putting more into its products than its competitors do. This gives it a reputation for quality that enables it to outride temporary cuts in inferior products. Secondly, it has carefully used its franchise system to protect the price level. Johns-Manville's dealers realize that they have a valuable privilege, and the company watches their inventories and helps with their selling. Hence, they are unlikely to initiate price cutting on the company's products.

In building materials, price cuts start at the dealer-contractor level and are transmitted backward to the manufacturer. Thus, if Johns-Manville can remove pressure at the dealer level, it can protect its manufacturing margins. It is convinced that improving quality, even if it increases costs, is cheaper than having to meet price cuts.

Price cuts on the products that the company maintains at a margin above most competing items are, of course, possible; but the company is usually the last to move, and it tends to maintain a price above the average of competing firms. Its policy of preserving a margin means that it will not move until either its lower-grade competitors have taken a substantial volume (no definite percentage was supplied), or first-line competitors have engaged in a dangerous amount of undercover cutting. Then Johns-Manville will reduce its published prices.

Many of the company's products are not protected but have to fight their way against a large number of almost completely substitutable items. Asphalt roofing, asphalt tile, and insulation board are cited as examples of products vulnerable to keen competition, entailing immediate adjustment to competitors' prices.

The feasibility of having a number of different price policies is clearly demonstrated in the case of Johns-Manville. When the company has a free hand and pioneers the product, it is able to earn a maximum return; when it can maintain a quality differential, it does so. With its preference for steady prices, it usually confines price changes to adjustments for shifts in direct costs. But the company's interest, like that of International Harvester, in maintaining a full line—in doing *all* the insulating jobs—inevitably brings it into lines in which it has little opportunity to obtain a target return. When there is an opportunity to move into a larger market, the company on occasion has done so with price reductions, the relevant policy still being, apparently, to earn a given return. However, when it does not see a future of quick expansion—as presumably in the case of asbestos pipe—the price remains close to the original level.

In outlining broad company policy, Johns-Manville officials spoke of keeping the company on the offensive and of their interest in fighting for a larger share of the market for new products rather than in striving to increase their share of a market in established products where they already have a substantial percentage. They were even prepared to say that 20 per cent of a market was as large a share as the company strongly desired. This aspect of company policy, however, does not appear to be determining in its pricing. For one thing, the problem is applicable only to those areas in which Johns-Manville is not the price leader. It has not, therefore, found expression in price, being simply a reason for intensification of sales activity along traditional Johns-Manville lines of working with customers on specifications and dealers on service.

UNION CARBIDE CORPORATION

Until about 1952, it would have been appropriate to classify Union Carbide among the companies subordinating price competition to product differentiation, although pricing for volume when new products or uses were promising was important. The firm still places great stress on custom-made products to meet particular needs, on servicing and sales engineering, and on continuing research, both basic and applied, in all product areas. In the past decade, however, increasing attention has been given to "return on utilized investment."

No minimum target return figure has ever been formally adopted by the corporation or assigned as a guide to the operating divisions of the corporation's multiproduct business. The fact that several of the operating divisions joined the parent corporation with fully developed pricing systems, plus the obvious diversity of product markets involved, would lead to great difficulties if a uniform target policy were imposed on all divisions. In practice, while the management of a division is conscious of a target for pricing purposes, considerable variation in targets and return exists.[29]

A unifying aspect of corporate policy that may affect pricing at the divisional level is the general use of standard procedures for the interpretation of the profits performance of a division. Four of the five

[29] The annual reports of Union Carbide Corporation for the ten-year period 1947-56 indicate a range of return on invested capital (before taxes), from a low of 15.5 per cent in 1954 to 35.6 per cent in 1951. See App. Table 11.

major divisions of the corporation use standard or built-up costs as a basis for pricing, certain important chemicals being the exception. However, the conditions affecting the implementation of policy objectives vary within each division and among the different divisions, and this is recognized in the corporation's policy of divisional pricing autonomy.

As is typical with chemical companies, some definite patterns have emerged in the pricing of established products as against new products. New products developed from original research have been priced under a typical procedure for market development.[30] Pricing, under the "test tube to carload" approach for synthetic organic chemicals, involves initially a consideration of upper limits to price as set by the natural products or substitutes, a sufficiently low price to stimulate volume, and then an orderly stepping down of price as cost reductions develop with volume. Once "maturity" is reached, chemical products tend to fall into a fairly distinctive pattern of cost-plus pricing with a target return objective, showing relatively less sensitivity to fluctuations in demand.

The target return for gas products is normally lower than for chemicals. The major fraction of the Linde gas output is taken by large customers like du Pont and Detroit Steel—a situation also found in some chemicals and alloys. In addition, Linde installs and services the necessary equipment for storing and dispensing the gases. For these services, it is occasionally able to obtain a somewhat higher price than the competition.

A policy has been followed of letting wholesalers handle sales to small volume customers. This applies not only to gas and apparatus, but to important lines of consumer goods marketed through the National Carbon Division, where wholesalers are permitted to handle not only small volume accounts but large accounts as well. In volume of sales, the most important of the products sold through National Carbon are "Eveready" flashlights and batteries, and "Prestone" antifreeze.

---

[30] This was illustrated by the pricing histories of triethanolamine, propylene glycol, methanol, ethylene oxide, ethylene glycol, acetic anhydride, and acetone discussed earlier.

Even though the company does no retailing itself National Carbon must concern itself with the retail price of its major consumer items. Fair-trade pricing is employed in some cases at the retail level.[31] The levels set in the retail fair trade contracts are based on the suggested list price, which in turn reflects what National Carbon conceives to be a sound margin for maintaining adequate retail outlets.

In the consumer goods lines, the attitude toward dealers is similar to that of General Electric: both are careful to see that the dealer is allowed a "living wage." Thus, National Carbon in early 1957 increased the suggested retail price of its most popular type of flashlight battery from fifteen cents to twenty cents, while some competitors were offering their batteries to retail as low as ten cents. It was explained that, in order to get wholesalers and retailers to carry greater inventories and push "Eveready" brand batteries, a more attractive markup was required. Accomplishment of the desired objective without impairing the company return entailed a complete revision of the price structure for this line of products.[32] For "Prestone" antifreeze, Union Carbide's most important consumer product, "postage stamp" pricing is employed—a uniform suggested price to consumers whether in New Jersey or Oregon.

It is evident that Union Carbide, by tradition a technologically oriented manufacturer, places greater emphasis on its role as supplier to industry than it does as supplier to the consumer. It obviously prefers stable pricing for its consumer goods and is concerned with giving the distributor the inducement of a reliable product he can handle with an adequate margin, thereby serving to keep Union Carbide's production at optimum capacity.

For industrial carbon products, of which National Carbon has long been the leading producer, prices are fairly standardized. Although industrial products account for less of National Carbon's dollar volume

[31] The company has obtained a number of permanent injunctions against some large retailers using "Prestone" antifreeze as a loss-leader.

[32] As a precautionary measure (indicating its uncertainty as to whether its revision of the price structure would be supported by the distribution channels), the company set aside a contingency fund to provide for a possible readjustment of price to distributors, should retailers not choose to sell at the twenty-cent price suggested by the company.

than consumer products, the average return on investment is said to be greater than on the consumer items.

As in the industrial carbons, most of the products manufactured by Electro Metallurgical are made to standard specifications and hence lend themselves to the use of standard or built-up costs. The policy for these products is to maintain sales primarily on a contract basis with prices guaranteed for ninety days.[33]

Under Union Carbide's decentralized pricing, the only way the corporation gets its view of price policy is in terms of profits. The principal criterion applied in deciding among the various requests for capital expansion is the prospective return on investment. To the extent, then, that this consideration is controlling in the corporate decisions of the Appropriations Committee, it can afford a means of forging a corporate profits policy and indirectly serve as a broad guide for price policy at the divisional level.

Perhaps no other company in the sample studied is more target-return conscious than Union Carbide. The approach is still new to the company and because of this, its pricing provides an interesting study of corporate price policy in the making. The company could be viewed as in an intermediate stage, where it may move toward a more co-ordinated pricing policy via the application of a profit-return test to its operating divisions.

Union Carbide, however, very much like du Pont, is a long way from having a monolithic pricing policy. The targets and earnings vary widely among the several divisions, with chemicals—the principal and always new line—averaging higher than the others. New products that are eventually duplicated normally follow a pattern of relatively high initial prices, with reductions in prices as new uses are found, volume expands, and competition appears. When, however, the company has what it regards as a unique product not yet widely duplicated in spite of age, it may rely upon continuous improvement and refinement of the product rather than on price reductions to maintain its position of leadership.

All divisions are involved to one degree or another with large

[33] Some changes in this policy were being made in 1957 to modify the quarterly provision on price changes.

buyers who purchase substantial quantities of the products of Union Carbide. There still is no overriding corporate policy to guide the divisions; each resolves the problems in terms of its own market setting and particular circumstances.

As the preceding section has just indicated, rate of return pricing (standard cost-plus target profit) requires a willingness on the part of management to make the necessary studies of costs over a long period, in order to translate the company's operating experience into realistic norms of volume and unit cost and realization on investment. The target return normally selected is one it is hoped can be adhered to fairly consistently.

While some firms adopting a target return policy were able to realize the target price or something very close to it, others found that they could use it only as a guide. Some, such as International Harvester, have to price some products well below the target in order to meet competition; others, like General Motors, may be able to price well above the target for years on end. The target still influences price, however, tending to prevent it from skyrocketing in periods of shortage and collapsing in periods of over-supply.

The companies selected to exemplify target return as a guiding price policy are by no means the only ones in the sample that make use of this method. Others, however, appear to have put less emphasis on it than those mentioned above. As we shall see, the nature of the product and of the market may force pricing policy into other molds.

Stabilization of Price and Margin

A majority of the companies in the sample probably favor a policy of stable pricing, if only because the scale of their operations requires forward planning in which price assumptions have a significant part. But frequently this policy only fits into what the company regards as more important pricing objectives, such as target return. Two companies in the sample, however—United States Steel Corporation and Kennecott Copper Corporation—appear to have placed high priority on maintaining steadiness of price in their industries, which by their nature are subject to wide fluctuations in demand. These companies have therefore been selected as representatives of the stable pricing objective, although in fact several other companies (American Can, Aluminum Corporation of America, and the chemical companies, for example) have come closer to achieving stable prices.

UNITED STATES STEEL CORPORATION

The markets for steel have been characterized by the convention of price leadership, implemented at least until 1948 through a formal basing point system. Factors considered essential to realization of certain major objectives of the steel industry are, first, stabilization of prices; secondly, protection of steel mill investments in the older, less favorably located centers of production vis-à-vis the more favorable locations of newer producers, and third, enlargement of the competitive market area of each steel plant. The focal point around which these objectives revolve is the United States Steel Corporation, which is generally recognized as the industry's price leader. The principal explanation of this situation lies in the history and market philosophy of steel producers and ownership by U.S. Steel of over one third of the basic steel capacity, within reach of all the important markets. As a concomitant of the strategic position it has occupied for many years, the company carries a mantle of responsibility that none of the other producers in the industry attempts to shoulder.

As a price leader, however, U.S. Steel regards itself as being hemmed in by limitations on its price policy imposed by followers who may not conform and by competitive products within or outside the steel industry that are beyond its control. The company has traditionally refused to nibble at its announced base prices by undercover price cutting but prefers to wait for its competitors to make the first move. It then decides when and how far to bring published prices into conformity with actual bids. Although these considerations may help explain the laggard tendencies of the corporation, they have not prevented it from setting the pricing pace for the steel industry.

That this leadership has carried over to the period since the Second World War was shown by: the lead of U.S. Steel in abandoning basing point pricing; its lead in raising steel prices after the unsuccessful attempt of the chief producers to hold the line against the postwar shortage; the announcement (October 1953) of its intention to meet delivered prices of competitors (and its effectiveness in firming prices); and priority in subsequent price moves to take account of increased costs.[34] Although in the postwar market, some of the smaller competitors of the company broke away from uniformity on finished steel products (plates and sheets) to exploit their customers' shortages, these deviations can justifiably be termed abnormal.[35] The premiums disappeared several years ago.[36]

Leadership of the steel industry has not resulted in a consistent, well-defined pricing policy for U.S. Steel. Company officials differ in their views on what constitutes pricing policy, not only on the level at which pricing of an individual product is determined but also on the level of company-wide decision. They were not in agreement on the purposes or functioning of the basing point system, although it was on the basis of this system that they built their policy of stable pricing. One high-ranking officer, long in the company's service, questioned

[34] *New York Times* (July 8, 1948); (July 21 and 22, 1948); (Oct. 1, 1953); (July 6, 1955).

[35] *Study of Monopoly Power,* Hearings before a Subcommittee of the House Committee on the Judiciary, 81 Cong. 2 sess. (1950), Pt. 4-B, Steel Exhibits, pp. 629-36. This deviation paralleled that of the years following the First World War. Arthur Burns, *The Decline of Competition* (1936), p. 82.

[36] ". . . this last frontier of premium prices is feeling very strong pressure from a highly competitive market. . . . The new base prices are the same as f.o.b. mill prices of major producers in others areas." "The Iron Age Summary," *Iron Age* (Sept. 16, 1954), p. 219. In 1954, National Steel, with a favored location at its Great Lakes steel plant, reduced by $2 per ton the effective price, in the Detroit area, of sheets and strip required in the automobile industry. "Steel: The Price Pot is Bubbling," *ibid.* (Dec. 23, 1954), p. 21.

whether "stabilization" accurately expressed the corporation's price policy. He preferred to speak of it as its "public utility" approach, conditioned by the desire to realize a satisfactory average return on the capital invested. In another general statement, the company's price policy was described as embodied in its sales objective:

> To obtain as a minimum that share of all markets for the products sold, product by product, and territory by territory, to which the Corporation's capacity in relation to the industry as a whole entitles it, and to accomplish this participation ratio through the exercise of judgment so as to insure the maximum continuing return on investment to the Corporation.

An additional complicating factor in the corporation's price policy was the gap between the public statements made by the corporation's president, regarding broad company objectives, and the development of price policy at the Commercial Department level, which has the direct authority over pricing matters. Testimony by executives of U.S. Steel before the TNEC and the Celler Committee, taken in conjunction with the interviews, suggests that the corporation's pricing policies are compounded of a variety of sometimes divergent elements. At least two explanations of the company's pricing practices can be distinguished, from which has emerged a mode of conduct constituting a price policy. The first is that the company aims at the "ideal" price, that is, pricing that is believed to be "just, fair, and economic" in consonance with a general target of return on investment. This rationale is colored by a concept of the corporation as the industry leader vested with the responsibilities and subject to the inhibitions of a public utility. The second is expressed in explaining the difference between the "ideal" system and what officials recognize to be the practical exigencies of steel price-making—capacity to be utilized, concentrations of competition, availability of substitutes, fluctuations in demand, etc. The pricing policies of the company may be regarded as a fusion of these two approaches. When viewed in this perspective, a price policy emerges that seems to characterize accurately the company's current operations and at the same time to indicate the impact of the objectives mentioned above.

Place of the "Fair Return" Ideal. According to public statements by Mr. Fairless and other officials of U.S. Steel, the corporation aims at a "fair return" at assumed norms of operation; its policy is to sell "at the lowest price consistent with cost and reasonable profit."[37] Mr. Fairless' definition of a fair price when he testified before the TNEC is quoted because of repeated reference to it by management representatives:

> A price is reasonable if it nets a reasonable return to our company; if it permits us to pay good wages to our employees, to keep our facilities in excellent condition, to keep our equipment abreast of the developments within this industry, also if possible to pay a fair return to the owners of this business.[38]

Mr. Fairless reiterated this theme in testimony in 1948, when he argued that U.S. Steel had not "made a fair return on its sales or investment at any time during the last twenty years."[39]

Confirming the testimony of Mr. Fairless that price quotations were based on assumed levels of operation, a marketing official, in an interview, summarized the company's pricing policy as bottomed on the expectation of earning over the years a net return, after taxes, of around 8 per cent on investment. Since the end of the Second World War, U.S. Steel has increased its prices from time to time and in each instance has based its action on the increases in costs, especially wages.

Acceptance of no more than it regards as a reasonable profit has meant that U.S. Steel has not increased its prices as rapidly as other steel producers in times of shortage; and it has lagged the market in the downswing. A sales executive, long with the corporation, stated he could not recall any period of upward price movement "when U.S. Steel was not a laggard," nor has he known a period of downward price movement "when it wasn't lagging the market," other than the few days between a public price announcement by U.S. Steel and the

---

[37] *December 1949 Steel Price Increases,* Hearings before the Joint Committee on the Economic Report, 81 Cong. 2 sess. (1950), p. 124.

[38] *Investigation of Concentration of Economic Power,* Hearings before the Temporary National Economic Committee, 76 Cong. 2 sess. (1949), Pt. 19, p. 10526.

[39] *December 1949 Steel Price Increases,* Hearings, p. 7.

issuing of formal quotations by the other steel companies. In both situations, he said the corporation has consciously lost revenue because of its price policy.[40]

Margin Stabilization Objective. The subordinate position of target return in pricing by U.S. Steel, in contrast with that of General Motors, reflects its reliance on a policy of stabilization. Although its pricing is similar in that each change uses the previous level as a take-off point, there is less evidence that U.S. Steel has realized a fair return objective for any particular product. At times, the corporation has been subjected to more severe competitive pressure than has GM. Even under the basing point system, competitors seriously undercut U.S. Steel's delivered price in slack times, and in 1953 the corporation threatened to match reductions in base prices by competitors. This proclaimed flexibility is somewhat at variance with its earlier practice of delaying price movements, either upward or downward, longer than other members of the industry. The corporation put an end to market deterioration under Fairless by making a firming price cut, and since the end of the Second World War its prices, with certain exceptions,[41] have been the same as those of competitors.

With the inflation that has, in spite of the deceptive stability of the wholesale price index, permeated industrial prices during the past few years, costs of replacing and expanding steel capacity have steadily risen. The industry now claims that new basic steel facilities cost over $300 per ton of steel capacity, as against $100 in 1939. Thus the

[40] This policy was said to go back to President Farrell (1911-32), who made himself a bottleneck by insisting that all price changes come to him. Under the leadership of Fairless, this situation was changed—Fairless apparently seeing the danger of a gradual market deterioration with U.S. Steel continually losing customers in the face of a price decline. Under his regime, the central office was immediately informed of price cutting, and it was one official's opinion that U.S. Steel would take the lead in the future in firming a deteriorating market with a decisive price cut. However, since the Second World War, there have been many instances when competitors of the corporation were selling steel at higher prices than U.S. Steel. This situation is explained, in part, by the leadership responsibilities and certain other unique obligations assumed by the corporation, discussed below.

[41] Amounting to roughly 5 per cent of its business and when the company's prices have been below competitors' prices.

books of U.S. Steel, with depreciation on an original-cost basis, could show current prices yielding the relatively modest return that it has regarded as adequate in the past. Although most of those interviewed did not name a specific figure, it was stated that 8 per cent, after taxes, on invested capital would be fair. One officer maintained, however, that, under present conditions, if earnings were limited merely to this return, replacement of plant would have to be financed with new capital, and expansion could not be financed at all except by foregoing dividends; even then there would be insufficient funds. United States Steel has taken the position that there must be some increase in prices to cover depreciation and replacement costs; and it has urged that the government grant more liberal depreciation allowances.

The concept of "reasonableness" can be said to govern the changes in prices of basic steel products. When the corporation announces a rise in the base price of ingots, sheet, plates, etc., it usually justifies its action in terms of direct costs, not the rising capital costs that have been agitating the industry since 1950. The announcement by President Hood of an average increase of $8.50 per ton by U.S. Steel in August 1956, following the settlement of the thirty-four day steel strike, stated:

> The new prices do not provide a solution to the problem that United States Steel faces with respect to inadequate depreciation allowances for the replacement of obsolete and outworn facilities, nor do they attempt to provide a solution to the many problems attending the expansion program upon which United States Steel is currently engaged.

However, Hood made it clear that the wage settlement was the immediate reason for raising prices at that time: "In determining the new prices, consideration has been given to steel-making costs, including the initial costs of the new wage agreement." The impossibility of further delaying the increases was suggested by Hood's explanation that another factor influencing the increases was "the new prices established for many steel mill products by competitive producers who have been operating during the period of the strike."[42]

[42] *New York Times* (Aug. 7, 1956), p. 10.

With the pressure to cover replacement and expansion costs taking precedence over other pricing policies, it may be asked whether the company should not be placed among those depending on target return to measure price adequacy. It has always, however, stressed the concept of a "reasonable price," affording a "fair return" with the implication of a minimum of fluctuation; the current inflation has merely given special weight to one element in the concept of reasonableness—the recoupment of mounting replacement costs as a charge against sales. The corporation in 1955-56 earned substantially more than 8 per cent on investment. It earned or bettered the target in five years of the decade 1947-56.

Adjustments to Varying Market Elasticities. Although U.S. Steel stresses its right to a fair profit, it realistically modifies the margins it accepts on different products sold in different markets. According to Mr. Fairless, the closer the item to the ultimate consumer, the greater the profit. In the interviews, however, other company officials listed those items on which the corporation enjoyed the largest profit margins as being, in general, those facing less intense competition—steel rails and cable, for example. Stainless steel, galvanized sheets, and tin plate on the other hand, which are in direct or potential competition with substitutes from aluminum to lumber, had narrower profit margins. Tin plate prices have been negotiated with an eye to threatened or actual competition with glass, paper, plastics, and other packaging materials for oils, beer, paint, and special foods. Moreover, some products, like cold rolled sheets, are sold to buyers (*e.g.,* automobile and farm equipment manufacturers), who are able to exert strong pressures because of size and ability to threaten, at least, to make their own.

The influence of product market differences must be recognized as a basic consideration in steel pricing. Price behavior is uniform neither within given product groups, nor between semifinished and finished steel products. It was observed that during the 1930's the prices of hot-rolled sheets and cold-rolled strip showed a much sharper decline than standard pipe, rails, or tin plate,[43] and in the period following the Second World War, prices of cold-rolled sheets have increased by a

[43] TNEC Hearings (1940), Pt. 19, Exhibit No. 1392, p. 10718.

smaller percentage than prices of hot-rolled sheets, hot-rolled bars, cold-finished bars, wire rods, merchant wire, wire nails, or standard pipe.[44] In short, there are products for which the demand is quite elastic, and for which there are close substitutes;[45] there are others for which the demand is inelastic because (as in the case of steel rails) nothing else will serve.[46]

Generally, margins on products for which demand is elastic will tend to be relatively low, and vice versa. Nonetheless, it was noted that the company has realized a more uniform profit return on its products in the sellers' market of the period since the Second World War than it was able to achieve in the prewar years. In the opinion of one official, the result is attributable to the greater emphasis on standard cost determinations plus the policy of holding closely to its price lists. Even in tin plate, where the price is subject to long-range potential competition of substitutes, there is still lodged in U.S. Steel, in the short run, an ability to earn not less than the average "reasonable return" on this business. At the same time, the net effect of the bargaining position of tin plate users like American Can and Continental will, of course, impose limitations on the ability of the corporation to extract high profits in this market.

Thus, the pricing policy of U.S. Steel can eventuate in upward shifts when considerations of expansion and fair return seem to warrant. Such shifts usually occur when management believes that using direct costs would leave too narrow a margin. But these alterations in the general level of steel prices do not determine the level

[44] *Study of Monopoly Power,* Hearings, 81 Cong. 2 sess., Pt. 4-B, Steel Exhibits, pp. 530-32.

[45] The statement by one executive of the corporation that "modern conditions provide for a much wider and more rapid substitution of materials than in pre-World War II days," was confirmed by President Hood when, in announcing the 1956 increases, he included substitutes as a factor limiting the increases on specific products. *New York Times* (Aug. 7, 1956).

[46] Of course, the assumption of inelastic demand for such items as rails presumes a certain price policy by competitors. A sales executive of U.S. Steel generalized that historically every price reduction of the corporation has reduced its gross revenues, and every price increase has increased its gross revenues. "But this," he explained, "has been due to the timing of price changes with respect to shifts in the level of business activity and expected shifts in that level; it has no relation to the character of demand over normal times."

of particular prices. Most of the quotations are related to the ingot price by what are roughly cost differences.

Market Penetration. In balancing low- and high-profit possibilities against the management's concept of a fair return, the corporation has sought to increase its "penetration" of certain product markets, which are more profitable than those in which it has had a commanding share. United States Steel, for example, might not be averse to a declining share of the market for semi-finished steel and certain types of heavy plates and structural shapes, in which its share has been dominant, if it could increase its proportion of the market for the newer types of light sheets and strip, in which its share is low and in which growth and profits look more promising.

It should be noted that U.S. Steel has gone on record as not only determined to meet head-on any attempts by rivals to steal its customers, but also as anxious "to increase its share of various product markets."[47] It was explained, however, that U.S. Steel intends to accomplish this greater "penetration" through the creation of additional capacity in strategic areas, to attract new customers or to increase sales to old ones. The company will not indulge in price undercutting to increase its share. In a declining market it will satisfy itself with such defensive measures as are necessary to maintain the position it has gained. The argument against penetration by price concessions followed the conventional line: "We know full well that others would follow, leaving us worse off than before." Finally, the point stressed was that, with only minor exceptions, availability has been the crucial factor throughout the period since the Second World War. Customers are said to think more in terms of dependable procurement than of the inducement of a couple of dollars off price with less assurance of continuing guaranteed supply.[48]

---

[47] Meeting competition, in the manner indicated in the announcement in the fall of 1953 of an intention to absorb freight when necessary, seems to be regarded by U.S. Steel as deviations enforced by conditions beyond its control.

[48] In the view of one company spokesman, the Fairless Works was completed too late to provide his company with a higher percentage of the growing sheet market; actually, the corporation has made small progress toward increasing its share in sheets.

The high level of demand for steel products that has persisted almost without interruption since the end of the Second World War has given U.S. Steel an opportunity to revise its price structure. Undoubtedly, continuous pressure for higher wages has contributed to the interest of the corporation in gearing prices more closely to costs, though considerations of plant replacement and expansion have complicated the picture in recent years. The thoroughgoing review of extra charges the corporation undertook in 1949 was said to have resulted in prices that "reflect an honest effort to arrive at the 'theoretically perfect' extra charge—one based on actual cost of rolling a given size, doing a specific job, or supplying a special analysis."[49] The hope of the corporation was that thenceforth alterations would be made only in base prices, unless technological changes shifted the costs of extras. As U.S. Steel knows, the industry keeps close watch on extra charges. Adjustments in extras, contrary to its expectations, have not infrequently been necessary. This ordering of the price structure is said to have been of great assistance to the corporation in following through with its present policy of transmitting changes in direct costs from time to time to changes in base prices—changes that appear to be more a response to variations in direct costs than would be indicated by an insistence on earning a particular rate of return.

Although the company does not insist upon an unvarying rate of return—in fact, one official stressed that the so-called profit target must be related to changing circumstances and differing products over time—some officials have believed that the policies of the corporation are explicable only if this is assumed as a goal. It seems more reasonable to assume, however, that the company is extremely conscious of its role as price leader; that it does not want to disturb the structure, and vastly prefers, unless impelled by sharp increases in direct costs or dangerous sniping by rivals, to avoid either price increases or decreases. The persistence of prices between shifts in costs testifies to the affection of the company for stability, which is sacrificed only when the decision is unavoidable.

[49] *Iron Age* (April 28, 1949), p. 123.

KENNECOTT COPPER CORPORATION

Kennecott Copper Corporation has consistently and strongly advocated greater price stability for refined copper. It has not been noticeably successful in achieving this goal, in spite of the fact that its output of domestic copper is greater than that of any other producer. Copper, unlike aluminum, its closest competitor, has been subject to extreme changes in price.

The domestic copper industry, from mining, smelting, refining, to fabrication, is concentrated largely in three integrated companies producing virgin copper—Kennecott, Anaconda, and Phelps Dodge. A number of independent producers, smelters, refiners, and fabricators are to be found in the industry, but the big three account for the major share of all copper activities.

The Kennecott Copper Corporation, the largest single factor in the domestic refined copper market, has reflected the interest of the producers of ore and the fabricators of refined copper in achieving price stability. The late Mr. E. T. Stannard, president of Kennecott, summed up the philosophy of the company in his testimony before the Temporary National Economic Committee in 1939. He expressed similar views when interviewed in connection with this study in 1949. As he saw it, the instability of copper prices accentuated buying waves by customers and led to over-expansion in the industry on the upturns. When the price of copper skyrocketed, customers lived off their stocks, and demand fell off very sharply. Stannard told the TNEC:

> . . . if we could have uniform business, and let us say the price of copper was 21 cents per pound, it would be a fine thing for the copper industry and a fine thing for the fabricators and the consumers of copper if the price of copper did not fluctuate more than an eighth of a cent per pound per month.[50]

Efforts of Kennecott to bring about a steady price situation have been defeated because of the inability of the big three to control the

[50] TNEC Hearings (1940), Pt. 25, Cartels, p. 13257.

independent custom smelters, the contrasting cost patterns of the industry, and the influence of the world market.

The custom smelters exert an influence on prices out of all proportion to their percentage of the total output. Buying on a spot quotation basis and selling correspondingly, they can force prices up or down with great rapidity. The custom smelter has two sources of supply, both independent of the big copper producers. It obtains primary copper from the small mines, and scrap copper in the open market. Its supply from the mines tends to be steady. The small mines selling to the custom smelter are for the most part run on a full-production basis or shut down, and, since they will shut down only reluctantly, their output is not very responsive to changes in price. Scrap, which provides a large source of supply for the custom smelter, comes to the market unevenly. When large quantities are offered for sale, the custom smelters will buy it cheaply, and, since they do not care to take a speculative position, they try not to pile up inventory but to sell as they buy. The big producers can control neither the supplies of copper available to the custom smelter nor the amount of refined copper that is put on the market.

The cost patterns of the industry contribute to price instability. For a primary producer like Kennecott, the proportion of overhead to direct costs is substantial because of the immense investment necessary to develop and provide for the operation of the low-grade ore mines. Kennecott has fixed a residual in its direct mining costs that is incompressible, in contrast with the custom smelters, whose offering prices for scrap would determine most of their costs. The custom smelters can depress the price of copper in periods of slack demand (or heavy supply) below the point at which it pays Kennecott to market its production. When the independent custom smelters face a sellers' market, they will try to charge what the traffic will bear. Kennecott may lag the market for a time but eventually will be forced to follow the trend. When prices fall, Kennecott can withdraw from the market and hasten the restoration of a higher price level, but it is helpless to prevent such initial sharp falls as may be created by dumping large amounts of scrap.

Domestic prices are influenced by policies of foreign, particularly Rhodesian, copper producers. Unlike Kennecott, the Rhodesian companies do not seem to be interested in price stability. Not included in the copper export cartel that functioned in the late twenties, they increased their output and brought about a price collapse. Today, when the United States imports copper on a large scale, the willingness of the Rhodesian copper producers to see prices on the London Metal Exchange rise to unprecedented heights has made it impossible for Kennecott to enforce any degree of price stability in the United States. The Chilean government insists that the United States-owned mines and smelters charge something close to London prices for their copper, and United States prices have responded accordingly.

Fabricators are naturally loath to suffer the drastic inventory losses that sometimes issue from sharp declines in price. Kennecott's concern with the price to fabricators is partly due to the fact that it has large fabricating subsidiaries—Chase Brass and Copper Company and Kennecott Wire and Cable Company.

Refined copper is a highly standardized product sold on both international and domestic markets in substantial quantities. But the number of important buyers is few.[51] Kennecott had less than forty customers in the 1930's; by 1949 the number had grown to eighty, but a few accounted for most of the sales. The practice of Kennecott in domestic sales is to sell on the basis of quoted prices, which it maintains is also the policy of the controlled fabricators.[52] A vice president of the company who indicated that this policy was strictly adhered to by Kennecott questioned, however, the degree to which it was followed by some of the company's competitors.

[51] There are about thirty important customers for refined copper in the United States, including such manufacturing concerns as General Electric, Westinghouse, Western Electric, and General Motors, as well as the copper and brass fabricators. Federal Trade Commission, *Report on the Copper Industry* (1947), p. 8.

[52] Mr. Stannard (in 1949) stressed the point that copper fabricators were usually more interested in stable values for their inventories than in price reductions, since the copper itself was often a minor element in the price of their fabricated product. But this cannot justify an assumption of inelastic demand for copper in general. High prices for copper prevailing in 1955 and 1956 led to widespread substitution of aluminum for copper cable and for other purposes.

There are certain obvious reasons Kennecott should be rather scrupulous about its adherence to published prices: it is the biggest factor in the domestic market, and by far the largest seller to independent fabricators—all independent fabricators are largely dependent upon the custom smelter or Kennecott, as both Anaconda and Phelps-Dodge sell only a small fraction of their product on the open market, most of it being absorbed by their own fabricators.

There was little mention of cost in Kennecott's discussion of its pricing policy, which suggests that the company gives greater consideration to demand in determining a feasible price. But it was indicated that a minimum "peg" is thought of as a cut-off point, below which no sales will be made.

Kennecott has on occasion tried to introduce some stability into its customer relations by pulling out of the market when the price dropped below its cost realization figure. During the downward movement in copper prices in the postwar period, there was an interval of heavy inflow of scrap copper from the public utilities seeking to replenish equipment worn out by wartime use. Custom smelters in the spring of 1949 forced down the price of copper refined from scrap below 13 cents a pound, as against Kennecott's estimated cost of nearly 16 cents on refined virgin copper. During this time, Kennecott was making no sales on the open market. Its policy was designed to allow the independent fabricators to draw off rapidly the supplies of the custom smelters. When that had been accomplished, Kennecott re-entered the market at a price of 17 cents a pound—a level it felt the market would sustain and its costs would permit.

Kennecott resisted for several months in 1955 the Chilean pressures to raise its price. It cannot, however, maintain prices far below the world level when the United States is an importer of copper, and it would have to resort to rationing if other companies charged substantially more.

It is difficult to trace the logic of Kennecott's thinking on the extent to which the company itself should curtail the market. During the period that its prices remained above the market, its controlled fabricators were, of course, faced with serious competition from other fabricators who were buying low-priced copper. In these circumstances, it was the policy of Kennecott to allow its fabricators to reduce prices, thus narrowing the differential between the price of fabricated products and Kennecott's price on refined copper. Kennecott took the position that any significant downward movement in fabricated prices by competitors should be met by the company's controlled fabricators or else they would lose the good will of their customers. This meant, of course, that in the downward movement Kennecott delayed in reducing the published price at which copper was available to fabricators, although it did reduce the prices of its fabricating subsidiary, Chase Brass and Copper Company.

In the case of upward price revisions, Kennecott sometimes leads and sometimes follows the market. The company views the situation as one of adjusting to the state of demand, the total supply of independent smelters, and the extent to which Kennecott wishes the market to rise. To the extent that Kennecott is willing and able to supply customers at a given price, independent smelters are not in a position to take the market up very far. However, if the market gets tight and deliveries are delayed, the independents may be led to initiate upward price movements. Kennecott is then forced either to move its price up or to refuse orders temporarily. It would be somewhat reluctant to do the latter. In the circumstances, Kennecott is almost forced to follow price changes upward. Hence, as the largest open-market seller of copper, Kennecott may be regarded as a price follower rather than a price leader, despite its avowed aim to keep the fluctuation of copper prices in bounds.

Chase Copper and Brass has followed the policies of the parent company. In March 1956, it delayed raising its prices until several weeks after independent mills, forced to pay London Metal Exchange prices for copper, had lifted their prices 3 cents a pound. Chase prices went up by only 1½ cents, and then only after Kennecott had been forced to raise its Chilean price. In fact, Chase, like most brass fabricators that are subsidiaries of the copper companies, has absorbed some price increases and shows a more stable price history than its parent.

Kennecott's position of favoring stable rather than fluctuating prices seems by and large to have been the consistent attitude of the dominant firms in the industry, at least since the First World War. As is generally known, the industry launched various programs in the twenties and thirties designed to stabilize prices in both foreign and domestic markets, which have had some carryover to the period since the Second World War. According to Kennecott officials, a major reason for desiring to stabilize copper prices is to develop a better competitive position vis-à-vis aluminum, which, as pointed out above, has been sold at a relatively stable price level. That the industry is not always unanimous with respect to stable prices, however, is evident from the fact that while Kennecott was unwilling to adjust its United States prices to the gyrations of the London Metal Exchange in 1955 and 1956, Anaconda announced that domestic prices would be tied to London prices.

Kennecott, despite its goal of giving greater stability to prices, has been unable to achieve it against the unstable world-wide market and drastic fluctuations in both foreign and domestic supply and demand. U.S. Steel, by virtue of its traditional leadership and integrated full line coverage of steel production, stands out as a more effective stabilizing influence on the price pattern of its industry. A factor in the continued maintenance of its leadership—which means the willingness of the other large steel companies to follow—is apparently a realization that U.S. Steel prices (at least in recent years) have on the whole accurately reflected the consensus of the industry's estimation of the market.

Pricing to Maintain or Improve Market Position

Some of the companies interviewed did not stress a particular target return or even allude to the achievement of a definite rate of return as a primary consideration in pricing. This means not that these organizations were indifferent to the level of profits but that pricing was related initially to other policies, which assumed major importance. One of these other policies, implicit or overt, is that of maintaining or improving market position.

GREAT ATLANTIC & PACIFIC

TEA COMPANY

The following discussion of A. & P.'s pricing policies is based primarily on company statements in antitrust proceedings.

The pricing policies of this company have altered over the years to conform to changes in over-all company policy. In developing its chain of economy stores between 1912 and 1925, A. & P. concentrated on reducing its retail prices to match the savings in cost resulting from elimination of credit and delivery. In the next phase, it relied primarily on cutting the gross profit margin to pave the way, through an aggressive sales policy, for an increase in volume and a rise in total profits.[53] Beginning in 1937, the company became absorbed in expansion through development of supermarkets to compete in variety as well as price. Thenceforward, the primary aim seems to have been to achieve a larger market share, and to gear that price directly to this objective. A rising volume explicitly took precedence over return on the investment as a basis for programing.[54] In any event, it is clear that the Hartfords, who enjoyed unquestioned command of the company, were not interested in raising the dividend rate. In 1941, they set as a goal for the divisional executives the attainment of at least 20 per cent of the grocery business of each A. & P. district subdivision (unit), and the divisions were asked to adjust prices and profit rates until this target was reached.

Given the keen price competition conventional in grocery retailing,

[53] See excerpts from the minutes of a board meeting of the directors, cited in *United States* v. *The New York Great Atlantic & Pacific Tea Company, Inc. et al.*, No. 9221, U.S. Circuit Court of Appeals, October 1947, Defendants' Brief, p. 40.

[54] *Ibid.*, p. 47.

A. & P. inevitably had to price to meet competition, although this, too, could be fitted within the market share policy. Since district officials were given considerable freedom in setting the prices of individual items to attain given volume and profit rate, they cut where necessary to meet the price competition of rivals. When A. & P. had lost volume to a competitor in a division or unit, it sometimes picked out a single department, like meat, and kept all prices there at an especially low level; and on occasion, in response to competition by a local chain, instructions would go to either division or unit managers to bring in customers through price cuts.

Although the company has been pressed by competitors from time to time in scattered localities, it generally is regarded as the price leader—constantly exerting a general downward pressure on the structure of retail prices in those areas where it operates. The company does not, however, assume the usual responsibilities of a price leader in initiating short-term upward or downward revisions in specific product areas.

The emphasis on continuous low pricing, rather than on meeting short-term competitive pressures, is illustrated in the company's method of penetrating a new neighborhood or market region. A. & P. starts with a general level of grocery prices representing its low-cost, low-margin, low-price policy. The pattern is thus introduced long before sufficient volume has been attained to make the low-price policy show a profit. A. & P. pricing is not dramatized, however, by the use of loss leaders. Officials of the company also pointed out that it does not price individual items at a loss, to be used as "come-ons." Until 1950, at least, 3 per cent was the minimum mark-up on a product, unless specific authorization was given from headquarters to meet a special situation. The minimum mark-up is approached on certain high expense items that must be carried in a full line, or on items of high turnover in which it has been customary for the grocer to take his lowest margins. Among the low-margin items, sugar was cited as taking a mark-up of 6 per cent and butter of 4 per cent. Dry groceries, on the other hand, generally take rather wide over-all margins. Among dry groceries, it has been possible to develop specialties under the label of A. & P.—such as its own brands of coffee—

in which the volume-getting value of the item permitted a lower than average dry grocery mark-up.

In many of its prices, for example, those of sugar and canned milk, A. & P., like all other grocers, has to accept what have come to be prevailing margins. The patterns of grocery retailing have also led to customary mark-ups on certain classes of goods. In the case of fresh vegetables, this is partly due to spoilage losses, and in others it may be a reflection of their prevailing use as a "come-on." A. & P. has also followed the recent tendency toward reliance on non-food items for a growing share of earnings. Even though the presence of A. & P. in a community usually exerts downward pressure on prices, its pattern of margins does not vary widely from that prevailing in supermarkets throughout the United States.[55]

The reduction of costs through private brands promoted for volume and fast turnover frequently makes it possible to add margins that are not below those obtained in lesser stores with inferior purchasing power or operational skill. But the over-all low-margin price policy is indicated in the company's average return after taxes of between 1 and 2 per cent of sales over the past two decades.

SWIFT & COMPANY

Swift's pricing of meat as described in Chapter II pointed up the limited maneuverability of the large packer in both its buying and its selling prices for fresh meats. Swift regards meat packing as a field allowing little scope for anything that can be dignified as pricing policy. Its major job is to see that sales outlets are fully supplied, that their clientele is held, and that their growth keeps abreast of the industry. The buying policy of the company is formulated in terms of bids that will best serve to keep its supplies in equilibrium with demand at the going prices.

[55] This pattern appears to have derived from the supermarket pioneers who in the midst of the depression forced everyone, including A. & P., to revise levels of mark-ups.

Wholesale prices, according to Swift officials, have a strong tendency to establish themselves at the level currently required to clear the market, frequently under conditions in which costs—the prices paid for livestock and the costs of plant and branch house operations —have little or no influence. Any attempt to sell with a strict eye to costs would put the company either in the position of being unable to supply its customers, if it attempted to buy at less than the "going price" at the stock yards, or of having meat spoil if it disregarded the current retail price. On products other than fresh meat, however, the company has more leeway for pricing policy. On canned goods, Swift'ning, and similar items, the company tends to follow the same pricing policies as other grocery manufacturers, selling on a price-list basis, with relative stability in mind, but nonetheless with a keen awareness of the prices of competitors. But since nearly 70 per cent of Swift's total sales is still in meats and meat products, the company's pricing policy is largely concerned with the spread between livestock costs and the going market prices of the meats.

A company policy that seeks to dispose of a perishable product at prices to clear the market and to maintain, at the same time, a semblance of order in the spread between its costs and market prices requires a high degree of co-ordination between central management and the far-flung network of local plants and branch houses through which the company operates.

Swift treats as many of its units as possible as though they were individual enterprises, each concerned with its own profit and loss statement. Thus, a branch house, selling to retailers and institutions at the wholesale price, will try to buy the dressed meat from the product department of a packing plant at a price that will return a profit. If the price quoted by the plant department is too high, the backing up of meat in the plant coolers will cause a downward revision of price to a level at which branch houses and others will be willing to take all of the current supply of meat. The product department on its part will try to buy livestock at a price to provide a profit to itself. A considerable degree of autonomy is given to each local plant or branch house in determining its local needs or in making prices that will dispose of the product for local consumption.

The company is also concerned, however, with supplying its national market. Some of its plants are located in areas in which a surplus of livestock is available, and these plants transfer a considerable portion of their processed meat to the large markets of the East Coast, where only a small part of the livestock is obtainable and a small part of the beef is produced. The interchanges between the variously situated plants and selling branches require that the direct interest of each plant or branch house in its own profit be compromised, where necessary, with the interest of the company as a whole.

In the programing of plant operations, the purchases and transfers of live animals must be likewise so co-ordinated that supplies can be moved to plants that are seeking to employ their capacity while others are seeking to dispose of surpluses. The opportunities for conflicts of interest among different parts of the total company operation have been minimized through long experience with this process of reconciliation.

The company's position with respect to the balancing of meat supplies and market demand through price, as explained by one of Swift's commodity vice presidents, may be summarized as followed:

All meat, excepting a small percentage canned or frozen to even out supplies from winter to summer, must be sold within a few days after it is ready for market. Beef, for example, in the average western plant cannot be held more than 4 to 5 days after slaughter. Of Swift's total meat sales not over 5 per cent is canned meat, and frozen meat sells substantially below fresh meat, particularly when incomes are high.

Likewise, the company must sell its pork loins at the going market prices, regardless of what the hogs cost. If the hogs cost so high that we do not have a cut-out profit, it will try to buy them lower, if it can; but if it cannot, then all that is left is either take the loss or cut back on the number bought.

Meat is actually sold on practically an auction basis. Suppose we shipped 200 cattle as usual to be sold, through the week, in Washington, D.C., where ordinarily we would sell 50 on a Monday. If 75 were sold on the Monday of this shipment, the demand would show up to be higher than it was the previous week and the meat would probably sell at a higher price because it was bid up. It is not at all out of the ordinary for us to have trade say to us . . . "I will give you half a cent more for beef, but double the order." That is how we find out when we get under a market, and we get under it at times. If we get over it, then we do not sell our meat. If our sales by Tuesday night are so heavy we see we are going to be sold out, we will raise our prices Wednesday.[56]

According to Swift, therefore, the profit from its operation is essentially a residual; the going market determines whether the packing plants cover their direct costs[57] on sales—and often they don't— or whether the branch houses realize their expected profit on purchases from the packing plants. Pricing policy in the sense of a formula, or long-run principle, other than that described above, which seems to consist mainly of adjustment to the market as rapidly as possible, does not exist. The employment of the cut-out procedures by which the going dressed meat prices at the plant are converted into projected profitable livestock buying prices represents a kind of pricing policy. But the interactions of fluctuating supplies of livestock, proportion of available supplies taken by competitors, shifts in consumer demand, requirements of optimum plant operation, and satisfaction of steady institutional, chain, and retail customers are so complex that any precise price conversion is clearly out of the question.

Swift therefore operates within narrow boundaries for formulating policy, although one would expect a big company catering to a nation-wide market to have a concern for maintaining or improving its standing in the industry. It has to dispose of its meats; it is continuously threatened with spoilage and at the mercy of the unpredictable vagaries of consumer taste. On that basis, it can justify the position that Swift can have no pricing policy.

Yet the fact that Swift's position in the industry has changed little over the past three censuses of manufacture suggests to the outside observer that overtly or subconsciously the company's activi-

[56] From Statement of Paul C. Smith, Vice President and Director of Swift & Company, *Utilization of Farm Crops,* Hearings before a Subcommittee of the Senate Committee on Agriculture and Forestry, 81 Cong. 2 sess. (1950), pp. 2387, 2389, 2394, 2398, 2399.

[57] *Ibid.,* Exhibit No. 7, p. 2404. Apparently a direct cost includes only expenses such as killing, dressing, and cooling less allowances for sales of by-products.

ties stem from the objective of remaining a leading factor in the national market. The longer-term policy involved in this approach may manifest itself in the company's response to long-term expectations of growth in consumer demand with plans for sharing in that growth. Rapid plant expansion could result in a relatively larger percentage acquirement by Swift of the total market. The current attitude of the company appears to be, however, that it is less concerned with the percentage increase of the national market than it is in the most economical disposition of its plant locations and selective expansion with a view to lowering costs and increasing returns on investment. In sum, the mainspring of Swift's pricing policy, if it be said to have one at all, is the maintenance or improvement of its position in the meat industry; and beyond that, the development of specialties that can be differentiated so as to win a market at price levels that will yield a margin above the company's average return.

SEARS, ROEBUCK AND COMPANY

The price policy of Sears is predominantly affected by the niche the company has carved out for itself with consumers, as a large distributor representing aggressive price competition on comparable merchandise. This is company tradition, for almost from the inception of the business, Sears has exerted pressure on prices. Today this price consciousness expresses itself through concern of the company for its share of the market.

The company gives, as an underlying objective, "maximum sales in every line consistent with the realization of its traditional return on investment of 10 to 15 per cent after taxes." At the same time, Sears is conscious of its share of the national retail market, particularly in lines on which national data enable it to maintain a close check on year-to-year changes. In other words, Sears price policy is designed to perpetuate the public belief that the company can be relied upon to be as low in price on most items and lower on many than any other retail supplier. This has required, among other things, that Sears have its own system of brand names well distributed across its merchandise lines. More important, it has meant working through manufacturers for lower buying prices and realization of economies in mass distribution.

In the process of striving for the economies of scale in distribution, Sears has developed a close link between price policies and buying policies. Indeed, the rationale of its price policies and practices cannot be fully understood without an examination of its buying policies.

Buying Policies. Merchandise buying is one of the two highly centralized functions of the Sears organization. Auditing and finance constitute the other. Following the major moves into store retailing in the late 1920's, the company placed increasing emphasis on the systematic development of working arrangements with manufacturers for items to be sold under the Sears trade name. The growth in volume has enabled the buyers of the company to become less dependent upon the open lines of manufacturers, and has permitted the company to extend the practice of contracting for products with exclusive features and design sold under a Sears private label.[58]

Sears relies on several sources of supply: (1) company-owned plants, *i.e.,* those in which Sears has a majority control; (2) plants in which the company has a minority ownership; (3) independent manufacturers with whom the company has continuing contractual arrangements; and (4) independents with whom no such arrangements can be made. The company-owned factories (22 in 1954) making stoves, plumbing fixtures, paints, farm equipment, television, and sewing machine cabinets, developed out of certain situations in the past when buying arrangements satisfactory to both existing manufacturers and Sears could not be made on merchandise that Sears believed could be sold in large volume through its outlets. The stock interest in partly

[58] The company had, before the move into retailing, carried hundreds of products under its own brand names but had not effectively associated the Sears name with them. From the 1930's on, it began to be more selective in its choice of brand names and to promote their use until they became synonymous with the name of Sears. In 1945, it reduced the number of brands to around fifty, and began a policy of grouping related product areas around one brand name, *e.g.,* Homart for heating, plumbing, and builders' supplies; Harmony House for home furnishings.

owned companies (46 companies in 1954, with 109 factories producing a wide range of merchandise) was usually acquired in exchange for financial assistance. These two groups of factories—the wholly owned and partly owned—account for a substantial percentage of dollar value of Sears products.

The group of independent firms with which the company has long-term buying arrangements—what the company refers to as "basic buying"—accounts for over 35 per cent of all its merchandise and for the bulk of its major appliance lines. The principle underlying these contract arrangements, which apply also to the partly owned plants, is that the price to Sears shall be the direct costs to the manufacturer plus a gross margin to cover the general overhead of the manufacturer and provide him with a profit on the capital investment deemed applicable to the Sears business.

This kind of arrangement means that prices will vary with the cost experience of the manufacturer. Conceivably, in the event of low-volume operations or miscalculation of costs by the supplier, the price to Sears might rise materially above the expected level. Sears protects itself to a certain extent by a "competitive" or "saving clause" designed to keep the cost-plus prices of its suppliers in line with prices of other suppliers. This proviso has the effect of encouraging suppliers to watch their costs and to be alert to opportunities to modernize their processes.[59]

These basic source contracts have been particularly effective with smaller manufacturers; Sears has found that, by eliminating seasonal swings in production and concentrating on a fairly standardized product, it can realize the economies associated with large-scale production and at the same time eliminate many of the expenses of distri-

[59] Sears officers stated that very rarely have they exercised the privilege under the competitive clause, but instead they usually work out some acceptable arrangement. This may involve simply an elimination of certain features on a product, which are not deemed important, as a means of offsetting unexpected increases in material or labor costs. Both parties may agree to take a smaller gross margin in the interest of keeping the final price within the desired level. If the higher costs are due to inefficiency in management, Sears may make some suggestions for changes in personnel. Whatever the difficulties, Sears takes the position of working them out with suppliers on the basis of a partnership arrangement rather than holding rigidly to contract terms.

bution characteristic of large manufacturers, *e.g.*, salesmen, advertising costs, wholesaler and jobber margins, factory representatives, etc.[60] These small firms ordinarily are not large enough to finance adequate engineering and development departments and look to Sears for technical help.[61] The company management prefers small factories concentrating on production and relying on Sears for a substantial part of their distribution. Under these arrangements, Sears feels there is "a natural interdependence of small business and so-called big business."

Sears wide array of products, involving some forty merchandise departments, may be broadly differentiated for purposes of pricing analysis according to the size of the company's purchases in relation to manufacturer's volume. At one extreme, are the items that are typically produced by a few firms and one manufacturer producing more in a day than Sears can sell in a year; at the other, are those of which Sears takes the whole of the supplier's output. In between are the products of which Sears buys more than a small fraction but less than the whole of the manufacturer's production.

When Sears purchases represent only a small fraction of the market, it can do no better than review all offerings of competing producers and make the most intelligent choice in terms of price and

---

[60] Sears officers stated that not only does Sears assume the full expense of these various distribution steps, "but when this expense is added to the cost of operating a Sears retail store or mail order department, the total distribution cost is less than the costs of a typical independent retailer."

[61] In this connection a high officer of Sears, addressing the firm's merchandising personnel, expressed the company's view as follows:

"There is no reason why the initiation of merchandise ideas should be left to the manufacturing organizations of the country, and all studies, analyses and data kept secret there. There is no reason for a Sears buyer being in the dark as to how goods are produced, what approximate cost should be, and what it would take to work out some contemplated new product or design. When the manufacturer alone does all this, he has to guess at the market and wonder how he will get a given volume distributed to the public. Here in Sears, a buyer, through experience, has a pretty sound idea of what the volume will be under assumed conditions of a given quality and price. So, if the buyer knows both the market and all that can be known in advance as to manufacturing design and production cost, he has the whole picture. He knows what kind of manufacturer to deal with, what costs ought to be for a given volume, and therefore the proper price to pay."

quality. While it may buy in large volume, its purchases in relation to the total output are not big enough to permit it to work out special arrangements, and it is subject to manufacturers' price schedules. White goods are bought in this manner, as are most staples. Sears management explained that in these cases the company's policy is similar to that of other large retail distributors such as Penny's, Montgomery Ward, and department store chains. Goods are purchased on a normal order basis. Sears has no special cost advantage over its major competitors and can sell at prices lower than theirs only if the items are not fair traded or it sells under its own brand name.

Top quality brackets of a line, such as the higher priced wallpapers and the top grades of its furniture, which Sears sells in small amounts only but carries to satisfy a few customers, come within the above area of goods for which Sears has no influence on the market. On these items, Sears may even be at a disadvantage in relation to major competitors selling in large volume, since it may not be able to buy on equal terms. Management pointed out, however, that Sears often sells at the same price as its competitors.

When Sears takes the whole of a manufacturer's production, it will work out a basic-buying (cost-plus) arrangement. When it takes a substantial fraction, it may enter into such an arrangement, or it may negotiate a special contract. In selling manufacturers' brands, such as the Corona typewriter, the Winchester gun, or 1847 Rogers Brothers silver, Sears is tied to the sellers' policies governing discount, allowances, and fair trading. The only advantage the company has is in the possibility that the large quantity it buys will reduce some of the manufacturer's expenses and permit him to sell at a lower price. Sometimes manufacturers are found who are sympathetic to the idea of supplying an item for sale under the Sears brand—and Sears will then get special terms; but officials of the company said that more often manufacturers prefer not to produce for private label.[62] Sears then has to find some other supplier to do the job and will normally

---

[62] The obvious reason given by manufacturers is that they fear sales under their own trade name will be injured if they sell at a lower price to Sears for retailing under its own trade name. They also fear criticism from their distributors and dealers, who might turn to some other brand.

enter into a basic buying arrangement with him. Sears has such agreements, for example, with King-Seeley and Emerson—King-Seeley supplying Sears with Craftsman woodworking tools, and several Kenmore appliances; Emerson furnishing Sears with bench saws and arc welders.

With respect to the large proportion of merchandise secured under a basic buying arrangement, Sears may be looked upon as the merchandising department for the manufacturer. The two are "integrated" in the sense that the supply contracts bring Sears into the design, planning, and production of the merchandise it purchases. The significance of this buyer-supplier relationship for Sears pricing policy may be indicated by a comparison of its costs and margins with those of its competitors.

Competition, Costs, Margins, and Prices. The table on page 194 presents a breakdown of the production costs, distribution costs, and retail prices of Sears brands and the corresponding brands for nine representative products.[63] It will be observed that Sears *factory costs* —both in total and by individual type—are approximately on a par or higher on four of the products, lower on the other five. The *factory margin* representing the unit profit provided for in the contractual arrangement with affiliated Sears factories and a comparable figure for the competitive manufacturer, is in most cases lower on the Sears brands. The net result is that Sears is able to buy (see *manufacturing cost*) at figures closely approximating those of other distributors in the least favorable cases and to have an advantage of as much as 18 per cent on featured items.

Sears points especially to the elimination of, or savings in, certain distribution costs as the area in which the company gains its principal cost advantages over manufacturers' brands. Sears' cost break-down in the table shows no separate national distribution costs or jobber margins (*i.e.*, costs of factory representatives, advertising-promotion, collections, and bad debts, etc., plus wholesaler and jobber margins), since the company's buyers are the manufacturer's sales representatives; the control stores or pool stocks are his jobbers, and the catalog

---

[63] The data are several years old, but are submitted as illustrative of Sears current pricing policy.

Factory Production Costs, Distribution Costs, and Retail Selling Price, Selected Products, Sears, Roebuck and Company

Cost Item	Water Heater		Refrigerator		Men's Shoes		House Paint		Dress Shirts		Silverplate		Garden Hose		Shot Gun		Girdle	
	Competitors	Sears	Competitors	Sears	Competitors	Sears	Competitors	Sears	Competitors	Sears	Competitors	Sears	Competitors	Sears	Competitors	Sears	Competitors	Sears
Raw Material	$30.52	$30.92	$77.02	$77.12	$3.45	$3.36	$1.72	$1.90	$1.02	$1.15	$10.70	$11.70	$1.32	$1.51	$4.85	$5.20	$2.39	$2.16
Direct Labor	3.20	3.17	15.91	15.93	.96	.99	.08	.08	.33	.37	6.36	6.57	.51	.46	10.33	7.29	.65	.59
Factory Overhead	12.60	12.51	36.82	38.67	.74	.45	.29	.29	.25	.20	7.63	7.98	.86	.71	23.52	18.64	.78	.70
Administrative Expense	3.27	2.10	2.55	2.55	.32	.20	.26	.06	.02	.03	.86	.75	.10	.06	1.30	1.18	.23	.21
Factory Cost	49.59	48.17	132.30	134.27	5.47	5.00	2.14	2.32	1.63	1.75	25.55	27.00	2.79	2.74	40.00	32.31	4.05	3.66
Factory Margin	16.41	12.73	33.53	31.70	.54	.44	.41	.38	.06	.07	3.20	2.25	.66	.35	9.33	8.14	.41	.37
"Manufacturing Cost"	66.00	60.90	165.83	165.97	6.01	5.44	2.55	2.70	1.69	1.82	28.75	29.25	3.45	3.09	49.33	40.45	4.46	4.03
National Distribution Cost	6.11	—	10.73	—	1.09	—	.52	—	.54	—	3.20	—	.35	—	3.25	—	.59	—
Jobbing Margin	21.85	—	29.42	—	—	—	.53	—	—	—	10.65	—	.90	—	11.12	—	—	—
Retail Mark-up	43.70	44.05	103.77	103.98	3.85	2.51	1.79	1.59	1.42	1.16	28.40	26.75	2.05	1.89	21.25	24.50	4.95	3.95
Selling Price	137.66	104.95	309.75	269.95	10.95	7.95	5.39	4.29	3.65	2.98	71.00	56.00	6.75	4.98	84.95	64.95	10.00	7.98

and retail advertising are at once his advertising and the dealers' sales aids. But these are indeed costs to Sears and must be provided for somewhere. In practice, these expenses are split among the parent organization, retail stores, and the mail order department. It will be noticed that the company's retail margins are essentially the same on most items (somewhat lower on shoes, paint, shirts, silverplate, garden hose, and girdles, and slightly higher on shot guns) as the margins allowed retail dealers by competitive manufacturers. In so far as these must cover part of the intermediate expenses of distribution, the effective margin is lower than that shown in the table.

The net result of Sears' method of operation is to produce selling prices ranging from about 15 per cent to 30 per cent below the retail *list* prices of the comparable items shown in the table.[64] It should be noted that the prices listed in the table for Sears brands and those of its competitors are not necessarily actual selling prices in the market. They are "suggested" list prices to the retail outlets, which the retailer or Sears store manager may or may not follow although because of its control over its retail outlets, prices suggested by Sears are likely to be more closely maintained.

The retail prices of manufacturers' brand merchandise (especially household electrical appliances) have been reduced to the point at which today the spread in price between Sears and other brands has been appreciably narrowed on many items. Sears attempts to strengthen its own position by watching costs closely and by what it calls "even better merchandising." Like others, Sears offers models at several price points, from stripped to de luxe, the former being used in part as a means of bringing in customers. Sears believes that it is more successful than competitors in trading customers up to the higher priced models, which carry a higher gross profit rate. Another practice followed by Sears is to carry over a previous year's high-price-point model and sell it at a lower price-point. Since tool and die and

[64] Price-quality comparisons are ordinarily not easy to make. However, in several cases listed, the Sears brand and rival brand are manufactured by the same company, the Sears brand being made to specifications as high as or higher than the rival brand. In other cases, the company subjects its product and rival products to various tests in order to establish comparability.

design costs have been written off on the previous year's sales, Sears prices these items much lower (*e.g.,* $169 as compared with $200 the previous year). Little concern was shown for the possible undermining of new models; in fact, it was indicated that such merchandising may even help push the sales of new models.

Sears has been able to establish price-points on its big ticket lines in particular, and to some extent on other lines as well, but has not enjoyed the same degree of success in soft lines. In women's and men's wearables, for example, it would like to get away from traditional price-points in order to give Sears products some distinctiveness on price but has found it difficult to do so. For example, in a consumer's mind a shirt priced at $3.30 may be a $2.95 shirt overpriced, or it may represent a discount on a $3.95 shirt. The general policy of following customary price-points in soft goods and not in hard goods has resulted in a tendency for the prices of the latter to take account of changes in costs while those of the former have been maintained and quality changed.

Mail Order and Retail Pricing. Mail order prices are basic in the company's price structure. Actually, mail order and retail prices are established at the same time on the recommendations made by company buyers. In setting these prices, an attempt is made to maintain on mail order prices a differential under retail store prices to allow for differences in selling costs, transportation costs, the purchase of merchandise "sight unseen," and the delay in delivery of the goods. The prices finally decided upon represent the buyers' evaluations of the traditional mark-ups and price-points of the trade, the estimated differential below manufacturers' brands necessary to assure a desired volume, expected price changes, and related matters. In the process of revising prices for the general catalog, prices may be cut in the expectation of stimulating a sufficiently higher volume to provide a better return on investment. In other cases, when management regards the prevailing differentials as larger than necessary to hold volume, it may raise prices. Decisions on such matters are based on buyers' recommendations, periodic comprehensive reviews of company and competitors' prices, quality testing, frequent comparison shopping surveys, and analyses of year-to-year changes in market shares of the company for different products.

Sears grants wide latitude in pricing to individual store managers. The central office suggests prices to the stores, but the managers are free to, and on some items do, modify these prices for the local market. This discretion is tempered by an effective performance test— the profit responsibility of the managers, whose compensation is based in part on the profits of the store.[65]

On certain lines the central office encourages the maintenance of suggested prices. Over the years, a delicate balance in price relationships has developed in retail competition in lines like tires, roofing, guns, paint, refrigerators, and other large appliances. Sears is especially conscious of just about how far it can go in giving price advantages to the consumer on such products without precipitating a price war; and it feels that nothing is more detrimental to the company than a price-slashing promotion in such lines of merchandise.

Sears chief advantage in pricing is in the saving it can effect through low distribution costs. By manufacturing for itself or through its direct buying arrangements, it is able to eliminate some of the advertising and distribution costs of competitors who operate through the normal distribution channels. Since, on a large percentage of its merchandise, Sears can also make arrangements with suppliers whereby considerable economies are effected in manufacturing, it can realize total savings that bring the retail price on many lines well below that of other merchants, even while permitting Sears to realize its target return. The company has thus acquired a general reputation for selling quality goods at low prices. This price policy is the instrument

[65] The retail stores and mail order plants in a sense are in competition with one another. This shows up particularly when one or the other is engaged in a special sale. Each part of the organization has "complained" from time to time about not being able to meet the prices or having its position undermined by the sales prices of the other. The retail stores have a greater degree of flexibility on such sales, since they can prepare a special sale within a short time, whereas mail order plants require several weeks or more to prepare and mail circulars. Generally speaking, the prices of the retail stores and mail order plants do not get far out of line with one another, and variations are relatively short-lived.

through which the company tries to accomplish its primary objective of expanding volume to maintain or increase its share of a nationwide market.

Sears has not been equally successful in all product areas in maintaining what it considers a satisfactory share of the market. In big ticket items like freezers and washers, where it has basic buying arrangements, it has traditionally held a substantial share, whereas in lines like soft goods, many of which it has to buy in the open market, it has been hard pressed to hold the fraction it has. Sears management has indicated that in 1957 it tended to obtain about twice as large a share of the market in durables as in soft goods. No fixed percentage of the national market is set up as a goal, although the management has said that when it obtains a share of 8 to 10 per cent it considers it is doing a very successful job.

STANDARD OIL COMPANY (INDIANA)

The procedures by which Standard of Indiana has, in the past, arrived at its tank wagon gasoline price to dealers were discussed in the preceding chapter. There, it was apparent that in 1950 the company virtually renounced responsibility for price leadership within its territory and stated its intention of meeting competition wherever it was to be found. A late variant of this development was reflected in the action taken in the Twin Cities market when the company set quotations to dealers "at a discount from suggested competitive resale prices."

Although the company has been quite forthright in disassociating itself from its former role of price leader, it remains the largest single seller in the Midwest territory. If it refuses to go along with a price increase, that increase is not likely to be successful; and a price reduction by Standard will ordinarily put severe pressure on its competitors to follow suit. Nevertheless, as Standard points out, there are so many possible sources of product supply in its marketing area that it can no longer use a price based on Oklahoma refinery quotations plus rail freight, as it did before 1949. It now uses no formula price but prices primarily on the basis of local competitive conditions. In practice, this means that its prices take into account the prices actually charged in each district by its competitors, the refinery quotations at different points plus known transportation charges, and the company's estimate of competitors' costs.

Because Standard occupies a position of primary importance in the midwest local markets, it is frequently the first to change its price when such action seems to be warranted. It meets competitive conditions as they locally prevail in the sense that the company formulates its judgments of what competitors would do in the light of the local competitive situation and prevailing economic conditions.

Standard usually justified upward adjustments by pointing to changes in direct costs but does not claim to shoot at any given or presumably fair rate of return.[66] This "posted" price is normally adopted by its smaller competitors to whose prices Standard theoretically is conforming its prices. Moreover, when it has to reduce a price locally to deal with a price war, it indicates—or has indicated in the recent past—that this quotation is "temporary" in nature. Thus, it appears to subscribe to the belief that there is some price that has more justification and support in objective conditions than the price which it has to charge temporarily because of local competitive conditions.

Throughout the shifts of policy that have occurred since Standard began, in 1934, to react more sensitively to competitors' pricing, the company's major purpose, in the face of a history of losses of market share, has apparently been to regain its market and protect its product against continuance of market share loss by more realistic adjustment to the competition in local markets. This aim explains the successive modifications in the basing point system and the development of flexible

[66] Over long periods, the price has remained unchanged in some cities covered in the trade press, suggesting that while Standard does not have a formula of refinery price plus transportation, the quoted tank wagon price probably takes into consideration, so far as the local competition permits, delivery costs to various points.

pricing policy (even to supplanting of tank wagon price by suggested retail prices), as in the Twin Cities case. Standard's policy does not contemplate a level of prices designed to attain a fixed target return. "Price levels depend entirely on competition; profitability is determined by continuing efforts to improve efficiency and lower costs so that the market price may yield a satisfactory return."[67]

It can be urged, of course, that merely maintaining a market share is not, for Standard of Indiana, or indeed any other company, an ultimate goal. Obviously a company with heavy fixed investment—*e.g.,* that of the oil companies in crude production and refinery facilities— must continue to find an outlet for product or suffer serious losses. But keeping a position in a market involves growth, not merely keeping existing facilities employed, and hence cannot be easily resolved into a method of stabilizing volume and profits.

None of the companies included in the study views with complacency a drop in the percentage of a market it enjoys. For the companies classified here as motivated by considerations of maintaining or increasing a market share, this seemed to be a goal of major import; but so classifying them has not meant other goals may not have taken precedence in the past or may not take precedence in the future. A firm like Swift, so long as it is chiefly dependent on meat, will inevitably regard the holding of its present markets and keeping up with their growth as fundamental company policy. Yet given wider opportunities for diversification in the future, it may well reduce its dependence on meat and the emphasis on its share of the national meat market.

It appears also that the nature of the business led some companies, classified under other categories in this chapter, to place special emphasis on their market share. General Foods, for example, was so sensitive to this goal as almost to warrant placing it in this category.

---

[67] "Obviously," the management also notes, "changes of industry costs, such as may result from a crude oil price increase, and wage and other cost increases, are factors considered by Standard in holding or attempting to increase its judgment price levels. Meeting competition is uppermost in mind when the company reduces its prices."

Pricing to Meet or Follow Competition

In many cases, the large companies faced what they regarded as a market-determined price over which they could exercise no measurable influence. There were, however, several varieties of market-determined prices differing with the market. The term "following competition" serves well enough to indicate the broad classification but is imprecise when for instance, Goodyear and National Steel are compared. Following the price of a dominant firm, which in a particular product line may be a small firm, is not the same as reaching, by trial and error, the price that will clear the market. What essentially unites the companies discussed in this section is their belief that many of their prices are fitted to conditions outside the company's control rather than to one of a number of positive pricing policies that the firm itself might decide to adopt.

GOODYEAR TIRE AND RUBBER COMPANY

Pricing in the rubber tire industry has been shaped by several forces that the tire companies regard as beyond their immediate control. These forces, in turn, have had an impact on the organization of the industry itself, as evidenced most noticeably by the decreasing reliance of the large firms on tire sales. There has also been a decline in the importance of the independent tire dealer and of the manufacturer's brand. In the evolution of the industry, there is little to show that Goodyear's pricing has differed in any substantial fashion from that of its immediate competitors. Indeed, the company is not aware of anything that could significantly differentiate pricing policies among the Big Four, unless it be Firestone's refusal to enter the private label market, or the failure of U. S. Rubber to set up its own dealer system.

First in the influences that have shaped the present tire market has been the difference between the original equipment demand for tires and the replacement demand. These two types of sales have been influenced by distinct and diverse forces. In the original equipment market, the powerful automobile manufacturers, capitalizing in part on the advertising provided by the selection of a tire as original equipment, have been able, by negotiating with a few firms, to force prices to levels well (perhaps 50 per cent) below those charged to any customer for replacement purposes. These prices cover also the spare tire, which would otherwise be sold in the replacement market. The original equipment market has expanded and shrunk with the market for new automobiles and is linked, via new car sales, to shifts in "supernumerary" income. There is practically no elasticity of demand for this tire; a reduction in its price may not affect in the slightest the quotation on a new car to the consumer, but Goodyear (or any other large tire manufacturer) may face a substantial loss in business to a competitor if it does not keep its original equipment prices low.[68]

The original equipment market thus serves as a pricing floor, and the volume of original equipment business provides a measure of security for the large firms that are able to take advantage of this opportunity. Original equipment sales constituted 30.75 per cent of total tire sales in 1925, 37.86 per cent in 1940, and 43.69 per cent in 1955.[69] The manufacturers are therefore becoming more and more dependent on original equipment sales.

The rising proportion of original sales indicates the rapidly improving quality of the automobile tire, which is capable of running an ever-increasing number of miles. With a ceiling on original equipment sales enforced by national income and highway capacity, and a continuous downward pressure on replacement demand, the tire manufacturers continue to be threatened with excess capacity.

Even though strong bargaining pressures have kept the price of original equipment low, the tire manufacturers might have been able to extract an assured return from the replacement segment if market-

[68] For comparison of costs and operating profit on original and replacement equipment, see Office of Price Administration, *Survey of Rubber Tire and Tube Manufacturers*, OPA Economic Data Series, No. 10 (May 1947), Tables 6 and 7.
[69] Data furnished by the Rubber Manufacturers' Association.

ing patterns had remained fixed. But improvement in tire quality has been accompanied by the growth of large buyers—mail order houses, auto supply chains, and oil companies—who have undermined the position of the independent tire dealer and the high margin for manufacturer's brand.[70] The importance of these brands in imparting fluidity to the price structure has been overwhelming. In the replacement market, there has been constant juggling of prices because the mail order or other private brands have jeopardized the structure of the prices of the manufacturers' brands. The private brands have undercut the factory brands and necessitated a continuous procession of sales and special discounts, allowances, and so on—some authorized, some not—which would have been present to some degree in any case. In addition, private brands have led to a succession of changes in tire quality, innovations that have upset the precarious stability of tire "levels" as a framework for a price structure. The standard, or 100-level tire has come to play a relatively minor part in replacement sales—so that fighting brands and premiums play a part, with price changes, in market strategy.

In fact, having created a marketing problem by selling 100-level tires to mail-order and other large customers at lower prices than those charged for factory brands, Goodyear—like other tire manufacturers—has tried to compensate by introducing a new tire to make the product mix more attractive. It has also changed the margin on a non-100-level tire from time to time, with a view to shifting the reactions of consumers so as to increase its own sales. Variety, novelty— attention-getting devices—seem to be as much if not more a part of tire marketing than shifts in the price charged on tires to the ultimate purchaser. Dealers are strongly urged, and since the margin in dollars rises with the grade of the tire, have an inducement to "trade-up" the prospective purchaser—who may have been brought into the store by a special offer—from a third-grade to a 100-level tire, or even to a premium tire.

Historically, Goodyear has generally led tire prices upward, while

[70] According to a 1947 study, private brands account for about 30 per cent of the replacement sales. Warren W. Leigh, *Automotive Tire Sales by Distribution Channels* (1948).

Firestone has been the leader in the downswing. The ever-changing price picture in tires, however, makes it difficult to assess responsibility in recent years for price changes. It is regarded as a misuse of the term to speak of a price leader in tires. It is for this reason that it has seemed desirable, in spite of Goodyear's leading position in the industry, to characterize its policy as that of "meeting competition," although it does not precisely match the price of its nearest rivals or attempt to do so.

NATIONAL STEEL CORPORATION

The pricing policy of National Steel is one of matching the market. It has disregarded costs in pricing, because (at the time of the interview), it has assumed that it is at least as efficient in its field as any of its competitors. Therefore, it is able to meet a competitor's price no matter what that price may be. If Mr. Weir protested U. S. Steel's failure to raise steel prices, it was not because he believed that Weirton was more expensive to operate than any of U. S. Steel's plants but because he thought U. S. Steel was accepting prices that would not permit plant expansion and improvement, which he—in common with business leaders in aluminum, steel, and oil—believes should be financed internally.

The officials of National Steel pointed out again and again that there are no secrets in the steel industry, that competitors are familiar with each other's costs. Consequently, it would be absurd to try to price on cost; the thing to do is to get the order—which for 75 per cent of the business of National is done by top management—and then compress costs if possible to make a profit.[71] The company has specialized in a few items—notably, tin plate and cold-rolled sheets for the automobile business. It believes that this specialization, plus speedy installation of all technological improvements, will serve to keep it ahead.

[71] The aggressiveness of Mr. Weir was evident almost from the establishment of National Steel. See "The Corporation," *Fortune* (March 1936), p. 191.

National has 19 per cent of the tin plate capacity and simply quotes the price of U. S. Steel (with 36 per cent).

In this connection, Mr. Weir testified before the Celler Committee in June 1955 as follows:[72]

> Mr. McCulloch. In recent years has this uniform price [for tin plate] been the price as fixed by the United States Steel Corporation, for instance?
>
> Mr. Weir. I would say in the majority of cases, yes. But there is no necessity, except that it would be a normal, natural price.
>
> Mr. McCulloch. Does your company ever fix prices or announce prices that are lower than your competitors' by reason of your more efficient operations?
>
> Mr. Weir. Well, we have made prices that differ from our competitors' based on reasons that we thought were good reasons.
>
> Mr. McCulloch. Does that happen often?
>
> Mr. Weir. No, it doesn't.

In summary, the few brief pricing rules enunciated by Mr. Weir for National Steel were as follows:

1. Follow the lead of the price leader, which is U. S. Steel, while sweetening the base price a little when, as in Detroit, the company has a considerable freight advantage.

2. Absorb freight if necessary on a single order, but watch closely the annual bill.

3. Never manipulate extras to get an order; reduce the base price if necessary to meet a competitive cut.

4. Price is never built on cost; pressure is backward on cost.

The policy of price followership appears to have undergone a modification following the elevation of Mr. T. E. Millsop to the presidency of National Steel early in 1954. In July 1954, National reduced prices on steel products at its Great Lakes Division by $1.00 per ton and again by the same amount in December 1954. This was done at a time when Great Lakes was running at capacity. One reason given was that it represented an effort to cement good will with the automotive manufacturers.[73]

---

[72] *Current Antitrust Problems,* Hearings before a Subcommittee of the House Committee on the Judiciary, 84 Cong. 1 sess. (1955), Pt. III, p. 2219.

[73] *Steel* (Dec. 23, 1954), p. 21.

GULF OIL CORPORATION

It was not possible to hold sessions with price officers at the time of the interviews with Gulf. References to price policy made in connection with other aspects of company policy indicated that in general the pricing policy of the company is to keep its prices on the same level as their competitors. They never lead in price changes and are not considered a "reference seller" in the industry, as is Standard Oil of New Jersey. Consequently, Gulf follows rather than leads in any price change.

KROGER COMPANY

In the discussion of A. & P.'s pricing for market share, it was pointed out that A. & P. is generally the price leader in the territory in which it operates. Where this coincides with Kroger territory, *e.g.*, in the East Central states, it is clear that Kroger is usually a follower. Kroger disclaims any attempt aggressively to meet competition; it emphatically denies a price leadership role. There has never been any talk of Kroger putting pressure on a local grocery retail price structure. Its pricing is, as for so many operators, largely a matter of finding out what A. & P. charges on the most important food items and then coming very close to A. & P.'s prices. Kroger has not used "week-end specials," and it avoids price-cutting as a means of initiating a new line. The company has endeavored to avoid the most severe forms of price competition, however, by featuring nationally advertised brands and notably by carrying quality meats at a relatively low profit margin as a business-getting device. In meats it does not carry the lowest price lines. In interviews, the company officials pointed out that Kroger had no interest in geographical expansion and that it stressed selling and research.

Kroger has obviously lacked the dynamic volume-minded management of A. & P.; it has sought to insulate itself—to the extent that it is possible to do so in the retail grocery business—from direct price warfare. By pushing nationally advertised merchandise, it has tried to differentiate its merchandise from the private brands of A. & P. But it also carries private labels and products of less well-known brands when it is important to cater to several levels of trade by price lining. In 1955, the chain began to show signs of moving closer to the A. & P. pattern; it decentralized its management and began to expand geographically. The company still depends for its profits mostly on "merchandising"—baking and coffee roasting are as far as it has gone toward vertical integration. This policy, of course, limits the company's pricing flexibility.

Of the three companies included in this section as price followers, two exhibit a followership that appears to be the logical result of being well below the industry leader in size. Goodyear, the third company, does not yield to its competitors in size, and it does not follow the pricing policy of any one of them; rather, it follows a market that feels the pressure of large and influential buyers and of changes in the nature of the demand that tend to create excess capacity.

Goodyear appears to have been trying to offset complete followership through the development of innovations enabling it to differentiate its products. In this effort, it has also gone outside of the tire field to develop a diversified production with greater opportunities for differentiation. National Steel has apparently put its emphasis on selection of those steel products in which its location and specialization will give it market advantages without price deviation. Kroger, as a distributor, has likewise attempted to choose a combination of lines for special promotion, with different margins, to reinforce its general followership of the leader in chain store food marketing.

Pricing Related to Product Differentiation

Few companies in the sample depended on price policy alone to maintain their competitive position. In nearly all cases, the effort to differentiate their product by qualities that could be associated with the name of the company was a factor in price policy. Three companies have been selected for inclusion under the present heading, not because they are the only ones that have stressed differentiation of their product, but because they serve to exemplify the product characteristics and position in the industry that are conducive to putting the emphasis on the value of their brand name and enjoying some price premium in consequence.

AMERICAN CAN COMPANY

The structure of both the canning and the can industries, and the nature of the contractual relations between the can companies and their customers, have served to focus the concern of the suppliers and buyers alike on the provision of service. The price of the can represents an appreciable fixed item of the packer's costs. A packer is concerned that all of his competitors shall be equally burdened; he recognizes that, unless he is one of the very few giants of the canning industry, a special concession is out of the question. With two major sellers dominating the industry and with American Can as the price leader, each canner would be assured that all canners would have the same can costs. From this premise, Canco's management argued that the canner wanted above all the assurance that cans would be available when he needed them. Since crop behavior is always unpredictable, a requirements contract obviously served his needs. It was claimed that the contracts between can manufacturers and the canners provided this necessary insurance against a shortage of cans at a strategic period during the canning season.

Because American Can dominated the can-closing and can-making machinery business as markedly as, if not more than, it did the can business, it also stood ready to rush its engineers and service men to any spot where the machines might develop trouble. In addition, the company worked closely with customers in improving the quality of the canned goods, in devising new types of containers, and in methods of packing.

In these circumstances, Canco tended to minimize the importance of the price of the can. Under the standard packing contract, prices to every buyer fluctuated with tin plate and labor costs, on a standard formula basis, while the total price covered most of the rental of the closing machines and the servicing and development expenses of American. The company looked on itself as the technical assistant to the canning industry as a whole, and the price of the can was expected to include an amount sufficient to finance technological improvement. The absolute amount of the company's research has been small, however, when compared with total sales: before the Second World War, it spent no more than about one third of one per cent of its revenues on research and technical sales service.[74] The company also tried to satisfy the desire of the canners for price stability during the canning season by preserving a constant differential between the price of tin plate and the price of the can. These were the primary considerations that it stressed prior to the postwar government suits in 1947 and 1950. The company did not appear to think in terms of a specific return on the investment. At any rate this was not sufficiently prominent to be brought out in discussion.

The company's pricing, at least until 1950, was also affected by its efforts to use its control over can-closing machinery to tie in sales of cans. It charged low rentals on the closing machines and low or nominal amounts for service and had the same terminal dates for the can and the closing machine contracts. Thus, the price of the can covered many items other than the cost of the can itself. A goal of the company, in addition to financing and furthering research, was undoubtedly maintenance of its share of the market through this tie-in device.

The court decree of 1950[75] has had a marked impact on pricing in the can industry. The pricing policy of American Can, like that of Continental Can, has been altered in several aspects covered by the decree. Contracts with canners are for a year only. The closing machines have to be available for purchase as well as rental by custo-

[74] Charles H. Hession, *Competition in the Metal Food Container Industry, 1916-1946* (1948), p. 284.
[75] 126 Fed. Supp. 811.

mers, who are thus free to buy their cans where they wish. Discounts to large purchasers have been virtually eliminated.

Continental Can is pressing American Can and has apparently been able to divide the business of big customers. The fact that the largest canners may undertake their own manufacture of containers must mean that American and Continental have to keep the price of the can and the servicing of customers under the "roll your own" costs of canners in manufacturing. It is not certain that other large customers will not emulate such large can users as Campbell's Soup,[76] Heinz, Pet Milk, Carnation, Sherwin Williams, and Texas Company, which are manufacturing their own cans in whole or in part.

Approximately one third of the more than one hundred tin can manufacturers are can users making their own containers. Most of the smaller can companies have local territory in which they are able to give the leader vigorous competition, especially in the general line.

The general line is the area in which larger margins may be taken than in the packer line, because orders in this field are more frequently on a custom basis, with each order meeting the specifications of the particular customer. Here the competition rests not merely on prices and on the ability of the supplier to provide immediate service on special orders but on the opportunity for research and planning to meet customers needs. This is where smaller and localized can manufacturers have their greatest opportunities to take business from the big companies.

The present contracts used by Canco provide at the seller's option for possible upward price changes in November and May. According to the company, prices have been reduced during the life of a contract —apart from the formula adjustment for changes in tin plate and labor prices—because of the competition of other can companies, while the opportunity to raise prices is seldom used.

Once the industry abandoned the long-term contract, under the terms of the antitrust suit decree, the canners seemed to lose some of their desire to protect themselves by a requirements contract, so that open-order buying has increased. By thus shopping around, the

---

[76] Campbell's Soup is currently the largest can manufacturer after American and Continental.

canners sometimes succeed in bringing down prices for everyone, because a concession made on one order will have to be made available to all.

American Can, therefore, has altered its pricing stress since the original Brookings interviews. It comes much closer to following a policy of "meeting competition" than to pricing to finance service and technological progress and ensure stability in market shares. Meeting competition—or using the cost of a substitute product to determine the price it charges—has also been the company's policy in marketing paper milk containers.

GENERAL ELECTRIC COMPANY

General Electric, like du Pont and other multiproduct companies whose output goes into many distinct markets, exemplifies a variety of pricing practices and objectives depending on the nature of the product and the market that is served. Hence pricing as a direct responsibility has been relegated to the product divisions, and the corporation serves as co-ordinator by setting general policies with which pricing is reconciled.

A common thread is discernible in the more than average emphasis on designing products that can be differentiated as G.E.'s particular solution to the requirements of users, with pricing approached as the necessary adjustment to estimated limits of market acceptance and the company's ability to bring costs in line therewith. But the pricing of products as different as major power units and small household appliances necessitates the decentralization of price management.

At one extreme, when the sale is essentially a contract to meet specifications—where the "product" is a group of generators for a massive public utility installation—the "price" will emerge as the resultant of efforts to meet a problem in which the customer has already placed a ceiling on price. Here G.E. may, in effect, be pricing its ability to offer a combination of equipment at a price that will serve to meet the company's objective of supplying power at or below a plant cost of a specified figure per kilowatt. At the other pole, are standardized traffic items such as fractional-horsepower general-purpose motors, or electric lamps, in which the competition may have to rest primarily on meeting the market price. In between, are many forms of industrial equipment or consumer appliances in which G.E. serves in varying degrees to assert its prestige and to sell on the basis of its product differentiation without necessarily matching the prices of other companies for the same general type of product. Nevertheless, if a generalization is to be made, the pricing goals of the company can be said to cluster about the company's first emphasis on supplying a product designed to serve the needs of its producer or consumer customers and to get the combination of quality and cost that will give a price that the customer will be willing to pay.

Management speaks of pricing to cover development and service costs, but here again the determinants of the costs to be covered will vary by type of product. When G.E. has promoted a new product—Disposall or a dishwasher, for example—it attempts to feel out the market to determine what combination of price and quality will result in the largest sales. It thereupon addresses itself to the problem of cutting costs in an effort to make as much as it can from large-scale output of the product. In this respect, there are obvious similarities to International Harvester, which also believes that costs are adjustable after the basic product design has been determined. In any event, G.E. appears to think of pricing in terms of stating to the customer what it will cost him to get the features of efficiency and potential output he believes are desirable. The large industrial customer has a more precise idea of what is "desirable" in terms of production costs and efficiencies, whereas the consumer tends to make a more intuitive decision, involving some degree of dependence on the reliability of the company. Yet there is a certain similarity in the pricing goal for products designed for mass consumption and for such products as custom built transformers or rolling mill controls; in both, G.E. management says that it finds out what the customer wants and then builds it. It does not think of itself as producing for an existing market that it could enter by cutting the price of an identical product.

While putting emphasis on design and differentiating product and service to meet consumer requirements, the company has at the same time tried to build volume by reducing costs and prices on mass production items like the major electric appliances. The drive for volume has meant a substantial fall in the average margin obtained by G.E. on sales, but the earnings per dollar of investment have tended to rise.[77]

General Electric does not regard itself as a price leader for all the products it makes. The company did attempt in 1948 to lead prices of electrical equipment to a lower level—a move that was not sympathetically viewed by its competitors. The company thinks of itself particularly as a price follower in the small appliance field. Here the company has made some attempts to set for itself a target market share; and in endeavoring to maintain the required volume, it relies on a body of dealers with satisfactory margins rather than on price-cutting. It would prefer, however, to push for market expansion rather than to defend an overwhelming share (except, of course, for situations in which it has the full benefit of patent protection). As one executive said, "The company would rather be pushing to expand the 25 per cent than to defend the 50 per cent share." Its wide range of products include both standardized items and custom built products, wherein G.E. finds a place for the application of a standard cost-plus-reasonable profit approach. The company executives in general are emphatic, however, in denying that cost-plus thinking determines the company's new product pricing. Consideration of the price at which the consumer will take the company's new offering is more likely to be a benchmark for the company's effort to incorporate the features it regards as essential, at the lowest cost that will accomplish this objective.

Since 1951 General Electric has undergone radical changes in organization to invigorate an entrepreneurial approach in making each product group a profitable enterprise. In the 1955 *Annual Report to the Stockholders,* Ralph E. Cordiner, president, said:

> . . . General Electric's organization has been changed from a centralized structure to as broad a decentralization of responsibility and authority as can be found in industry.

[77] See App. Table 20.

Today, General Electric's products are engineered, manufactured and marketed by nearly a hundred decentralized Operating Departments, each of them bearing full operating authority and responsibility for the Company's success in a particular product field. The special skills and knowledge required for each product are thus brought to bear by a local business management team which can concentrate on the opportunities of a specific product or marketing area.

GENERAL FOODS CORPORATION

General Foods has an important interest in specialties and in the price premiums they can command. It does not have any strong influence on prices of those of its sales items that cease to be specialties, except in so far as it can, by improvement or promotion, delay the total loss of specialty status for the product. In its origins, there was an attempt to have the company concentrate on specialties. General Foods was to restrict itself to food products that were at the other end of the spectrum from "commodities" or "trading items." It was to promote novelties in the expectation of making more profit than was customary in the manufacturing of food staples that General Foods, as a conglomerate merger of food companies, was launched.

As its products have been imitated and lost their novelty, margins have shrunk, and the old formula of one third of the price for manufacturing cost, one third for marketing, and one third for profit has had to be abandoned, even for new items. The company's gross margin has shrunk from 50.4 per cent of sales in the specialty product mix of 1931 to 29.8 in 1955. Many of its products, such as livestock feeds, family flour, and frozen fish, are sold at the market as "trading items," the company having little or nothing to say about price. On specialties like Minute Rice, Postum, and Birds Eye Frosted Foods, margins are much lower than at the time the products were launched.

In the view of one officer, only Postum, Sanka, and Jell-O sold at margins as comfortable as the company would like. There are some items for which General Foods is in a position to hold the umbrella over its weaker competitors. Jell-O is a good example. Because of the flavor-fixing research carried on by the company, there appears to have been a renewed swing of consumer preference toward this brand of gelatin dessert. In addition, through its own gelatin manufacturing plant, it appears to have been able to introduce manufacturing economies. If General Foods were to price Jell-O on a low-margin basis in light of these developments, some smaller competitors probably could not survive.

The officers of General Foods consider gross margins as high as the original company working rule "one third to make, one third to sell, and one third for profit," to be an unwise business policy, shortening the life of a specialty and an untenable policy for an item that has been duplicated by competitors. While the belief is held in the management of General Foods that a reversal of the price policy of the constituent companies was part of the original plans of General Foods, it seems likely that analysis by General Foods of the acquired companies following their purchase—and later the impact of the depression—have had more to do with changes in pricing policy. The company delayed a substantial slash in coffee prices until well along in the depression.

In price policy for specialties, where the management has a zone of discretion, emphasis is placed on a longer-term view of profits than seems to have been taken earlier. The company is very sensitive to the effect of high prices and long margins on a sustained strong market position, and on long-term favorable earnings of specialties, particularly as those items become part of the accepted food products of the country. They feel that now only Postum, decaffeinated coffee, and Minute Rice can be called "unique."

Because of the losses in specialty position, General Foods exercises little power as a price leader in general grocery lines. In coffee, Hills Brothers is the dominant brand on the West Coast, and in some other areas Chase and Sanborn (Standard Brands) is more important than Maxwell House. A. & P. probably equals General Foods in importance as a nationwide coffee roaster. In determining price changes, the dominant influence is raw material costs. The company problem is, therefore, largely a question of timing of price changes. No evidence was found that General Foods occupies a unique or uniform role in initiating changes. Moreover, although the company is by far the largest producer of frozen fruits and vegetables, and has a well-established national brand, it can get only a small differential over competitors selling products of equal quality. Thus, it cannot obtain the kind of gross or net margins that ordinarily accompany food specialties. It finds its market position much restrained by the competition of other frozen foods producers, some of whose product is of uncertain quality, and by the availability of fresh and canned fruits and vegetables. On the other hand, General Foods has a zone of discretion in setting and adjusting the prices of those items that have managed to retain their specialty status. The chief restraining influence is a full realization that a high price will restrict the volume and that it will speed up the process of developing competition. Aside from the frozen foods field, the greatest threat of competition is from private label selling by the chain stores.

Discussion by the company executives both with Brookings interviewers and before the Joint Committee on the Economic Report in 1949 made it plain that, on the non-trading items, the company was forced to take potential competition into account and that it has been hesitant to raise prices when costs have increased. There is a significant contrast here to the recent behavior of the steel and aluminum firms, which have regularly advanced prices with a rise in direct costs. Clarence Francis, former chairman of the board, thought in terms of what he called a "stable franchise" for General Foods products that would be jeopardized if the company were to raise prices to enjoy what must be inevitably a temporary increase in profits; subsequent losses would more than offset gains.

Therefore, while General Foods might perhaps be classified as a company that strives for a target return, it has expectations in this regard only for new products. It feels obligated to develop these at frequent intervals, in order to rejuvenate the product mix, as the older items become subjected to more intense competition. Following this strategy, the company acquired and began large-scale promotion of a salad dressing mix in 1955; it also developed new instant cake mixes and Kool-Aid flavors. The purpose of introducing these products is obviously to offset reducing the margins of products that have become staples.

Product differentiation is a significant aspect of price policy when a company features products that can offer the purchaser special satisfactions for which he will pay a price that yields a better than average return on the capital invested. To exploit this policy successfully, a company must have a product line that lends itself to innovations with marketable advantages over comparable standard products. Beyond that, the emphasis on making a product "different" in the consumer's estimate may be an indication of the research-mindedness of the company's management or its strong inclination to develop opportunities for upgrading product rather than cutting price.

American Can (also, in recent years, Continental Can) has felt able to maintain prices on its established lines because of a premium placed on the dependability of its product and the credibility of the claims made for its frequent innovations in containers. General Electric has also emphasized, for a substantial percentage of its products, special features that make the product a desirable buy at the quoted price, whether or not competitive products are available at lower prices. The specialty-mindedness of General Foods is a tradition on which the company was founded. Because the staples in the food line so quickly reach a low-margin level, there is an urge to bring out new specialties to sweeten margins and prevent the return on over-all investment from declining. To some extent, a successful reaching for volume at reduced cost can be an offset to the settling down of the product line to the staples class. The specialty represents the conscious effort to find a fresh approach to the product—its ingredients or the convenience of its use—for, which, for awhile at least, the consumer may be willing to pay an additional price. The desire for product differentiation to obtain higher than average margin can be regarded as a universal characteristic in the companies in the sample. The particular companies that were selected to exemplify this aspect of pricing have made it an important part of their appeal for market favor.

The classification of company policies used in this chapter, which results in identifying a company with one major type of pricing goal, is at best an arbitrary device to facilitate the description and interpretation. The foregoing accounts indicate that most of the companies surveyed follow different goals for different products and product groups. Their size and their product diversity require that product groups be administered through semiautonomous divisions. The common factor in determining prices seems to be the ability of the product and division to show a profit record that satisfies the central corporate management. Thus, the management of a chemical company on the one hand appears to have planned carefully to have profits of a unique product finance other research and development in textile fibers, while at the same time it pays little attention to the pricing of the heavy chemicals in a division that mainly serves to supply other divisions. The fact that some pricing problems are carefully resolved at the highest executive level, while others are relegated to subordinates, in itself is enough to produce dissimilar standards for setting prices.

It would be possible, without excessive distortion, to assign some of the companies to other categories than those in which they are placed. United States Steel and General Electric could be fitted into the target return group, or Johns-Manville, because of its interest in keeping a full line, to the market share group. Esso and Alcoa could with some justification be put in the price stabilization category, although this is not such an unqualified goal as it has been for Kennecott, which actually finds the goal very difficult to attain. Furthermore, since most of the companies think of research as an important function, a cost that must be covered and justified by revenues, they tend to price with the goal of product differentiation also in mind. Several of the companies in the sample have, indeed, questioned the appropriateness of the classification selected for them; but it was found that they would have been no less critical of being assigned to any other category that was meaningful for interpreting the practices of the company or the outlook of the management.

Moreover, company goals change with circumstances. Standard of Indiana, after much internal debate, shifted from what could be described as a high-margin, low-volume, shrinking-market-share concern to a firm with a primary interest in building up its market share. American Can, because of antitrust action by the Department of Justice, lost the power to achieve price stability and hence the interest it had formerly maintained in it. Esso, which once seemed to have little or no interest in strengthening its position in the market, has more recently become markedly aggressive in promoting its brands.

Hence, this discussion of the nature of goals, and of their relative rank is not intended to indicate any permanent coloration for any of the firms discussed. It can select only what seemed to be the major policies at the time of the interviews. But the ephemerality of goals is a quality that needs to be brought out, because it, too, is a characteristic of big business behavior. Company policies toward price do not exist in a vacuum and change as the influences that help to formulate them change.

3 / *Pricing Organization*

AN EFFORT IS MADE in this chapter to single out the procedural aspects of pricing as they manifest themselves in the administration of corporate pricing policy. Such a discussion is useful in understanding price policy in action since, among other things, it discloses the general lines of authority, the necessary referrals, and the levels at which pricing decisions are made. The earlier analysis of pricing particular products inevitably touched upon this subject, but the emphasis so far has been largely on the bases for price making. Here the stress is on procedure. In addition, this discussion is helpful in gaining an insight into the pricing practices of certain companies that did not provide enough information to justify a discussion of how individual products of the company are priced.

The pricing procedure, or administration of pricing, is not uniform among the large corporations in the sample. Usable information is not available for all companies covered in the interviews, but certain marked differences in the organizational arrangement and responsibility for price determination will be noted among the firms considered below. The case studies disclose a wide variety of arrangements from the closely held power on every price change at the top management level to instances of almost complete delegation of pricing authority to product sales manager and salesmen.

ALUMINUM COMPANY OF AMERICA

Heading the sales organization of Alcoa is the Vice President, General Sales Manager. Under him are a vice president in charge of sales offices, who handles direct sales through twenty-three district sales offices, with forty-two branch or resident offices reporting to them, and a vice president in charge of product sales, who makes the price decisions for the company. The latter has charge of fourteen product sales managers whose functions are analogous to those of a vice president in charge of an operating subsidiary. There are also three industry sales managers, who are responsible to the vice president in charge of product sales. In describing his duties, one product sales manager stated that product managers are on the sales department payroll, have both sales and manufacturing functions, and operate as liaison between the sales force, production, and product development, and as adviser to the sales force.

The product sales managers have the main price-making responsibility. New product prices, however, require the approval of the vice president in charge of product sales and of the vice president, general sales manager. The accounting department is also drawn in on pricing matters. As a guide in making decisions, each product sales manager and each production manager, as well as the top executives, receives every month a summary for each product line, giving among other things the total output, sales, unit costs, unit profit margin, capacity utilized, and rate of return on investment. Daily market reports are also received by the product managers from the sixty-five sales offices of the company regarding the developments in competition and any significant shifts in the market strength of particular products.

Alcoa is admittedly organized informally at the top, with division of authority among the principal officers not clearly defined, although certain key policies are apparently followed closely by all the product sales managers. There seems to be little question, however, that Alcoa's top executives, including the product managers, have a great influence in deciding what new products the company shall develop and hence can be said to determine roughly the initial price of products. Within this framework, subsequent changes by product sales managers are modifications of original prices approved by the vice president in charge of product sales. This means that in certain cases the product sales managers may act independently in adjusting prices.

But although the Alcoa management encourages the assumption of responsibility by the product sales managers in price matters as necessary to meet changing market situations, the product sales managers ordinarily will bring a recommendation upstairs, where it will be accepted or rejected.

AMERICAN CAN COMPANY

American Can does little bargaining with its customers, and its pricing with all but a few canners has been, as far as the cans are concerned, determined by a standard contract providing American with a standard mark-up over cost. In more recent years, this contract has been elaborated to pass on to the customer savings accruing in the cost of tin plate and labor. Decisions on the level of prices for cans and on the range of discounts, both before and after the Robinson-Patman Act, appear to have been made by top management. Dr. Baker, President of American Can at the time of the TNEC hearings, assumed responsibility for the company's pricing. The sales department of the company is essentially a service department; salesmen do not try to sell cans in any direct way.

GREAT ATLANTIC & PACIFIC

TEA COMPANY

A. & P. undertook a formal reorganization to decentralize fiscal operations and decision-making in 1925. The controlling decisions remained in the headquarters office, largely as personal decisions of the Hartford brothers, until the Second World War. In more recent years, the decentralization has become more meaningful. Headquarters operates as an over-all policy-making body consisting of the president and four top level associates. It offers general policy guidance on location of stores, selection of merchandise, and price and profit objectives. The operating decisions are left to the divisional managements and their local representatives.

As now constituted, the nationwide A. & P. chain is divided among seven divisions, each covering a major area of operation. Under each division are a number of district units. Each division has its president and one or more vice presidents, a director of sales, director of purchase, and director of operations.

At the head of each district unit is a general superintendent.[1] The unit usually has as its other principal officers an office manager, sales manager, buyer, and warehouse superintendent, who together form the executive committee of the unit. Within the district unit are superintendents and assistant superintendents, each of whom has charge of a zone containing a number of individual stores; the store managers, as a rule, are immediately responsible to a supervisor.

The responsibility for the store location rests in practice with the division management, although final approval from headquarters is required for rental above a given level. It is the unit management that provides the basis for selection by appropriate surveys of population, territory covered, surrounding industries, existing competition, and other factors supporting the estimated sales and profit potential of the store.

Prices to be charged in the individual stores are under the general oversight of the sales director of the division, but the operational responsibility rests with the sales manager of the unit. There is a general conformity in the price structure for stores of the same type, by size, character of the areas, etc. Merchandise is ordered by the store manager but in pricing he must adhere to the price levels set by the unit sales managers for the given type of store. The store manager's discretion in special pricing, as in disposal of perishable items, is only within the limits set by the unit sales manager.

Operating results of the stores and zones are collated and analyzed by the unit general superintendent for the division president. The quarterly meeting of the division president reviews the operational

---

[1] Several of the superintendents, in charge of major markets, are also divisional vice presidents.

situation of each division and presents a general operational program for the ensuing quarter. Pricing policy receives consideration at this level as part of the profit performance, which, in turn, is reviewed in total company terms at headquarters.

E. I. DU PONT DE NEMOURS

AND COMPANY

It was indicated earlier that the executive committee of du Pont has always set a fairly strict earnings requirement for the various departments of the company. Its viewpoint in purchasing and operating new departments, as the company diversified from explosives, has been akin to that of an investment banker. The interviews have indicated that in recent years the top management of the company has concerned itself only with general upward or downward movements. Pricing is apparently done far down the chain of command. Departments are composed of divisions, which in turn are organized on a broad product basis; thus, the Fabrics and Finishes Department has a Fabrics Division and a Finishes Division. Yet, the general manager of this department has only an advisory role in setting prices for paints. Price setting is the responsibility of the director of sales in the Finishes Division, who is subordinate to the division manager, whose superior is the general manager of the department.

Du Pont, like other companies in its size bracket, attempts to establish machinery for continuous price examination to minimize the number of crisis situations demanding emergency action or quick improvisation. The aim is to sense a trend or change in costs or demand before the situation reaches a point at which the possibility of careful planning is lost. To this end, the responsible administrative official for each functional aspect of the product operation is kept in touch with the problems and the thinking of his colleagues. The procedure may be illustrated by reference to one of the major product group departments—the Film Department. (See accompanying chart.)

Organization, Film Department, E. I. du Pont de Nemours and Co.

General Manager
 Assistant General Manager
  Control Manager
   Assistant Control Manager
    Accounting Section
    Office Service Section
    Accounting Section
    Planning & Scheduling Section
    Standards Section
  Personnel Manager
   Assistant Personnel Managers (2)
  Director of Production
   Assistant Director of Production
    Production Manager ("Cel-O-Seal" & Sponge)
     Columbia (Sponge)
    Yerkes (Cellophane, Polyethylene Film, "Cel-O-Seal" Bands, Sponge Yarn)
    Circleville ("Mylar" Polyester Film)
    Clinton (Cellophane)
    Old Hickory (Cellophane)
    Spruance (Cellophane, Acetate Film)
    Cellophane Technical Section
  Research Director
   Assistant Research Director
    Development Section
    Patent Section
    Wilmington Research Laboratory Director
   Assistant Research Director
    Yerkes Research Laboratory Director
  Director of Sales
   Special Assistant
   Assistant Director of Sales
    Promotion & Advertising Section
    Sales Development & Technical Service Section
     Associate Manager
     Assistant Manager—Sales Development
     Assistant Manager—Technical Service
    Trade Analysis Section
   Assistant Director of Sales
    "Cell-O-Seal" Sales
     New York District Manager
    Converter Film Sales
     Assistant Manager
    Export Sales
     Associate Manager
    Industrial Film Sales
     Assistant Managers (2)
    Packaging Film Sales, by district: Central—Chicago; Eastern —Philadelphia; New England—Boston; New York— New York; Pacific Coast—San Francisco; Southern—Atlanta; Southwestern—Kansas City
    Sponge Sales
     Assistant Manager

The ultimate responsibility for the price of a product within the department rests with the general manager, who depends on the director of sales for the pricing operations. In building a price or making a price change, the general manager has frequent informal meetings and a formal monthly meeting with those directors of functions in the department who can contribute to a pricing decision. These include: (1) the control manager, a staff officer who represents the sections of accounting, planning, and scheduling, and the formulation of cost standards; (2) the director of production for the department, under whom are the separate product managers or plant managers, for example, for cellophane, acetate film, polyethylene film, spun yarn, "mylar" polyester film; (3) the research director, whose office embraces a product development section, a patent section, and the research laboratories; (4) the director of sales, whose division embraces the district offices for product subgroups, as well as sales promotion, including technical services, advertising, and trade analysis.[2]

A price proposal for a new product or product development may have its start in separate analysis of basic requirements and market opportunities by all four of these divisions. In the case of an established product, the price consideration may develop from an analysis of production costs by the control manager, or of sales experience by the office of the director of sales, who in turn may receive warnings, complaints, or recommendations from district or product sales managers. Any price action that suggests itself to one of these functional departments can be tested or re-enforced by analysis in the accounting or other appropriate section.

A minor price change may be effected by formal consultation between only one or two functional directors and the general manager of the department. A major decision will be reserved for a more formal meeting in which all the directors of the department may participate.

The general manager makes a monthly report on the progress of his department to the executive committee of the du Pont corporation.

[2] The group may include the personnel director, if the basis for the change lies in an increase in wage rates or other factor affecting the labor force. The personnel director also attends the monthly meetings, where he listens in for information rather than participates in the decisions.

The report presumably notes any appreciable price changes. When the probable effect of the change is a need for new financing or the change is a response to the financial problem brought before the corporation, reporting the price action is required. In practice there would also be consultation with the appropriate member of the executive committee whenever the general manager felt the need of consultation, or at least believed that preliminary discussion of a special pricing problem with an executive committee member would be prudent or helpful. Thus, it rarely happens that any significant price change will have been made before coming to the attention of someone in the central corporation, who is recognized as a policy consultant appropriate to the area of the problem.[3]

A factor in pricing of du Pont products, developed over recent years, is the maintenance and regular examination by departmental executive groups of a system of charts, which reveal trends in the level of activity for business generally and for the industries on which the particular departments are dependent, the purpose being to determine the effect of these trends on the returns to the corporation. These are in addition to the internal charts kept by a department concerning its production, sales, profitability, expansion trends, and financial requirements. The analysis and discussion of these factors may contribute to a general upgrading or downgrading of the price structure

[3] In connection with the running battle in recent years of the various acrilic fibers developed by competing chemical companies, the introduction of one competitor's product was pushed by a sharp price reduction that enlarged the differential between it and the corresponding du Pont product. In the case cited, opinions in du Pont on effective countermoves ranged from a strict holding of the line at du Pont's higher price, with continuing emphasis on du Pont quality, to a direct meeting of price at the expense of profit margin. (The spread in price between the two products was roughly between $1.40 and $1.75 per pound.) The price decision had to resolve this question: How far could awareness of the superiority of the du Pont product be carried over into consumer willingness to accept a spread between the prices of the du Pont and the competing fiber? In this case the product manager's first determination, resulting from a department conference, was tested in an informal consultation with a member of the corporation's executive committee. It resulted in a final determination by the general manager of a price approximately 7 per cent above the figure to which the competing fiber had been reduced. The formal decision was that of the general manager.

of the department apart from any price change made on a specific
product.

Discussion with the Rayon Department suggests that, within the
general procedure outlined above, there may be considerable diversity
among departments in the procedures used in keeping with the investment philosophy of top management. It may be that the authority for
pricing rayon, nylon, or cellophane may rest at a different hierarchical
level from that of the products pricing authority in the Fabrics and
Finishes Department. The manager of one department was forthright,
however, in saying that the determination of prices and rates of return on the large variety of products under his control rested entirely
with him, top management supervision being at a minimum.

GENERAL ELECTRIC COMPANY

The products of General Electric come under four general product
groups, each headed by an executive vice president, viz.: Industrial
Components and Materials Group, Consumer Products Group, Apparatus Group, and the Electronic, Atomic, and Defense Systems
Group. The groups are divided into product divisions, each headed
by a general manager who may also rank as a vice president. These
in turn are separated into about one hundred product departments.
Typically, the product department is charged with operating as a
separate business, making its decisions on prices, as well as channels
of distribution and other policy areas connected with its operations.
For example, the Medium AC Motor and Generating Department is
an operating department of the Motor and Generator Division of
the General Electric Company.

The head of the product department is responsible for sales as well
as production, and prices are quoted in the name of the department.
Supervision over the department manager is termed educational and
advisory. It may take the form of bringing department policy into
line with more general policy of the company, such as the corporation

effort to resist inflation by holding down prices generally during the campaign of 1948. Subject to such general policy checks, the department heads have complete authority to determine the pricing of their product line.

One over-all factor imposing a discipline on the pricing policy of the product department relates to its capital commitments. The pay-out period on capital commitments, in the case of cost reducing improvements, is only two years. This pay-out test influences both the selection of products and the pricing policy of the department heads, who must justify their proposals to central management for new or improved facilities.

Department heads appear to have less independence in pricing new products than in changing prices on established products. At least this is true in the sense that the introduction of a new product requires considerably more consultation with divisional executives and ultimate approval by the divisional or, in cases of major import, the group vice president. Thus, a number of different prices were used in testing consumer reaction to a new dishwasher before a price recommedation was made, and the final decision required approval at both the divisional and group level.

Since the corporation operates a number of service divisions, which advise all product groups and in some cases are charged with appraisal of operations, the direct lines of operational authority occasionally have to be crossed in the interest of expeditious and effective action. This is true of pricing as well as of other activities of the product department. On this point, the organization chart of the corporation has the following interesting footnote:

> *Channels of Contact*—While the organization structure and chart define lines of responsibility, authority and accountability, they do not indicate or limit Channels of Contact, or flow of information, between or among members of the organization. Organization policy permits and expects the exercise of common sense and good judgment, at all organization levels, in determining the best channels of contact for expeditious handling of company work. Contacts, and flow of information, between people and components of the organization should be carried out in the simplest and most direct way practicable. In making such contacts, however, it is the

duty of each member of the organization to keep his superior promptly informed regarding any matter:

1) For which his superior may be held properly accountable by others;

2) As to which there is, or which is likely to cause, disagreement or controversy, especially between different components of the organization;

3) Which require the advice of his superior or coordination by his superior with other components of the organization; or

4) Which involve recommendations for change in, or variance from established policies.[4]

GENERAL FOODS CORPORATION

In General Foods, the location of authority to set or change prices appears to have considerable flexibility. It depends upon the character of the product, whether it is a new specialty or an established standard item, the frequency of price change, the product market, and in a few cases the experience and capabilities of particular company officials. Price changes contemplated by one operating vice president are characteristically discussed directly with the president, while analogous price problems in another vice president's jurisdiction are discussed with the executive vice president.

The operating areas of General Foods are divided into two groups: the Jell-O, Birds Eye, and Maxwell House divisions, under the president; the rest under the executive vice president. Each of the divisions reporting directly to the president is headed by an operating vice president. The group reporting to the executive vice president includes (a) Bireley's Division, Electricooker Division, and the Perkins Products Company, in charge of one vice president for operations; (b) the Corn Mill, Franklin Baker, Gaines, and Walter Baker divisions under another; and (c) the Atlantic Gelatin, Post Cereals, and Institutional Products divisions, General Foods, Limited, and International Opera-

---

[4] National Industrial Conference Board, *Company Organization Charts*, Studies in Personnel Policy, No. 139 (1953), p. 65.

tions, the heads of which are directly responsible to the executive vice president.

Until 1953, all products except frozen foods, which had their own sales force, were marketed by the General Foods Sales Division. In that year, Maxwell House coffee and Post cereals set up their own sales organizations. In due course, other product divisions followed suit, and in 1955 the General Foods Sales Division was abolished.

Considerable autonomy resides with the division managers. They are responsible for their own profit and loss positions; hence, except as important new product situations require direct consultation with top management, the division managers make their own price decisions. In general, the following pricing situations prevail:

1. The authority to move prices resides in the managements of the respective product divisions and in some cases in the sales departments of those divisions. In the latter category, are bulk livestock feeds, which are by-products of the grain mills, family and bakery flour, and frozen fish, for which prices change frequently, perhaps even daily.

2. In the case of specialties, for which price changes are relatively infrequent, the change is likely to be made at a fairly high level, typically by the operating vice president, who in turn often consults with the executive vice president.

3. The authority to change prices is in the hands of the operating vice president, but he keeps the president fully informed of developments and often consults with him in advance. This applies to coffee, a large item in the General Foods business, in which important price changes occur, but less frequently than in such products as bulk livestock feeds or frozen fish, etc.

4. In the frozen fruit and vegetable line, for which the issue of prices arises once a year and the prices that are expected to prevail for the products govern what can be paid for raw materials (some of which are grown on contract), the size of the crop and probable price levels enter into the planning of the budget for the division. For that reason, the projected prices are reviewed by the president. Once the operating plan for the season has been set, however, adjustments in prices, such as those for slow-moving items, are made by the vice president and general manager of the Birds Eye Division.

INTERNATIONAL HARVESTER COMPANY

The International Harvester Company appears to be organized with more centralized control over price determination than the typical enterprise of its size. Pricing is the primary responsibility of the Price and Contract Department, a functional unit of the company, which serves all product groups. The department, after consultation with manufacturing and sales personnel, determines the price at which it believes a product should sell. With the exception of service parts, for which the Price and Contract Department is the decisive authority, the price recommended by the department is subject to review by the divisional vice president and approval by the executive vice president for the product in question.

International Harvester has three product divisions: Farm Equipment, Motor Trucks, and Industrial Equipment. Each division has its own manufacturing and sales departments. The divisions have their own vice presidents and are also under the jurisdiction of an executive vice president. The Farm Equipment Division is responsible to an executive vice president who also has charge of the Price and Contract Department, of Credits and Collections, and of the Canadian group. Motor Trucks and Industrial Equipment are under the jurisdiction of another executive vice president.[5]

Though the Price and Contract Department is under the general jurisdiction of an executive vice president, for pricing decisions, it refers to the particular executive vice president in charge of the products division concerned. In the case of farm equipment, this is its own executive vice president. In the case of motor trucks and industrial equipment, it is the executive vice president in charge of the Motor Trucks and Industrial Equipment Divisions.

The Price and Contract Department was established as a staff department to ensure co-ordination of the pricing of similar products made or sold by the various divisions, particularly service parts.

[5] There is also a third executive vice president, who is responsible for manufacturing and engineering throughout the company.

Many of these are common to the products of more than one division and must be sold at the same price by each division, since a dealer might buy from more than one division. In fact, on service parts, the department has final responsibility in pricing.

For the pricing of a complete piece of equipment, the Price and Contract Department obtains from the producing division an estimate of the factory cost, which is arrived at on the basis of policies and procedures laid down by the company comptroller. Working with sales, manufacturing, or engineering personnel, it also makes a first-hand study of the product, in order to assess its value in relation to competing products. The department itself assembles background material such as specifications and prices of competitive products, selling agreements of competing firms with their dealers and distributors, and trade and fringe discounts.

The department is expected to exercise independent judgment as to the optimum competitive price, acting as a balance wheel between sales personnel, who have a predilection for low prices, and manufacturing personnel, who tend to emphasize adequate margins over production costs.

When the Price and Contract Department staff has completed its study, it discusses the competitive price it expects to recommend with the sales member of the product development committee responsible for the product. The assembled data on the competition, as well as a price-cost-profit analysis are reviewed, using the above-mentioned approved factory cost and the estimated selling and administrative expense. The recommended price, nearly always agreed with the product specialist of the sales department, is then reviewed with a member of sales management and ultimately with the vice president and general manager of the division. The department submits its recommended price and relevant data to executive management for final approval. If any differences of opinion exist between the divisional management and the Price and Contract Department, the latter must also submit the views of the divisional management to the executive vice president responsible for the product.

In most instances, the executive vice president will make the final price decision. Most price decisions on major machines, however, are reviewed with the president and frequently with the chairman of the board. When final price approval has been given, the Price and Contract Department is responsible for issuing the price information in a form and at a time suitable to the Sales Department.

The procedure outlined here applies primarily to a new or redesigned product. A review of the price for an existing product may be initiated, however, at any level and in general will follow the same pattern.

The pricing of service parts is handled under authority delegated to the Price and Contract Department without review by sales or executive management. There are many thousands of parts, and usually the pricing of a new part fits into a pattern established for a similar or related part. Many parts prices are determined by following the price structure recommended by the supplier of the part, who probably sells the same or a similar part to competitors and through independent parts distributors. When requested by the sales or producing departments, the price of any part is reviewed in relation to cost and competition.

A semiannual analysis of each division by an operations review committee, consisting of executive and top-level management personnel, provides an opportunity for price review of existing and proposed products in relation to the performance of the producing division. Full data with respect to competitive prices, as well as costs and profits, are available at such reviews.

JOHNS-MANVILLE CORPORATION

Johns-Manville has a fairly clear organization of pricing responsibility with little overlapping apparent. General price policies are controlled by the vice president for sales, a functional officer of the corporation whose major decisions are made in consultation with the senior officers and passed upon by the board of directors.

Specific responsibility for pricing is vested in the general manager of a division. The divisions are organized mainly on a product basis:

Industrial Products (industrial insulations, pipe, packings, and friction materials), Building Products, Celite, Asbestos Fibre, Canadian Products, Dutch Brand (rubber) Products, and International. The divisional general manager delegates the pricing to a merchandise manager, who in turn may delegate part of his authority to a district manager, especially for meeting local price competition. Salesmen have no authority to change prices or quote special prices on their own responsibility; all concessions must be cleared with the office of the divisional manager. Salesmen and district managers keep close watch on competitive prices and report by telephone as well as in written reports. They are the eyes and ears of top management in meeting competitive situations.

  Although this organizational framework gives the merchandising managers a great number of products to handle, the problem is made manageable by the general price policy of the corporation of adhering to quoted prices and its practice of making price changes only infrequently.

NATIONAL STEEL CORPORATION

  The line of authority for pricing responsibility in National Steel is materially influenced by the range of products the company sells, and by the fact that it is essentially a price follower in the industry. Its two steel-making subsidiaries are Weirton Steel, about half of whose capacity is used for making tin plate, and Great Lakes Steel, which is primarily engaged in the production of sheets for the automotive industry and businesses with similar requirements.

  With respect to tin plate, the prices are made by negotiation between U.S. Steel and American Can, and these prices are as a matter of course accepted by National and the other leading makers of tin plate. This takes care of a sizable fraction of National Steel's pricing area. Sheets, which account for a large part of the business of this company, are with few exceptions so well standardized as to general specifications and extras that National Steel may follow the pattern of prices of U.S. Steel, except in so far as locational differences prevail on base prices.

The simplicity of its line and the fewness of its plants, combine to make it possible for National Steel to centralize its pricing authority at the very top. Thus the pricing responsibility resides essentially in the executive committee, which sets the general pattern of prices. Even the president of Weirton or of Great Lakes has final authority over only relatively minor price changes on specific products. The executive committee, however, is a small group consisting of five persons, two of whom are the presidents of Weirton and Great Lakes, the other three being, respectively, the chairman, the president, and a director of National Steel.

The office of the vice president for sales is apparently a policy-making office, which presents for approval of the executive committee the general pattern of prices and decisions affecting major contracts. Each of the divisions also has a sales vice president and a well-distributed organization of sales offices. But salesmen are in no instance permitted to make price concessions. The salesman is expected, however, to keep in close touch with competition in his sales territory and to advise his superiors with regular reports as well as informal communication. It is stated by management that approximately 75 per cent of the selling agreements are made by top management and are "open end" requirements contracts. (Actually they are not contracts in the strict sense, but represent informal understandings, which serve as guides to the expectations of seller and buyer.)

Within the high degree of centralization and standardization of National Steel's prices, there is always the need of meeting the special requirements of customers for specifications that are out of line with the standard schedule of basic prices and extras. National Steel regards itself as being a sufficiently small company to bring its engineering and technical staff as well as officers into informal conference with their opposite numbers for the customer, so that necessary adjustments in practice receive quick approval at both the divisional and the corporate level. The company prides itself on the fact that its sales staff is smaller and more active and able to get business with a less costly organization than is maintained by the larger companies or

those with greater complexity of product lines. This stress on simplicity of organization is said to be a general characteristic of the
corporation, which is reflected in its organization for pricing.

SEARS, ROEBUCK AND COMPANY

Price setting in Sears is fairly centralized, although there are distinct
differences between mail order and retail store pricing. The responsibility for establishing catalog selling prices for mail order and suggested selling prices for the retail stores rests with the "parent" merchandise organization, headed by the vice president in charge of
merchandising. In practice, price determination is initiated by the
company's 420 buyers in conjunction with the procurement of merchandise. The buyers are attached to fifty buying departments, each
under a merchandise supervisor, who reports directly to the vice
president.

With respect to mail order selling, price decisions are made by each
company buyer for his own line of goods, working with his supervisor and mail order sales manager. The merchandise supervisors are
guided by a particular percentage or dollar mark-up, depending upon
the custom of the trade and modified by the kind of market involved,
price differential from nearest competitors, including the discount
houses, and related factors. The vice president works very closely with
the merchandise supervisors. Ordinarily he makes little or no change
in their price recommendations, except that he views pricing more in
terms of prospective return on investment than on sales, and this
emphasis occasionally determines whether on given products he would
attempt to realize a higher return through greater volume, or conversely, to raise margins to secure a more favorable return.

The retail prices are determined at the same time as mail order
prices, with the buyers suggesting appropriate retail differentials for
the thirty-five retail price zones in the Sears geographic price structure.
The management pointed out that these are suggested retail selling
prices, since each store may alter prices depending upon local com-

petition. In fact, however, the stores follow the parent buyers' recommendations over 90 per cent of the time, and when changes are made
they are usually minor.[6]

The discretion of the individual store manager is affected in large
part by the particular class of store he manages. Managers of Class A
stores, of which there are approximately 120,[7] report to a group
manager, in cities where there is a group of A stores, who, in turn,
reports to one of five territorial vice presidents. In cases where there
is only one Class A store in a city, the manager reports directly to his
territorial vice president. The managers of Class B and Class C stores
also report to their zone managers,[8] who in turn report to the territorial officers. Store managers ordinarily consult with their immediate
superior in making price changes, and although the vice president in
charge of merchandising is notified, his approval is not necessary.

Each of the eleven mail order plants has its own catalog and
catalog supplements, which are issued by the parent organization in
Chicago. Regular seasonal and special mail order sales originate at the
central office, although different items may be stressed in different
areas. Also, from time to time, depending upon its inventory position,
the season, and competitive conditions generally, each mail order
plant may issue its own sales circulars. Similarly, retail store managers
decide upon the timing of their sales, which may be entirely local in
nature and bear little or no relation to catalog sales.

While it is clear that considerable leeway is permitted by Sears to
retail store managers, it is equally evident that the managers characteristically adhere to the suggested selling prices. Thus, since the
parent organization buys the goods and sets selling prices, which are

[6] Suggested prices are issued with a merchandise list containing every item
of merchandise that a retail store may require. No retail store is permitted to
stock any item not shown on the merchandise list. On the other hand, no
supervisor or buyer can order a store to carry certain goods.

[7] The Class A stores are complete department stores with selling space of approximately 75,000 square feet or over.

[8] There are three types of B stores (junior department stores, stores carrying
essentially appliances and hard lines, and those carrying lines usually found
in a hardware store). The C stores are small hardware-type stores with special
emphasis on farm equipment and a catalog sales department.

followed most of the time, the parent organization along with the stores is responsible for the sales and profits in all retail stores as well as in mail order.

SWIFT & COMPANY

In Swift there is more than one line of price responsibility because the company is organized on both a functional and product basis and because many of the individual units, both functional and product, are treated as enterprises with their own profit and loss statements.

The Sales Department of Swift is a functional division through which nearly all sales of meat to the trade are made; it consists of General Sales and Contract Sales and is headed by a vice president. Contract Sales sells to the government and to some institutions. Most of the meat processed by Swift is sold through the General Sales Department. Some of this is sold directly to customers through the Larger Buyer Division, some through the Hotel, Restaurant and Institution Sales Division, but the bulk is sold through Plant Sales units and Branch House Sales units to retailers, a few wholesalers, and certain institutions not covered by Contract Sales. The Plant Sales units, which are responsible not only to General Sales but also to their own plant managers, sell in areas where no Branch House exists. (See chart p. 240.)

Meat is sold to the Plant Sales units and the Branch Houses by the Commodity Department units at the plants. Each Commodity Department is headed by a vice president. Thus there is a vice president for the purchase and processing of hogs, another for cattle buying, beef and veal. Outside of meat packing there are vice presidents for plant foods, agricultural chemicals and feed, for dairy products and poultry, for margarine and vegetable oils, for table-ready meats, etc. Most of the packing plants will generally process all types of livestock, thus cutting across more than one commodity department.

Each commodity unit tries to sell at a price that will give it a profit.

Sales Organization, Swift & Company[a]

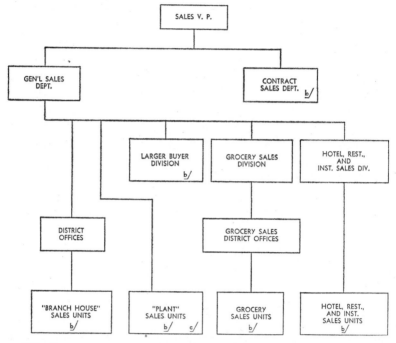

[a] This diagram covers only sales of meat and grocery products (but not, for example, feed and plant food) except export sales and those sales made direct by commodity departments.

[b] Sales to trade are made by these units.

[c] The plant sales units are plant departments and are also responsible, like the plant commodity departments, to their plant manager.

The Sales Department units, however, must try to buy from the plant at a figure that will permit them to realize a profit on the wholesale price. While the price is a matter of negotiation, and in theory the departments can bargain, in practice each has an understanding of the needs of the other, and there is little or no real bargaining. The Sales Department knows that the Commodity Department must cover the cost of livestock and the cost of processing; the Commodity Department knows that the Sales Department must dispose of its product at the going price and that the price at which it buys must be low enough to allow for selling expenses.[9] The Sales Department has some leeway in that its units are at liberty to take only what they think they can sell at the expected wholesale price.

From the standpoint of the plant manager, the profitability of the plant depends on its sales from all livestock. Each commodity unit in the plant, however, buys and sells independently. It is therefore possible for the plant as a whole to show a loss as a result of unprofitable operations in one of the commodity units.[10]

Of products other than meat, grocery products are sold through the Grocery Sales units of the General Sales Department. A number of other items, however, such as feeds and plant food, are sold by sales forces attached to the product department concerned. They are responsible to the vice president of the product department and are independent of the General Sales Department.

UNION CARBIDE CORPORATION

Union Carbide was essentially a holding company until after the Second World War. During the period 1948-1952, the leading subsidiaries—National Carbon, Bakelite, Electro Metallurgical Company, Carbide Chemicals, and Linde—were made operating divisions of the parent corporation. With increasing size and complexity, a major problem of the corporation has been the need for greater co-ordination of certain operations in what has for many years been a decentralized enterprise.

The Appropriations Committee is the key policy-making group,

[9] The Commodity Department aside from its transactions with the Sales Department, also does some direct selling to the Export Department and, in a few special situations, to other packers, to processors, or to brokers.

[10] The plant manager, as head buyer for the plant, can control this to a limited extent through instructions to the buyers on the price and quantity of each type of livestock to be bought for processing through his plant. In the case of an impasse between departments, a decision may be made at the vice-presidential level in Chicago.

controlling the corporation's purse strings. Apart from the annual budget sessions with the division heads, the committee receives copies of the monthly operations reviews that are prepared by the various divisions. These reviews do not discuss pricing as such but do include a presentation of the operating statements of each division, in total and broken down by individual products. These data enable divisional comparisons to be made, product by product, of the forecasted and actual returns on utilized investment and sales. If price changes are mentioned, they would be by way of explanation of operating results.

In addition to the above, the Appropriations Committee meets frequently in informal "Chart Sessions," scheduled so that each group of products can be reviewed at least once a year. These sessions provide an opportunity for the committee to meet with individuals in the operating divisions who are primarily responsible for the products that are the subject of the meeting. These sessions have nothing directly to do with pricing. If the subject comes up for discussion, it is principally to help explain the profit picture, or possibly to explain why a price change has taken place, or why one may be contemplated for the future. The Appropriations Committee likes to be kept informed of changes only in cases in which there may be sizable effects on profits, but there is no general requirement that the committee be informed in advance of any changes. It is the attitude of the corporation that the divisions are held responsible for profits and must therefore be given the right to determine their selling prices.

Another kind of corporation review of divisional operations is through actions on requests for capital expenditures. When additional facilities are under consideration, data covering sales quantities, selling prices, and related information must usually be reviewed in order to provide a basis for decision. In this process, both the division and the corporation may be alerted to problems of consistency between divisional prices and corporate profit objectives.

In so far as production, research, pricing, and sales are concerned, divisional autonomy is the rule. In the pricing of alloys and metals, for example, prices are reviewed by the vice president for sales of the Electro Metallurgical Company, who in the matter of major price revisions makes recommendations to a management committee (of which he is chairman) and to the president of the company. In the initial stages of pricing a new product, other departments are consulted, but ordinarily prices are set by the sales management. No delegation of price authority is made down the line to sales managers or salesmen.

In Linde, the pricing of industrial gases is the responsibility of the vice president and general manager. He consults with the gas sales manager and manager of apparatus sales on questions arising from monthly sales and cost reports. Regional sales managers are also brought in for consultation, but they have no authority to make price changes in the field. On general price revisions arising out of major changes in costs, the president is informed before the changes are effected. In the past few years, there has been an increasing degree of product line autonomy with respect to pricing, production scheduling, and development programs. The manager of gas apparatus sales has authority to make price changes without going to the vice president and general manager; only in cases of general price revisions cutting across product lines of the company would this referral normally be necessary.

In pricing chemicals, the organizational picture is much the same as presented above: divisional autonomy with little delegation down the line to salesmen. Because a large proportion of many chemical products is sold to large consumers on a contractual basis, negotiations on price matters are ordinarily pursued at the sales manager or vice presidential level.

The pricing of "Prestone" antifreeze is a special case in which the authority does not rest within a single division. Prices are recommended at the start of each season by a small committee from Union Carbide Chemicals Company, which produces the basic raw material (ethylene glycol), and National Carbon Company, which markets the final product. If agreement cannot be reached by this group, the matter goes to the two divisional presidents, or higher if necessary. The explanation for this special treatment for "Prestone" is that ethylene glycol has many possible end product uses, so the price established for this product, the most important end product, has implications cutting across several divisions of the corporation.

UNITED STATES STEEL CORPORATION

Pricing is one of the few functions in U.S. Steel that do not follow divisional lines. In earlier periods, the president had ultimate responsibility for matters of broad price policy, but the determination of product prices and price changes has now been delegated to the Executive Vice President, Commercial, who is the key man of the corporation in setting prices. It will be recalled that, under the regime of President Farrell, all price changes had to be cleared through him—a situation that resulted in his becoming a bottleneck in the pricing process.

The mechanics of a particular price change in steel products were discussed in detail in connection with the 1956 increases. It is clear that the executive vice president relies very heavily on the Price Division for basic analysis and recommendations. The product divisions, also under the Executive Vice President, Commercial, are responsible for distribution, and may make recommendations for price revisions, but have no authority to change prices without approval of the Commercial Department. Intracompany memoranda stipulate the conditions under which prices may be altered and make it evident that sales personnel have no discretion in this matter. Interviewers were told that no absorption of freight or price changes, on any product, may be made without the approval of the Executive Vice President, Commercial. In practice, this means that on the question of freight absorption the Executive Vice President indicates on which products, and the procedures under which, absorption may be made. The district sales managers interpret the limits for their own areas and the amount of absorption necessary for salesmen in their districts. It is company policy to absorb no more than the amount of freight needed to equalize with a competitive mill. It can be said generally that pricing authority is not delegated down the line to the operating divisions of the company.

The foregoing review of the organization for pricing and the distribution of pricing authority reveals differences in company history and in temper of the leadership. Nevertheless the administration of the pricing function tends to reflect the nature of the product and customs of the trade appropriate to it. The company organization may, in turn, exert an independent influence on the price treatment of the firm's products.

The responsibility for pricing a specific product frequently appears to be determined by its place in the company's product mix, the multiplicity and diversity of products handled, and the degree of interdependence among the product divisions. Thus "Prestone" antifreeze is made by Union Carbide's Chemical Division but is sold and priced in the Carbon Division, which distributes the consumer product. The interdependence is for a number of companies primarily an aspect of their integration. This is apparent when, as in metal production, the cost and price of a primary product provide the base for the series of price steps that apply to the succeeding stages of production.

Centering pricing at the summit, with little if any delegation to sales managers or department heads, is characteristic of one segment of the sample, represented by firms such as American Can, General Motors, International Harvester, National Steel, and U.S. Steel. Each of them is associated with a major durable product or group of related products, accounting for the bulk of sales, for which price quotations are issued at regular periods rather than short and irregular intervals. Top level responsibility at American Can is directly exercised in the strategic yearly negotiations with U.S. Steel on the tin plate price, as well as in the governing standard contract for packers' cans, with its formula for determining price changes. The integrated steel companies tend to tie the prices of final products to unfinished steel prices by more or less standard formulas, which are generally traceable to the leadership of U.S. Steel. National Steel, carrying a relatively narrow line in which sheets and tin plate predominate, can readily administer the company pricing from the top, with U.S. Steel prices generally followed.[11] The responsibility retained by top level central management for pricing the GM lines of automobiles can be seen to flow

[11] In this case the continuing personal leadership of one of the founders (Ernest Weir) has also revealed itself in the absence of delegation of price decisions to the product sales forces.

from the co-ordinated production of bodies and other key components, as well as the dovetailed price ranges of the car divisions, within the corporation. International Harvester's price lists for its main lines—farm machines, trucks, and earthmoving equipment—can also be set at the center because, apart from company tradition, the pricing of these major items is crucial to the success of the corporation as a whole. In these representative cases of centralized pricing the sales forces are chiefly service personnel without a direct part in price decisions.

In A. & P., the multiplicity and variety of items have necessitated putting the price responsibility within the manageable geographic limits of the district unit. But the delegation is limited; store managers have no discretion to modify the ground rules of uniform prices for the same products in the same zones and types of stores as laid down by the unit administration.

A second group, represented by Standard (New Jersey), Johns-Manville, G.E., du Pont, Union Carbide, and General Foods, discloses by comparison the large degree of delegation in price-making responsibility down the line of management to divisional sales managers and department heads. The product divisions of companies like G. E. or Union Carbide are, in the size of their operations, the equivalent of large companies; the delegation of pricing responsibility can still be within a framework of more or less strictly set targets at the divisional level, which conform in turn to over-all investment objectives of the corporation. In a mixed line such as that of General Foods, distributing merchandise that is subject to keen price competition and short-term changes, more direct participation of the sales force in pricing is required than for automobiles produced by GM, for which an integrated plan covering all car lines must be worked out well in advance for the model year. Johns-Manville is concerned with the distribution of a full line, which includes widely different products in which the company has a high degree of authority, and those which it carries to make up a full line with only a small share of the market. It is therefore necessarily flexible in the delegation of pricing decisions to those who are closest to the peculiarities of the different markets to which the products respectively cater.

Undoubtedly, the character of the company organization may exert an independent influence on the price policies and practices of a firm and, because these are giant firms, on the industry itself. Thus, the significant shift, which many of the companies have recently been undergoing, from a pyramiding organization based on the functions of engineering and production to a divisional- or product-based structure, should increase the degree of flexibility in pricing and eventually the independence of subordinates. This consequence may easily be exaggerated by taking the form of organization at face value. In some instances, the firm organization chart represents an expectation not yet realized, while in others the practices are well established in keeping with the formal organization.

PART
II / Analysis and
Interpretation

4 / *Major Influences on Pricing Policies in Big Business*

IN THIS STUDY a three-pronged approach has been used for examining the pricing policies of large companies. In the first approach, the discussion was restricted to a presentation of the techniques employed by management in pricing single products and product groups. The variety of products and market situations covered illustrated the diversity of pricing practices found among large firms, and demonstrated the manner in which the pricing policies were implemented. In the second approach, the perspective of the presentation was widened to include all the products sold by each company. An attempt was made to characterize the nature of the pricing policies of each firm as a single pricing organization, even though actual pricing decisions might be delegated, for instance, to its product divisions. At this second level of company policy formation, the material available from the interviews with the pricing executives was used to isolate and develop responses to the question: "What is your pricing policy?" and not, as in the earlier discussion, to the query: "How do you price wire or cable?"

In so far as it was in accord with the pledges to respect the anonymity of persons interviewed and to treat certain data as confidential, the material was presented as made available by the management, with a minimum of derived generalizations, imposed consistencies, or imputation of motives. How particular products are priced in the market and what the management stated it used as broad guides to their pricing have been indicated. The officials for the most part did not, however, indulge in generalizations cutting across firms; nor did they attempt to list and rank the determinants of their pricing policies.

Coming to the third approach, an attempt will be made in the following discussion to summarize those identifiable influences or variables that affect and serve to explain the pricing of large industrial companies. It should be made clear that, at this third level of inquiry, the obligation to restrict the treatment to a faithful reproduction of the stated views of management no longer applies. The statements and other pricing materials furnished by the companies will be appraised, as required, in the light of related information from other sources. The classifications of pricing influences with the appraisal of their relative importance must be to a large extent our own, although deriving mainly from the information supplied by the company managements.

The influences considered below cannot be of equal importance to all the companies studied, either because of differences in products and markets or differences in the bent of management. Attention will be focused on how the major influences manifest themselves in the pricing policies of the companies interviewed. First, several latent forces are examined that condition the general direction taken by the company's pricing—the nature of the product, the cost structure, the composition of the product mix or the pattern of integration, etc. These are followed up with certain influences on pricing that company policy is designed to exert. They may be reflected in the emphasis on quality, style, and service competition or in pricing for special market objectives like product promotion, penetration of new markets, or maintenance of what a company regards as its appropriate market share. The impact of the antitrust laws is dealt with from the standpoint of their influence on pricing. Finally, consideration is given to the consciousness of leadership as a factor in the pricing policy of big companies, and its expression in "administered" prices or in the rationalization of price stability as an essential feature of orderly competition.

Throughout this chapter, it will be found that the company history and the dominant personalities that served to shape general company policy have also helped to determine the pricing policies of their companies. The legacy of the past tends to accumulate, in the big enterprise, what may be termed the collective company personality: a complex mixture of organization and dominant personalities, antitrust suits, and marketing methods rooted in tradition, which together play an important role in modifying the effect of the conventional determinants of pricing policy that are discussed in the ensuing sections of this chapter. The interaction between pricing policies imposed upon the company by the nature of the product line, and those that the big companies have developed by their own traditions and policies, is central in the interpretation of big company pricing.

CHARACTER OF THE PRODUCT

The character of the product—the type of demand to which it caters, as well as its physical attributes, production requirements, amenability to differentiation, and stage of maturity—sets boundaries to the pricing discretion of the company, big or little. When interpreting the role of product characteristics, however, the possibility that reaction may run both ways must be kept in mind. These characteristics are not fixed or unadjustable. They themselves may be affected by price. But the basic concern at this point is with pricing policies that seem to be imposed by the nature of the product, rather than vice versa.

With a product like fresh meat, perishable and subject to unpredictable output and shipments of the primary commodity, even a firm of the importance of Swift & Company has a limited opportunity to bend wholesale prices to company policy. A durable product with controlled raw material output, and production based on orders, better lends itself to fairly stable price quotations, as in steel or crude oil. Copper on the contrary with its volatile price behavior points up the effect on the manageability of prices of a widely diffused raw material supply and a world market. Limitations on the transportability of the product (transportation cost in relation to product value) may give locational advantage in pricing even when there are business giants in the industry.

New products, with varying degrees of marketable uniqueness, provide opportunities for pricing discretion not generally available in standardized goods. Large companies whose resources are concentrated in established standard products are aware of the general unprofitability of price wars when confronted with similarly large and resourceful competitors; hence they keep in step with the competition on price and depend on such factors as favorable location, or availability of adequate supplies and satisfactory service to customers, for their competitive strength at the going price. In the use of these devices, however, product features (*e.g.,* vulnerability to substitution) may determine how successful a stable price policy can be, even for the large and resourceful company.

New Products and Matured Products. The natural frame of reference for pricing a new product is the price range of existing substitutes. For example, it was recognized that nylon was capable of penetrating the markets of a variety of textile fibers. The problem of effectively introducing this new fiber resolved itself through a compromise between pricing for the widest possible use and pricing for the more limited, but in the long run, more sustainable and profitable quality market. In cellophane, the same company reached more aggressively for more extensive market penetration without undermining the profit potential. Apparently, the cost elasticity of volume output and the price elasticity of growing demand were sufficiently high to permit a more rapid rate of expansion than was possible in nylon. The introduction of a major consumer appliance, for which demand is as yet an expectation rather than a reality, has entailed elaborate market research to select a price niche that will permit the inclusion of features required for optimum acceptance. In the pricing of a major piece of farm machinery such as the cotton picker, the decision settles on a middle ground between the estimated maximum economic value as a replacement for hand labor and a sufficiently low price to give assurance of widespread adoption. Prices determined in this manner may well limit the components that can be selected for incorporation in the assembled product; automobiles and other consumer durables considered earlier were cases in point. With the accumulation of know-how and the lowering of costs, subsequent pricing turns on whether the product can readily be imitated, whether the prestige acquired in its pioneering can be prolonged through improvement and product differentiation, or whether lower cost reflected in lower price will open up a highly profitable volume increase.

An established standard product, be it a metal, flour, or heavy chemical, does not entail such conscious balancing of alternative possibilities to fix its price levels. The price may start from a fairly well-recognized cost base, but the profit is a residual reflecting the current willingness or ability of the market to keep the capacity employed. Large firms with heavy investments in established areas of primary production have constantly feared that price changes will lead to hazards of unpredictable magnitude. This fear has often been justified in the past—witness the gyrations of price with accompanying demand fluctuations in copper, lead, or zinc; and even with price leadership, boom and depression fluctuations in steel prices have not been unknown. There is in consequence an undercurrent of antipathy in the firms interviewed to policies that would disturb the pattern of stable and infrequently changing prices. The instability of copper prices is certainly not due to lack of desire on the part of Kennecott and other primary producers to keep firm the price of their metal. The volatility issues rather from the fickleness of a world market, in which fluctuation is accentuated by extremes of overflow or scarcity in the supply of copper scrap.

At least until the Second World War, Alcoa supplied and priced aluminum in the United States with some regard to the fact that it had to penetrate the markets of copper and other metals as well as some non-metallic products. Its technical development in a capital-intensive form with integrated production and standardization of finished products now tends to assert itself; so that while product promotion remains vigorous, pricing in the basic aluminum lines is showing resemblances to steel's pattern of base prices and extras.

The type of use to which a product is put also has a bearing on the importance attached to price variations. The stable pricing of containers carried by American Can and Continental Can has met with little resistance by their customers, and this is not solely because of the duopoly leadership in can manufacture; it is largely due to the fact that what the final user is buying is not the container but the contents. Similarly, flexible packaging materials, aluminum fabrications, special electrical equipment items, and industrial gases permit the manufacturer a minimum of concern with price competition because these are products sold as part—an incidental part—of the larger end product in which the cost of the contributing item is not a prime consideration.

Cost Structure. Production and cost characteristics of the main product played a primary role in conditioning the pricing policies adopted by several companies in the sample. The overriding importance of certain materials in the total cost structure, as in the case of tin plate for can manufacture; the leanness of the ore, and the consequent magnitude of the mining operations of Kennecott Copper; the relatively small runs and large number of items, as in the case of Alcoa's fabricated operations; and of course the high proportion of indirect cost in basic steel production—all these distinctive features are transmuted into pricing policy. U. S. Steel seeks to avoid cutthroat price competition, and evolves a fair return philosophy. Alcoa finds a standard cost system unusable for many items. Kennecott, when prices drop, has to pile up inventory and await more settled prices; it looks with favor on stabilized prices. American Can, and perhaps even the oil companies, in the long run, become transmission belts for passing material and labor costs on to consumers with an inelastic demand. Thus a large part of price policy may be the response to the cost pattern inherent to the product.

INTERDEPENDENCE OF

THE PRODUCT MIX

The pricing of an individual product is frequently affected by the place it occupies in the company's product mix. Consideration was given to this influence in the discussion by management of product diversification, full-line pricing, vertical integration, and joint costs.

Many of the corporations studied have a diversity of output that puts them in a number of different industries. Johns-Manville, though one of the smaller giants in our sample, is listed in about twenty industries; Union Carbide is in at least five major industry groups, any one of which may be subdivided into market areas that are far from overlapping.[1]

The rank and presumable price leadership of a firm in one industry or market is not determined simply by comparing its assets with the assets of its competitors therein. The fact that General Electric may be one of the thirty-odd electric refrigerator companies or twenty-odd toaster companies, indicates the impossibility of stating with precision or in broad terms the considerations that might govern G.E.'s price policy for all of its products. Even if the company followed the same rules (based on market position) in pricing all products—a policy no management adopted—different products would inevitably be priced differently. But going further, it seems clear that enjoyment of a dominant position in one line may alter market tactics elsewhere. Profits or losses in one area may help to explain an intensification or moderation of marketing effort in another field. There are also cases in which policies developed for one product in the early company history have been carried over to other products, some of which are far removed from the original line.[2]

We have seen that, in the administration of pricing, homogeneity of product line makes for standardization of pricing, with authority at a high level, while wide diversification tends to vest pricing authority at the level of the product division. Firms that can focus on one product or which obtain their chief revenues from one product, such as National Steel, or from products performing the same function, such as American Can's containers, naturally tend to have more consistent pricing than is to be found in a firm, such as Union Carbide, whose

---

[1] It is of course difficult to bound an industry; but lack of product substitutability, difference in marketing organization and procedures, and difference in ultimate buyers can in combination serve to distinguish industries and justify the conclusion that different products produced by the same company do not compete in similar markets.

[2] International Harvester attempted to apply the pricing and styling methods of its original farm equipment to trucks and refrigerators. In these instances, it will be remembered, the market provided the company with its lessons, leading to a break-away from farm implement tradition in trucks and to an abandonment of the refrigerator line in favor of more promising fields.

products range from flashlight cells to industrial oxygen, or one, such as General Mills, that is selling airplane controls as well as Wheaties. In meeting both product diversity and product interdependence, the consistency in price policy may express itself by holding, as does du Pont, that some products on which it can earn only a below average return will be carried by the higher-margin items on which it concentrates its attention.

Full-Line Pricing. Companies that have built up a full line of related products for the same or similar markets frequently find themselves unable to make and change prices with the flexibility enjoyed by the independent producer who concentrates on one segment of the line. The various sizes in a line of motors produced to power farm machines of all sizes must be kept in some price arrangement that is internally logical. The eight-horse power motor, let us say, would have to take a price that in the full line is reasonably spaced between the six-horse power below and the ten-horse power above. The fabricator concentrating on one of these sizes, however, can supply it as a component for his machine at the price base that best suits him, without having to look over his shoulder at the price of related parts produced in the same factory. On the other hand, a full line of building materials, as carried by such a firm as Johns-Manville, may represent products that are complementary, in that they serve the same distributors. But they need not come under uniform pricing tactics. The company has opportunities for administered pricing with product differentiation in the field of its leadership, while in others it may follow the market price at an accommodation level in order to have a complete line for customers who bunch their orders with a supplier.

When the product mix represents different products emerging from the same equipment or process, pricing may be largely influenced by arbitrary allocation of joint processing costs among the prime and secondary items in the product flow. To the extent that such cost allocation has become rigid, the end price may likewise be stabilized up to the limits permitted by competition.

The vertically integrated company frequently concerns itself with pricing for successive stages of production represented by its product mix in a manner that has some resemblance to the problem of full-line pricing. Under the impact of antitrust legislation and court decisions, the integrated producer of a primary metal and its end products may find that he cannot freely price his products at a given stage of fabrication if his customers are also his competitors at that point. The integrated producer may therefore add to the transfer price from one product stage to the next the margin over cost used in billing the customer-competitor.

Thus the multiproduct company may be confronted with a range of both opportunities and inhibitions, as it devises policy for products that may be differentiated and priced independently and for those that must be priced with due regard for other items of the full line so as not to be a maverick in the pricing scheme of the product mix; and if it is vertically integrated, it must frequently price with an eye to the position of the non-integrated producer.

The shifts in organizational structure adopted by many of the large companies—from a pyramid based on the functions of engineering, sales, and production to a divisional or product-based structure—are a response to the dangers of over-centralization in price making for multiple product groups. The shift is usually designed to bring the responsibility for price making closer to the units that must make and market the given product line. The expectation is that a product-based structure will increase both the flexibility of pricing and, eventually, the initiative and efficiency of subordinates.

MARKET OBJECTIVES

REFLECTED IN PRICE

Managements, in response to their experience in the production and marketing of their main products, set up or adopt certain positive pricing objectives that have acquired the status of traditional practice. These company programs are perhaps the most direct and forthright of the influences distinguishing the pricing practices of several leading companies. They do not necessarily result in consistent direction of prices; but they do determine in fairly predictable fashion the typical responses of the company to new products, changes in costs, and change in market shares. The predilection for concentrating on the opportunities for style and quality emphasis rather than direct price competition is a major influence of this character. Two further influences prominent in company pricing policy are product promotion and maintenance of market share.

Quality, Service, and Style Competition. Pricing policy and "non-price" (quality and style) competition appear to be closely linked in the majority of the companies surveyed. There is a wide range of thinking on the importance of non-price competition. Those companies that stress engineering and sales services and play down price policy, or declare themselves uninterested in competing primarily on price, are selling goods with values lending themselves to successful differentiation.[3] This is especially so if the engineering and service needs of the customer are included with the product.

The clearest example among those surveyed, in its emphasis on non-price competition as a basis of price policy, was probably American Can. The policy of this company of automatically transmitting to its customers increases or decreases in basic costs—tin plate and wages —removed its prices from the executives' roster of items with which they must have constant concern. Possibly even more important was the emphasis of this company on routine and special services to its customers. American Can, having relegated price to the background, and having enjoyed a position as price leader, was able safely to concentrate on the provision of service and the devising of innovations. The peculiar cost structure in can making may also account in part for

[3] This kind of non-price competition was exemplified in testimony given by the assistant director of du Pont's film department in the Cellophane Case: "The main competitive materials . . . against which Cellophane competes are waxed paper, glassine, greaseproof and vegetable parchment papers, all of which are lower in price than Cellophane. We do not meet this price competition. Rather, we compete with these materials on the basis of establishing the value of our own as a factor in better packaging and cheaper distribution costs and classify as our logical markets those fields where the properties of Cellophane in relationship to its price can do a better job for the user." *United States v. E. I. du Pont de Nemours & Co.,* 118 Fed. Supp. 41 (1953).

the emphasis on service competition. When such a large part of the cost of the can is represented in the purchase of the tin plate, when there is little or no opportunity to shift overhead costs among products, and when the product takes up much space and is usually not stored but produced mainly on order, then it is unlikely there will be serious price cutting. This is particularly true when, as noted elsewhere, the canners are apparently more concerned with price equality than they are with price reductions.

Du Pont points out that, while heavy chemicals may sell mainly on a price basis, it is the missionary work with dealers and first-hand demonstrations to farmers that permit the company to compete effectively, in the sale of agricultural chemicals, insecticides, and fungicides. Union Carbide, perhaps even more than du Pont, appears to rely more on service and engineering auxiliaries than on price in competition for customers. Having attained leadership in the handling of industrial gases under great pressures, it is assumed to enjoy superior know-how in this field. Rather than wrestle with difficult technical problems and the unknown risks involved, customers who might otherwise be capable of turning out the product, buy it from Union Carbide.

The chemical companies spend on research as a matter of course. Their development of new products and the improvement of old constitute a familiar type of quality competition. Non-price competition, in the form of development of new products and product improvements that, for a time at least, may be bought without reference to price, is probably more prevalent in the chemical industry than in any other.

The contributions du Pont has made to the list of new chemicals —acetate rayon, de-greasing solvents, titanium pigments, neoprene, synthetic camphor, lucite and teflon plastics, 2-4 D plant growth regulant, etc.—in substance provide its *raison d'être*. Union Carbide, with a similar list of products, notes the importance of continuing efforts to provide better means of filling definite customer needs—as in the development of improved alloys; in such situations differences in shades of pricing could be overshadowed by the superiority of the improved product for specific purposes.

General Foods, many of whose products face severe price competition, feels the need for developing high-margin novelties that will serve to pick up sales and make more than a proportionate contribution to profits; Minute Rice, Swan's Down, and the increased range of Jell-O flavors are familiar examples. In the choice of a suitable metal for automatic transmission in automobiles, the battle between steel and aluminum moved back and forth on the basis of their respective properties, with current prices accepted. In this situation the advantage of easy machining with lighter metal was offset by the precision casting attainable on the heavier, until a new method of precision casting for aluminum turned the tide in its favor. The rubber tire companies, while engaged in vigorous price competition in every type of marketing outlet, attempt to pull themselves from the melee by introduction of value features such as the special tread, low-pressure, and tubeless tire, on which they may briefly rely for a favorable rate of return.

The role of style competition in the automobile industry dominates competitive relationships at the manufacturers' level. Executives did not stress this characteristic with the interviewers, but it is clear that style plays a strategic role in shifting customers from one make to another. In the postwar period the trend toward greater length, wider vision, and automatic operating features, represents the manufacturers' rivalry in capitalizing on the vagaries of consumer demand for new automobiles.

International Harvester officials, while speaking of the company's historical position as price leader, and dividing its competitors between those who matched on price and those who were price cutters, held the view that price has probably been less decisive an influence in determining sales than have credit terms. International Harvester attached greater importance to the qualities built into the machines: durability, economy of operation, and dealer service. When improved production methods reduced costs for some products, International Harvester, like G.E., transferred the benefits in new product features, but retained what was considered the optimum consumer-indicated price.

An interesting attempt to use non-price competition in grocery distribution appears in Kroger's policies. By stocking mostly nationally branded merchandise, which is somewhat higher priced than private brands, and by making tenderized meat a business-getting feature, it has managed to create the impression that its products tend to be of a higher grade than those customarily found in chain grocery stores. A. & P., with its greater size, features quality comparisons on its own specialty brands—*e.g.,* Bokar coffee and Ann Page Fine Foods.

The oil companies, by increasing octane number and proliferating additives with eye-catching names, have engaged in strenuous non-price rivalry—but they did not touch on this in the interviews other than to speak generally of continuing efforts to promote improvement in fuel and lubricant performance.

In this area, it has been possible to distinguish several varieties of quality and style competition. There is, first, a category of product lines in which non-price competition is consciously used as a technique for drawing attention away from price—as in automobiles and some home appliances—partly to relieve the company or the industry from the necessity of depressing prices or of changing them frequently. A second category takes the form of research expenditures to develop new products that can forge ahead of the old to attract new customers and new business. Such is the non-price competition of the chemical companies. In a third category may be put the featured provision of sales and service engineering; stressed by nearly all the manufacturing companies interviewed, the combining of product and services appeared to be relied on most heavily by American Can, Johns-Manville, and Union Carbide. The transmission of cost-savings into product improvements without change of established price, to which attention was called by du Pont, International Harvester, and General Electric, among others, may be regarded as a fourth species of other than direct price competition.

What stands out most clearly, perhaps, from the interviews is the infrequency with which any of the officials referred to advertising or merely superficial style changes as alternatives to price change. Indeed, the various forms of "non-price competition" could not very well be posited as an alternative to "price competition" because the latter, with rare exceptions, was seldom considered as an independent policy. The discussion of product pricing took note of the fact that substantial fractions of the products sold by these large companies were marketed under some variety of formula pricing, and that even those products sold "to meet competition" such as heavy chemicals, or refined petroleum products, were not typically subject to frequent price changes. Given a broad base of relatively stable prices, and the sense of security thereby afforded, the large firms have channeled expenditures into areas that would permit them to increase customer preference for their products.

Product Promotion. The process of new product development and marketing requires a wedding of capital expenditures with subsequent profitable pricing. The pattern often seems to be one of heavy and long-sustained expenditures to make the product practicable. Occasionally, the new product has been bought in the initial stages of development from a small company that apparently was unable to bring it to successful fruition. Thus, General Motors' engineering and resources were required to move the diesel engine to the point where it could do the job to bring out the railroad demand. Similarly, at the time du Pont acquired the basic process for making cellophane, this product was so expensive and of such poor quality that it had a limited market.

The experience of General Electric in pricing such items as garbage disposal units, dishwashers, and electric blankets is in some ways similar. An initial period of heavy investment is necessary to bring the product to the point where it can be commercially marketed. The company then attempts to find out, by controlled experiment, the price at which mass production can be achieved, taking into account the fact that in order to have large sales, extensive advertising will be required. Following this pattern, General Electric, instead of first marketing at a high price, begins commercial sales with the price that will enable it to get volume. International Harvester followed the same course with cub tractors.

Price reduction, however, is not always characteristic of the pricing of new products. General Foods, for instance, has aimed at maintaining its novelty items (specialties) at as high a margin above the run of the mill competition as is practicable, relying on continuous product improvement to prolong the specialty position—a kind of quality or non-price competition. Union Carbide has not notably reduced the price of Prestone to meet new competition, relying rather on improvement in the product and more pointed advertising to prevent market erosion. Du Pont has not relied on direct price reductions to widen the market for nylon but has continuously refined the product to make it more acceptable for different uses.

Market Penetration and Market Shares. The firms interviewed have often alluded to their concern, as administrative organizations, with keeping the staff alert. Management is afraid of becoming lethargic. In order to maintain a vigorous sales organization, it is impelled constantly to move into new areas, to avoid becoming the dominant seller in any market, and to feel oneself to a certain extent the underdog (except in terms of quality, of course), always fighting for a larger market that still will not place the business in a vulnerable position. How is this management policy reflected in pricing? With some firms, such as A. & P., aiming at a minimum market share in the sizable towns, it has resulted in downward pressure on prices. With others, the techniques for obtaining a bigger market share appears to be reconciled with a preference for steady prices. When a firm such as U.S. Steel or Esso has sought to expand its share in certain product areas, it has not featured price cutting—although in 1953 U.S. Steel threatened to do so. It has typically refrained from reducing prices until smaller rivals force it to do so; when there is danger of its losing ground, it will match the cuts of the "followers." Its recent market penetration has been sought primarily through making more of the product readily available in favorable locations, and featuring dependable quality or services.

The goal of maintaining a market share cannot be unequivocally said to result either in price stability or instability. Some large companies, in order to maintain their place have, like Swift, had to accept continuous price changes and have sought to keep customers supplied even when packers' buying prices left meager margins or deficits. Others, like Reynolds, have increased their prices in the primary metal while striving to raise their market share through featured finished products. In 1948, G.E. cut prices in the face of rigid if not rising direct costs, to combat inflation and at the same time to improve its competitive position.[4]

Small firms, too, aim for certain market shares and strive to insulate whatever position they may have gained from attack by rivals. They may, in some cases, be more willing to resort to price cuts than large firms, but, in other cases, they lay heavy stress on advertising of quality. General Electric's rivals in the small appliance field—Sunbeam or McGraw—are not price cutters. In fact, Sunbeam has gone to great lengths to fight for resale price maintainance.

The big firms are more easily able to aim at a given market share because they do not have to stake their future on reaching a given level in any particular market, having so many product lines to fall back on. This in turn enables them to use competitive techniques that, while they may not bring immediate results, may be more productive over the long run, in contrast with small firms that have to depend on price cutting.

INFLUENCE OF ANTITRUST LAWS

Cases have been noted in which company pricing policies and practices were obviously dictated by antitrust decisions and decrees, or reflected a special concern to avoid complications under the Sherman Act or implications of the Robinson-Patman Act. In those instances, companies commented directly on the effect that antitrust decrees had on their pricing. In other instances, officials did not include the antitrust laws as a significant pricing influence even though many of the companies surveyed in this pricing study had been defendants in antitrust cases. Reticence was occasionally encountered because of pend-

[4] *New York Times* (Dec. 31, 1947), p. 1, and *ibid.* (Jan. 1, 1948), p. 33. Mr. Wilson described the reductions as a continuation of the company's effort to combat inflation and said this was done at a time when his firm "could have obtained even higher prices than we had been charging for these products." *Corporate Profits,* Hearings before the Joint Committee on the Economic Report, 80 Cong. 2 sess. (December 1948), p. 473.

ing cases, counsel having advised officials in general to avoid comment. Nevertheless it is of some value to summarize the admitted effects of antitrust legislation on the pricing policies of the companies included in the survey.

Certain aspects of Alcoa's postwar antitrust experience were freely discussed by its management. There has been continuing re-examination of its pricing for antitrust implications, and the policy of the company has a general bearing on the pricing problem of fully integrated producers who are similarly dominant in a market and similarly vulnerable to action under Section 2 of the Clayton Act. In the last decade, Alcoa, for the first time in its long history, has had to take into consideration the effects on competing primary producers when contemplating changes in its ingot price. In addition, the company's range of discretion, its freedom to price solely with regard to its own costs of fabricated products, has been specifically limited by court decree. Under the decree the prices of fabricated products must cover reasonable costs of efficient non-integrated fabricators (who are both customers and competitors).

American Can and Continental Can have also significantly changed the pricing pattern for cans, in response to an antitrust decree. Whether or not the new fluidity may be exclusively attributed to the antitrust action, there is no question that there is more direct price competition in marketing both packers' and general line cans.[5]

Some phases of A. & P.'s pricing presumably have been directly affected by antitrust action. The court found that the company had intentionally sold selected items in selected localities below cost, with the intent of eliminating smaller rivals. The company later entered into a consent decree that enjoined such pricing practices.

The Robinson-Patman Act appears to have affected the pricing of several companies, mainly in the direction of reducing quantity discounts. The can manufacturing companies, in an effort to comply with the law, have extended to smaller accounts discounts approaching those extended to the larger customers. The steel companies discussed the possible impact of the Cement decision, as did du Pont. But in steel there is no evidence yet of definitive consequences of the aban-

[5] See pp. 209-11.

donment of the basing point system. The high level of demand, and the successive price increases with rising costs, have provided an environment in which direct price competition would be de-emphasized in any event. And the minor adjustments in chemicals do not indicate any significant change since the Cement decision in the pattern of pricing for those chemicals that had been under delivered price systems.

Alcoa, General Electric, and Union Carbide have been among the companies that have availed themselves of the legalization of resale price maintenance protection on some of their consumer products. Executives did not debate the pros and cons of such agreements except in terms of a "living wage" for retailers and the opportunities to increase distributive outlets by protecting dealer margins.

A broader impact of the antitrust laws may be their effect on market share policy. Many of the companies interviewed expressed a preference for making their way into new markets, wherein their shares would be a minor fraction, to dominating the market in the established product.

A further discipline attributable to the antitrust laws is seen in the independence that appears to surround the price-making—at least in the procedure—among the companies surveyed. Some of the executives indicated, by mention of specific competitors, that reactions of other firms in the industry influenced their companies' pricing. Yet, with the shift to f.o.b. pricing, a decision to equalize freight on a competitor's plant was regarded as an independent decision, not as part of an industry plan. When there was a price leader, the followers decided to follow for their own reasons; the price leader hewed to his policy, without attempting to justify it in terms of protecting or attacking a specific rival. This was as true of Kennecott Copper as it was of U.S. Steel, and it was enforced on A. & P. by court order.

The cumulative evidence of sensitivity to antitrust laws leaves little doubt that the large companies formulate pricing policies to conform to what they believe to be the current trends in antitrust policies. It goes without saying that open collusion with rivals is never considered as a possible pricing policy. The mechanisms for avoiding direct price competition have therefore taken shape as rules or reflexes applied independently, but as part of an industry pattern, to minimize price conflicts. Perhaps equally important has been the emphasis on product differentiation, which, as an alternative to price agreements or price warfare, has become pervasive in varying degrees among the companies examined here. To the extent that quality differences can be stressed, or actually obtained and maintained by continuous research, the income flow to the company is protected against cutthroat competition. Other than the examples given earlier of specific court directives, there seems to be little in the way of easily discernible changes in pricing policy that, from the interviews, could be directly attributable to antitrust policy.

INDUSTRY AND PRICING LEADERSHIP

Another motivation which is conducive to price stability remains to be considered. It is an aspect of big business that may be described as the desire of companies in the limelight to be respectable in the eyes of the public and of their business associates. The managements of such large corporations explained that they often avoided taking all the traffic would bear because from the standpoint of continuing market response it was wiser not to profiteer. The steel and oil companies, and General Motors, Alcoa, and Goodyear, among others, forsook short-term profits that they could easily have obtained immediately after the Second World War by allowing prices to rise to match the demand.

Reliance on a stable price accompanied by relative profit stability may be (and commonly is, according to advocates of the well-behaved price) accompanied by continuously improved quality, so that apparent price stability may in effect be real price reduction. With several of the firms in the survey, the self-discipline they exercised in pricing could be further explained on the ground that they regarded themselves as vested with a responsibility for the whole pipeline of production and distribution. These companies saw themselves in a similar relation with their suppliers, especially with those that might lack the bargaining power of the larger firm. It was deemed desirable to protect both suppliers and distributors against untoward sudden price changes; thus on occasion the big company cut prices to distributors, as in the case of gasoline, to prevent their being squeezed.

The resolution of conflicts of interest between established giants and newcomers, such as the problem of price structuring for non-integrated fabricators discussed above, may tend to modulate price policies of leaders. Alcoa's prices were explained by management not solely in terms of market shares, cost-plus, or target investment return, but also as a response to the claims of non-integrated competitors and customers. United States Steel's traditional low-margin policy in pricing semifinished steel required by small, independent fabricators could be similarly inferred from Fairless' TNEC testimony. Statements by U.S. Steel executives comparing the company's pricing approach to that of a public utility likewise appear to be in the same vein as the earlier statements of Fairless. Yet, U.S. Steel, as befits a giant with a multiplicity of products has, of course, anything but a monistic pricing policy. With a market share target of 30 per cent for standard steel products, it will, according to top management, reach for business through freight absorption if necessary, to hold its market; it is at the same time cognizant of the profits of its fabricators and end-product distributors; it has foregone short-term profit "to properly serve the country," and withal, "the company tries to earn a fair profit above cost."[6] From the standpoint of the interviewee, there was no "squeeze."

Leadership, to the firms involved in this study, meant something more than single market dominance. All the firms considered were sufficiently large, even though in any particular market they may have ranked only second, third, or lower, to feel the inhibitions of leadership as well as its power. Continental Can, for instance, did not assume that American Can made all the important decisions for the industry, any more than National Steel let bigger steel companies look after its dealings with the automobile industry. Leadership was not regarded as a method by which a single firm could impose its own judgment on the market. It was in no case advanced as an equivalent substitute for market forces in protecting the public interest, even though price

[6] *Study of Monopoly Power,* Hearings before a Subcommittee of the House Committee on the Judiciary, 81 Cong. 2 sess. (1950), Pt. 4A, p. 632, and *passim.*

administration, a conspicuous aspect of industry leadership, was defended by some executives as a rational interpretation of what the market could sustain.

The development of price leadership in large-scale industry has roots in the earlier experience of violent price fluctuation and cutthroat competition, which culminated in consolidation of competitors, as in steel, copper, oil production, tin cans, and farm equipment. Such experience has generated a distinct predisposition on the part of managements to avoid price changes except through periodic, well-considered, and well-publicized alterations in recognized base prices. By relating price changes to such formalized bases as changes in direct costs or style and quality changes, the firm attempts to avoid the extreme fluctuations in return on investment that were attributed to frequent, uncontrolled disturbances of the price structure.

This desire for systematic pricing, which is oftentimes described with a blanket adjective as "administered," usually implies that the company or companies set some kind of target conforming to their price policy. Hence, the price is presumably controlled by the firm acting as the price leader or by a select group of firms that make policy for the industry. Confronted with this interpretation of administered pricing, business executives who simultaneously advocate dynamic competition and disciplined pricing, contend that an administered price, such as the tank wagon price of gasoline, far from being an independent creation of the price leader, is in fact a device for approximating a market equilibrium. According to this view, there are so many possibilities of substitution of one product for another, or an off brand for a name brand, that the limits of discretion are much narrower than is generally supposed. Administration of prices in most cases merely avoids the decision to use cutthroat competition—which in itself would be another form of administered pricing; it also avoids temporary exploitation of shortages. Refraining from raising prices when a higher price is necessary to equate supply with demand can also be justified on the ground that over the long run the higher prices would disturb equilibrium by bringing into the industry unneeded capacity.

But this conventional justification for price leadership can be associated with genuine "equilibrium" only if the word is made equivalent to whatever is the decision of the leading firms. Their decisions are not the impersonal resolution of market forces except perhaps in the sense that if they are very skillfully adjusted to market response they may, in effect, register a close approximation to the values in an unmanaged market.

Another reason given for price stabilization as a company objective is that, for many products, price stability is preferred by the customer. By providing this stability, the producer may make his product more attractive than a competitive substitute that has a lower average cost but is subject to wider-ranging price fluctuations. For example, this is said to be one of the main advantages, apart from the technical product characteristics, of the artificial fibers. Manufacturers and retailers are relieved of some of their inventory worries, since they know that raw material prices will remain relatively fixed. From this standpoint, price stability is an advantage that primarily the large firm stands ready to deliver to its customers.

The expectation of the large companies administering prices—G.E. its dishwasher price, International Harvester its tractor price, G.M. the price of Chevrolets, Alcoa the price of aluminum—is that, at the administered price, the firm will, with all the necessary qualifications, attain its profit goal with production at or close to what the firm regards as a normal percentage of capacity.

Although the stabilizing and other leadership influences referred to above are associated with policies that are common in big business, they are not exclusively attributable to dominant size. Smaller companies also rely on standard cost systems in an effort to rationalize their price competition—particularly in situations where smaller business does not have to contend with the large number of unorganized competitors buying for a common market. In this, as in other aspects of pricing policy encountered, it may appear that differences between what big business does and small businesses do are frequently a matter of degree. The following chapter is reserved, however, for a consideration of those respects in which size of the firm can be said to be the significant determinant of pricing policy.

5 / Bigness and Pricing Authority

THE PRECEDING DISCUSSION examined the pricing prac-
tices and policies of the companies included in the survey from a variety
of viewpoints, and explored management's avowed pricing goals.
Finally, a broad summary was made of those influences that
seemed to have an appreciable impact on pricing decisions. There now
remains to be considered to what extent the pricing in these big firms
fits into definable big-business moulds.

In the selection of product case studies, in the isolation of management goals, in the summing up of pricing influences, there was a focus
on the role of size. For the survey from which this material was drawn
restricted itself to the industrial and merchandising giants. Each of
the companies participating and opening to the appraisal of outsiders
both its pricing experiences and its pricing philosophy was outstanding in its field. Even the firms, such as National Steel, that did not head
an industry were among the top companies in their main product lines.

The survey made it plain that a typical characteristic of the giant
firm was the construction of a pricing rationale, or overriding policy,
that had a bearing on price. The pricing philosophy has not been
the same for every firm; nor has it persisted unchanged through the
years for the firms in the sample. Nevertheless, most of the firms were
quite articulate in referring to guiding principles for their pricing.
These principles were linked with and often inseparable from other
aspects of a behavior code that the officials believed could be followed
only by big business.

The impact of size on conscious rules of conduct is a theme that
appears and reappears throughout the interviews. Because they were
big, these companies felt they had to follow certain courses in labor

relations, in management organization, and in moving toward new markets and products. It seems fair to say that the executives were, almost without exception, inclined to revert to their exposed position and consequent sensitivity to the public interest in the midst of discussion of almost any phase of policy from purchasing to research. This tended to be equally true of opinions expressed on pricing.

The articulate self-consciousness of the big firm raises questions of promise and performance. Has pricing, as far as we can discover it in action, followed the course or courses indicated by the guides the companies adopted? Has policy conformed to rationalization? Assuming, as the executives did, that large size generates it own standards for pricing and a unique set of long-run goals, what indication is there that the firms were, in actuality, able to escape the competitive market pressures that limit the choices of smaller firms? And, taking the reverse approach, just how much of the pricing does seem to be attributable to size? The latter approach involves us in the problem of whether certain policies may be ascribed to absolute size apart from relative size and control of supply.

IS STATED POLICY CONSISTENT?

Big company executives, apart from reserving the right to reexamine their stated policies from time to time, seem alternately confident and dubious of their ability to maintain a policy of their own.[1] At the end of the Second World War, with the relaxation of government price controls, the leaders, notably in steel, aluminum, petroleum, automobiles, farm equipment, and electrical equipment, assumed responsibility for holding down the threat of inflation. General Electric, for example, reflected the self-assurance of leadership in the electrical equipment field when it attempted, between 1946 and 1948, to depress prices, especially in major appliances, single handed. It cited as its motivation the desire to stem the tide of inflation; its

[1] This was evident in cases in which companies were interviewed in more than one year, or gave public expression to their views at various times.

competitors explained the effort as a move to recapture a part of the market G.E. had lost. But General Electric's top executive, early in November 1956, was quoted as saying that his company had abandoned the belief that it could guide the market; its inability to do so was demonstrated, he said, in the unsuccessful attempt to hold prices back in the years following the war.[2] Eleven months earlier the manager of the Housewares and Radio Receiver Department of General Electric, under the impact of discount-house competition, had said: "Realistic pricing, cutting costs of operation and selling, increased unit volume, doing business with dollars instead of percentages, accepting lower margin competition, must be the order of the day."[3] By September 1956, G.E. was leading the price upward, however, in industrial equipment.[4] In late November of 1956, a fortnight after the disclaimer of ability to influence the market, the chairman of the board of G.E. announced that the company was going to boost prices "in order to restore profit margins that prevailed before 1940."[5]

Prior to the war, Mr. Fairless of United States Steel, testifying before the TNEC, expounded a theory of pricing that came close to reliance on standard costs yet somewhat inconsistently called for, but did not result in, price increases in slack periods and reductions in booms to implement a "fair return." More recently, U.S. Steel has, in a fashion that has become almost standardized, raised prices whenever there is a wage boost, but without setting a norm for return to be earned as part of the standard cost. Unless the comments of other firms in the industry are discounted, U.S. Steel is sitting on the lid of the steel price pot.[6] At the same time, the company insists that to get orders it prices "competitively," though it was unable to provide

[2] "Electrical Industry Needs Higher Profits," *Wall Street Journal* (Nov. 14, 1956).

[3] *Business Week* (Dec. 31, 1955), p. 21.

[4] "G.E. Raises Prices 10 Per Cent on Steam Turbine Generators," *New York Times* (Sept. 25, 1956), p. 41.

[5] *Wall Street Journal* (Nov. 29, 1956), p. 2.

[6] "National Steel's Chairman Urges Industry to Raise Prices without Waiting to be Led by United States Steel," *Wall Street Journal* (Mar. 23, 1956), p. 22; "Bethlehem Steel Chairman Sees Price Rise Inevitable," *New York Times* (Oct. 26, 1956), p. 43; "United States Steel Dictates Prices that are Up—But Not Running Away," *Business Week* (Aug. 11, 1956), p. 24.

instances of undercutting competitors to get the business of particular customers. It seems probable that while, at an earlier period U.S. Steel, plagued by high-cost plants, accepted a low return, its competitors today face higher costs than U.S. Steel. The corporation therefore finds it unnecessary to resort to price competition other than what the rest of the industry regards as insufficient response to increases in costs.[7] But there is no sign that these considerations have been incorporated into the official pricing philosophy, or that the executives of U.S. Steel have abandoned the ideal of "fairness." Certainly, public pronouncements justifying increases still use the old terms of reference even though management believes that it is more "competitive" than it was a decade ago.

The courses of action in these representative companies bear out a commonly reported finding from our interviews that the policy— even when similarly stated—is variously interpreted within the firm.

IS COMPANY POLICY COMPREHENDED

AND CARRIED OUT?

It is not always evident that the price makers in the various big companies know there is a policy, even if an inconsistent one. There are gulfs between the policy formulation and the realities as viewed by those directly concerned with price matters. In the multiproduct firm, of course, the price maker in one sector may hew to the line of making his product salable, without knowledge of the over-all objectives of top management.

The chemical firms have tended to tie together an ideal of product pricing and the development of new products. Union Carbide and du Pont have each pointed to slashing price cuts made from time to time on new products, and to price stability in the face of overwhelm-

---

[7] ". . . exactly 25 per cent of a group which produced more than 90 per cent of our steel last year earned less than 4.5 per cent on sales in 1955—the fattest year in steel's history." *Ibid.*, p. 25. At the same time U.S. Steel was earning 9 per cent.

ing demand. Alcoa has likewise called attention to a policy of price reduction, when it promoted fabricated products like aluminum screen wire. These companies, however, have also priced dozens, if not hundreds, of products on a "non-promotional" basis. It is questionable whether the new products on which prices have been reduced to open up new reaches of demand have been sufficiently numerous to be representative of a given company's new product pricing policy as a whole. Managements can point with pride to sharp declines in the prices of products that they had nursed from test tube to carload; but there comes a time in the life history of every such product when its price becomes stabilized and in some cases, by the time the price is materially lowered, the maturity has already set in.

The true picture can easily be lost, however, by dwelling on the failure of some large companies to conform to a certain pattern of pricing, which may not have been explicitly adopted by the company as its ideal. Du Pont, for instance, has made no secret of its conviction that, when it has risked and invested sizable sums in varied product development, it is entitled, when it hits a product like nylon, to a commensurate return. Hence, until that goal is reached, it will not cut prices below the levels that have proved profitable with sustained demand. But while it is improbable that a company would sacrifice the opportunity to earn an exceptional return from a product highly rated by the market, the creed to which most of the companies in the survey subscribe requires big business to combine product innovation and venturesome pricing policies. One of the advantages of size is that the big-scale enterprise can afford both, and can follow through on its vision of the potentialities to carry out the policies designed to realize them.

Prominent among the examples of a divergence between the rationalizations, or official formulas for pricing, and the actual pricing process, are the standard-cost formulas that big companies have adopted. Through the years, General Motors has developed an elaborate technique for handling costs, which sometimes has been presented as its basic pricing guide. Yet, the selection of the price, as an examination of the company's earnings statements appears to demonstrate, must deviate by a wide margin from the level that would result from the use of the Donaldson Brown variant of standard cost pricing. The management is no doubt aware that the discrepancy exists; this is why it prefers to call the determination of the final price an "art." General Motors' deviation is by choice; International Harvester, by its own account, has been unable to price as it would like, in an industry in which its sales of specific pieces of farm equipment are often smaller than those of a close competitor. Still, the ideal persists, even when it appears to be related more to cost control than to pricing.

Some of the companies successfully carry out their explicit policies. This seems to be true of Johns-Manville, which when it is the price leader and not thwarted by the competition of substitutes, bases price on cost; but, in entering new areas, prices to reach a mass market, as it did with asbestos shingles. And there is little discrepancy between what Swift believes it should do and what it does in the purchasing and pricing of its sensitive product. American Can, until the antitrust suit, was in control of a pricing situation that enabled it to carry out its objective of devoting substantial resources to experiment and improvement of the product. Lately, it has had to abandon its fixed margin theory; no clear policy formulation has been substituted, other than that of meeting competition.

DID SIZE CONFER INDEPENDENCE

IN PRICING?

Many of the large companies did not pretend to price leadership, with concomitant responsibilities and orderly procedures. Others, while ranked at the top of their industry, had their leadership circumscribed by specific competitive pressures, or by the very prominence of their position, or both.

Susceptibility to Market Pressures. It is notable that so many of the firms chosen for examination regarded themselves as, and actually were, prisoners of market forces. Swift, although it must tread delicately in its buying program to avoid stimulating a runaway market (it must engage in continuous "market sharing"), is vulnerable to unpredictable shifts in consumer preference and shifts in the level of its own and competitors' inventories in pricing its meats to customers. Like sellers of perishables generally, it can do little more than hope that, on the average, a year's operation will see it in the black, with losses being canceled out by profits, but neither traceable to a standard for pricing.[8] Kroger, except for its featured meat differentiation, which it is big enough to capitalize effectively, has little if anything to say about its retail prices, and not much more about its buying prices.

Alcoa, when it had not only size but virtually all of American aluminum production, adopted a pricing policy that called for slow and small reductions in the price of the basic metal and its fabricated products—distinguishable from the drastic promotional technique. But when Reynolds Metals entered primary production, Alcoa, confronted with direct competition for the first time, responded with a sharp cut. Since the Second World War, Alcoa seems to have lost direct control of the market price, even though its total assets more than doubled in the postwar decade, and it is twice the size of Reynolds, its closest rival. Alcoa, too, though in a different fashion from Swift, has had to price with due regard to outside forces: imports, substitutes, the new competitors' costs and market tactics, and the more direct antitrust decrees. Its pricing therefore cannot today follow its own bent, with leisurely price reductions kept well under control. The newcomers, even if they do not force price reductions, can force price increases. Alcoa cannot—or could not during the period of acute aluminum shortage—refuse to go along with upward movements.

Others among the group of giants feel competition more sharply than Alcoa does. Kennecott has never been able to price as it would like. High pressure from the aluminum newcomers has disrupted the

---

[8] The meat and vegetable departments of A. & P. and Kroger are in a similar situation. However, a retailer can vary his meat pricing by changing the mark-up or margin assigned to the meat department. The First National chain during the 1930's apparently accepted a lower margin on meats than A. & P. had been accustomed to; the latter was forced to operate its meat departments in New England at a loss until it built up volume. But where the possibilities for shifting overhead are limited, as they are for Swift, the generalization seems justified.

cable market. In spite of its hopes, and exhortations, Kennecott has never been able to persuade the custom smelters to adopt stabilization policies. So copper, in contrast with aluminum, has exhibited rapid price gyrations (influenced by the London market) that Kennecott could avoid only by staying out of the market.

Their size has not protected the largest tire manufacturers from an almost uninterrupted series of price buffetings. Goodyear, big as it is in tires, has been extremely vulnerable to price competition. Diversification into more stable industries has proved the only solution. On the average, realizations of big firms were somewhat larger than those of the small, but with the exception of a differential maintained between new equipment and other sales, the tire market can only be described as chaotic.[9]

Market factors—embracing personal and impersonal forces that limit severely the independence of the large company's pricing—are present in the case of the three petroleum companies, Gulf, Standard of New Jersey, and Standard of Indiana, all among the ten largest industrials. Gulf admittedly is strictly a price follower at the tank wagon level, although its policies in selling to commercial accounts from its refineries or terminals may involve price competition. At all events, it watches inventories and competitors' tactics on a day-to-day basis. The other two oil companies should presumably be classified as price leaders. But their price leadership, as we have seen, is of a tenuous sort. Standard of Indiana, from the short-run standpoint, does preserve some semblance of price stability; but, taking the long view, since 1932 the company has had to make a never-ending succession of adjustments in its overriding formula. The picture is one of continuous change in competition, climaxing in the recognition by Standard of Indiana that it had to adjust itself to the tactics of small, independent brand marketers selling pipeline gas in Minneapolis.

Exposure to Public Pressures. Another type of pressure, aside from that of the market, stems from the fact that outstanding size makes the firm an obvious target for antitrust suits, legislation, congressional

---

[9] See the variety of discounts available listed in Federal Trade Commission, *A Quantity Limit Rule as to Replacement Tires and Tubes,* File No. 203-1, Findings and Order (Dec. 13, 1951 and Jan. 4, 1952).

investigation, and similar restraints that call for additional care in pricing. To a certain degree then, bigness itself entails vulnerability, and in consequence may actually generate a sense of *noblesse oblige*. Obviously, there is limitation on pricing independence. Recently, pricing restraints have been spelled out by court decree following antitrust suits, as in aluminum and in tin cans. Moreover, a disposition has developed on the part of the community to look on and appeal to these companies as "pattern setters" for industry, and in pricing they are expected to avoid taking full advantage of immediate profit opportunities. In this vein, the *Economic Report of the President,* January 1957, said:

> Specifically, business and labor leadership have the responsibility to reach agreements on wages and other labor benefits that are fair to the rest of the community as well as to those persons immediately involved. . . . *And business must recognize the broad public interest in prices set on their products and services.*[10]

Thus the exposed position of the big firm as a familiar institution contributes to pricing inhibition except as it is able to introduce and expand new products or processes, preferably those clear of involvements with others in like fields.

These pressures are not cast in the mould of classical pure competition, but they have the effect of market forces to which the pricing policies and practices of these large companies must in the end conform.

TYPES OF PRICING ASSOCIATED

WITH SIZE

The survey does not provide an adequate basis for a confident generalization on the influence of size on the pricing policies of the companies examined in this study.[11] There is indication, however, of

[10] P. 3. Italics supplied.

[11] We are not prepared to accept at face value the justifications of size as a means of maximizing value offered as presented by spokesmen for the giant

the influences of size on certain types of pricing customarily associated with dominant firms.

Administered Pricing. The survey has encountered administered pricing at least in one sense among all firms in the sample. The very size of a company, the length of its pipelines of productions, the requirements of communication with suppliers and distributors, would make for company quotations of price with an eye on costs, market shares, and returns on investment. In the main, quoted prices would stand so long as the market accepted them or until the company policy indicated an improvement of income possibilities through a change of price. The assumption cannot be made, however, that large size per se necessarily results in administered pricing if by administered pricing is meant the fixing of a price that is determinative for the market.

Giant firms do not have a large percentage of the market in all their product lines; and where their share is small, evidence is lacking that, by dint of size alone, they can measurably affect price. The firms in the sample did, however, command influential shares of one or more important product markets. In these areas, much of their pricing is administered not merely in the sense of equating a price that it is hoped the market will accept, but setting a price that appreciably influences the action of the market. Thus the crucial factor is the degree of control exercised over supply in a given market. By virtue of such control, companies have been in a favorable position to shape prices therein. The degree of pull they exercise on the market varies by product and, in the showdown, is determined by the response of competitors or of buyers who are potential producers and by the extent to which substitution is possible.

Administered pricing is not confined to the large firm; smaller competitors can also be parties to the administration. This is true of products sold on a freight equalization basis to meet local competition, of products fair-traded at the instance of the buyers, or of raw materials priced by primary producers to stabilize inventory values for

---

concerns. While they were supported in specific cases, to which allusions have been made earlier in this study, the evidence offered is not sufficiently pervasive nor consistent to justify equating size with superiority in value given, for the aggregate operations of the sample.

the fabricator. Nevertheless, codes of conduct and elaborate expressions of pricing principles seem to have issued mainly from the big firms (whether or not they are price leaders), while small ones depend more on rule of thumb.

Price Stability. Stability, in the sense of relatively infrequent price changes, is commonly associated with absolute size. Other things being equal, the big firm spaces its changes with an eye to the interdependence of suppliers and distributors and the continuity of its own production programs. Aluminum, steel, the various products that are priced seasonally by the manufacturer, and certain patented chemicals, tend to rise sluggishly, and then only after the industry in general recognizes the necessity of an increase. Price decreases, similarly, result from the willingness of other firms to follow the firm making the initial move. Rigidity, on the other hand, while it is reinforced by a high degree of domination of an industry by one firm or a closely knit coterie of leaders, is not necessarily associated with absolute company size—witness the price of antibiotics, the principal producers of which have not been of giant dimensions, albeit big enough to influence the specific product area.

It has been suggested that price stability is, in the final analysis, a consequence of an elastic, that is, manageable, supply. And when changes in demand are met with a relatively elastic supply, they are not so likely to result in sharp price movements. The output of steel, since it is mostly on order, is more elastic than that of copper, which gets a world supply that is hardly manageable. If increased output is not obtainable easily with a rise in price, changes in demand will be sharply registered in terms of price. Meat, which has extreme volatility, tends to confirm the hypothesis that commodities with the least elastic supply have less rigid prices.

When there are short-run shifts in demand, and supply does not respond readily in the short run, price variation would quickly follow were it not for the absence of a sensitive market; in other words, the fewness of sellers provides the opportunity for giving up short-run profits maximization. The gray market, in steel and aluminum, registers the price changes that in copper and, to a lesser extent, in gasoline are openly quoted.

Price Cutting. Big business does not as a rule engage in price cutting, at least of the day-to-day variety, and it has been noted that greater ability to control supply in the long run is a factor in stable price. But size does not give immunity from price wars. Price cutting has been a notorious feature of gasoline pricing. In 1955, it also appeared in heavy electrical equipment. It seems clear that price wars result largely from refusal of smaller firms in the industry, who are mainly short line, to follow the pricing philosophy of the giants, who have in mind the full line and the integrated pipeline. Hence, price wars are the complement of rigidity; but they are indicative of a lack of power of the big firm to maintain consistent pricing. United States Steel could not stem the pricing tide in 1938; General Electric had to cut in 1955; Standard of Indiana and Esso Standard have not had a powerful grip on the tank wagon price. Nevertheless, size in general means resources to implement the potentialities of mass facilities and production; in that respect bigness tends to impart a measure of elasticity to supply and, by the same token, tends to encourage stability to price.

SIZE AND PRICING CONFORMITY

Notwithstanding the commonly encountered preference for orderly markets and relative price stability that attaches to the long-run outlook of the larger firm, bigness alone cannot be said to have produced uniformity in big business pricing. Even the firms of greatest size, like GM, New Jersey Standard, U.S. Steel, would not fit into the same pricing pattern. There has been, as already noted, some clustering around a norm of target return pricing. But the discussions of policy also disclosed that among those that could be characterized in general as following an administered, stabilized, cost-plus system of pricing, the degree of precision and of compliance ranged too widely to make target return a master key to pricing. Within the multiproduct company, there are radical departures from the policy that is said to be overriding for the company. In many cases, there appeared to be no single standard against which policy was to be measured.

The attempt to isolate the particular ways in which size seems to shape pricing policies has demonstrated also that size may have opposing effects, depending, among other factors, on the maturity of the product. The big company can and does reduce prices rapidly in order to extend the market for a new product; the same firm may do its best to insulate a mature product from price changes, either upward or downward.

This is not to say that the foregoing proves, or even suggests, that size, simply because it has no uniform influence that is traceable to a single kind of pricing policy, can be dismissed as a determinant of pricing policy and behavior. In the first place, it is clear that most of the pricing policies and company goals are chosen by the firms using them from among a number of possibilities. Their very ability to make a selection, to decide to price for a target return rather than a market share, or to sell a service rather than a product, distinguishes them from sellers who, in different market situations, are unable to follow any policy whatever, save approximation of the "going price." Is the freedom to choose prices and price policy one of the consequences of size? If it is, then size is reflected in pricing policy, in spite of the absence of uniformity in the policy chosen.

This brings us back to the point that the management can select a price policy when it has some degree of control over supply. Whether a new product is to be priced promotionally or sold for reasons of prestige at a high established price is open as a choice only when the management, as in marketing cellophane and nylon, has a controlling output that encroachment of substitutes has not offset. A policy of gradual and cautious price reduction could be pursued for aluminum over decades because there was one domestic producer of virgin ingot. Because a firm had a controlling portion of the asbestos supply, the asbestos shingle was first developed for a limited number of buyers relatively indifferent to price and then, as the company explored the expansion possibilities, the price was rapidly brought down to compete with wood and asphalt shingles. However, where asbestos had no close substitutes, the company does not claim to have engaged in aggressive price reduction.

The companies just mentioned range from a corporation with billions of assets to one under $200 million. They are all sizable, like the rest of the sample, but degree of product control cannot be correlated to size; the product and the strength of competitors in, and on the fringe of, the industry, cannot be disregarded. The seriousness with which a firm regards the maintenance of its traditional market share in turn depends on its opportunities to diversify and grow with smaller shares of more product markets.

It has been suggested that where size is comparable, differences in pricing can be associated with the "nature of the product." This admittedly serves to distinguish the pricing, let us say, of the automobile, which receives annual examination as the model changes, from that of basic steel, which changes when direct costs substantially alter. Yet in both these cases, the seller—or the dominant seller—sets the pace, and makes the crucial if not the ultimate decision. In contrast, the discretion of the large seller is sharply limited in the marketing of meats, tires, gasoline, flour, copper, or specialty foods. The difference between these pricing experiences is explicable not so much in terms of nature of the demand for the product as in terms of controllability of supply. Both, however, may be related to the "character of the product." Where small competitors lack incentives to be price followers, differences of opinion will inevitably lead to price differences and adjustment.

The nature of the limits to the influence of size on pricing may now be recapitulated. The giant firm obviously has a much wider range of alternatives in pricing than the small firm. Its planning period is much longer. It can afford to wait in developing a new product, can invest larger sums, and can take risks in pricing a new product that a smaller firm could not afford to take. The larger the firm, the more effectively it can diversify; and diversification will permit it to follow, with each of the wide variety of products, a longer-range price policy. It should be able to place greater stress on improvement of quality. In all these areas, the absolute size of the firm is significant, granting the differences in industry and product opportunities. Only a du Pont could afford to risk the millions necessary to develop nylon; once the new fiber was available, the sizable profits could be used to upgrade quality of other products sold, like paint, under conditions of rather intense competition. Only an A. & P. could afford to absorb large losses in some sales areas in the process of penetrating or maintaining to a target minimum market share, because it had the resources to sustain the campaign. Only an International Harvester could afford to stay for years with an unprofitable tractor in its product line, or an Esso Standard a long-continued below-cost tank wagon price.

We have been applying the term *size* to individual companies, in contradistinction to the *relative size,* which is more closely linked with concentration ratios, with command of supply, and the enforcement of particular pricing practices.[12] But it still is evident that companies of great size, even when they do not represent a major fraction of a product or industry output, enjoy an important respect for their pricing beliefs and appraisal of the market, which shows up in the pricing of common products. Despite the substantial drop in its share of the steel market since its formation, U.S. Steel is still in a position to quote and obtain prices conforming to its goals; it can exercise pricing leadership because the other big steel companies recognize in U.S. Steel's quotations a basis of cost and price figures that they, too, regard as the one most tenable for the industry and its markets. American Can, whose percentage has likewise been reduced, can revise prices only twice a year, as long as Continental Can adopts the same tactics, and the small can companies are willing to minimize their undercutting.

The influence of size, reflected in pricing in a variety of ways, does not give us clear uniformities. Sometimes it leads to a stable price that brings with it an approximation of what the price leader regards as a "fair" return, as in steel. Again, as in GM's automobile pricing, it fosters such a combination of franchised outlets, engineering

[12] Our case studies were of individual large firms and the policies they individually avowed or followed; the broad implications of the concentration ratios by industries were considered in the general volume on *Big Enterprise in a Competitive System,* Chaps. IV, V, and VI.

and styling—a function of yearly risk investment—that it is difficult to postulate realistic circumstances in which a small competitor could affect the pricing decisions of the large company. But when, in spite of absolute size, the large corporation faces intractable or numerous competitors—A. & P., Sears Roebuck, General Foods, Gulf Oil, Esso Standard, Goodyear—size cannot manifest itself so directly in pricing. Conversely, when the corporation in terms of absolute size is far from being on the level with the giants, but is nevertheless outstanding in a field within the reach of its size, such as Johns-Manville, it can follow an independent policy.

Evidently, when an attempt is made to estimate the extent to which giant size confers on its possessor an autonomous pricing policy or freedom to choose price levels and returns, a spectrum or scale has to be set up. Some of the companies surveyed still enjoy a substantial degree of discretion. Others are far from this position. In fact, size seems to be uncorrelated with pricing independence for many of the firms. It would be pointless to examine the divergence between pricing theory and practice for these companies, because they have not been able to insulate themselves from market forces. Moreover, there are other companies of outstanding size that, where pricing independence in concerned, seem to have been recently downgraded; their size has been no protection against invasion of new and dynamic sellers. Absolutely, they may be bigger; relatively, they have slipped.

In industries in which, because of the nature of the product and its market, continuous huge investments were necessary to maintain market share—autos, synthetic fibers, steel (given a full employment economy), the giant corporation was bound to have a dominant influence, unless and until it met a new overriding development to which it could not or would not adjust. Even here, the policies of its management were not predictable except in so far as the historical patterns of the industry affected all member firms.

It might be expected, after probing as far as officials would permit into the pricing subconscious of the big business, that the Brookings study would emerge with one or more definite generalizations on how price is shaped by size that would be applicable to all the companies in our limited sample. What finally emerges, however, is an inability to fit their price policies into a common category.

One could repeat, of course, that the big company, because of the very size of its investment and operation, seeks in its pricing policy to comprehend the whole sequence of production and distribution from suppliers to final consumers. This is reflected in a preference for prices that will stay put through the length of the pipe line. Moreover, the majority of the companies have in mind an acceptable target return on their investment, and in gauging new investments the expected volume at a price must enter into the estimation of the outlook and hence into the investment decision. On many products a target price at standard volume is actually set down as the basis of operation. But when it comes to the evidence in the actual market, the pattern of price decisions offers no definitive correlation with size. One company, turning out a product of manageable supply and only slight vulnerability to substitution, will appear close to achieving its aim of building a price on costs and desired return. Another, equally big, will take its price from the level at which the market is responding, and will concentrate on costs until they are brought down to the point where at the going price the "satisfactory" rate of return may be visualized. A third firm finds that, though it is the biggest in its industry, it must buy in an uncertain market where supply is unpredictable and must sell in a market where the demand is similarly unpredictable; and since the product is perishable to boot, it must be sold for what it will bring no matter how big the seller. The company with a multiproduct line may have all three of these situations and base its corporate target return on an averaging out of the more and the less controllable product lines with a combination of market-determining and market-determined prices. Some companies stay with the same product through generations and may pin their hopes on stable pricing to contribute stability to the return on investment; others diversify into lines that promise pricing with higher margins or more assured returns than the original line yields.

The attempt to correlate these pricing policies with the total assets of the firm is fruitless because, for one thing, we don't get the "other things being equal" for isolating the size factor. Business has found opportunities for bigness in lines of varying promise and varying possibilities of price discipline. The companies differ in the nature of their product, the degree of innovative ingenuity of the management, the willingness of the directorate to gamble, and in competence of production and established prestige of firm name and product. Standard of New Jersey may be fifty times the size of Johns-Manville; but that does not reflect the relative ability of each to exercise market authority. Though all the companies in the sample are big, they are highly individual, each one distinguishable from the others. General uniformities in their pricing are wanting. Yet the apparently negative conclusion contains this positive implication with respect to the dynamism of the large-scale corporate enterprise in our day: that in pricing as in other aspects of big business operation, the stable solution is far from having been attained. There is no apparent slackening in the rate of presentation to management of new situations—ranging from substitute products and shifting consumer habits to legislative inquiries and judicial decrees—to compel periodic re-thinking and readjustment of company policy and of pricing as an inescapable part thereof.

Appendixes

Questions for Interviews with Executives of Large Industrials

The following questions relate to two overlapping but logically distinct problem areas: *First,* problems of evaluating the social usefulness of very large enterprises; *second,* problems of organizing and managing these corporations. Questions pertinent to the first problem area are particularly pointed at (1) evidence of competitive or non-competitive behavior; (2) economies and dis-economies of very large size; (3) roles of these corporations as innovators or conservators in their respective industries; and (4) their impacts upon investors, suppliers, customers, and competitors. Questions dealing with the second problem area attempt to uncover (1) the principal operating policies and practices of giant enterprises; (2) the forces that guide their development; (3) the special problems they confront because of large size; and (4) the ways in which top management seeks to solve these special problems.

It has appeared desirable to organize the lines of questioning upon a basis of the principal functional fields of management rather than upon a basis of problem areas.

The attached is a general check list for the interviewer's guidance. *Not all questions are applicable to every company;* the interviewer will select the pertinent questions, or reframe them to suit the specific case.

The field interviews ordinarily divided among ten major functional areas, are as follows:

Part   i. Opening Interview—Analysis of Growth and Size
        ii. Organization and Administration
       iii. Financial Policy
       iv. Research and Technological Progress
        v. Purchasing
       vi. Production
      vii. Marketing and Pricing

           (For distributors, special questionnaire for Parts v-vii, covering policies in Procurement; Production, including sponsored suppliers; Merchandising and Selling)

VIII. Personnel Policy and Labor Relations

IX. Public Relations

X. Operating Advantages and Disadvantages of Pre-eminent Size (Review Session)

(In the majority of corporations there will be a vice president or group of vice presidents corresponding to each of the above departments or functions. The questions will be adapted to the arrangement of operations and staff work in the given organization.)

MARKETING AND PRICING

(Interview with Executive in Charge of Sales)

1. What have been the principal changes in the marketing and distribution methods used by the industry during the past 25 years?

2. Which of these changes were initiated by the company?

3. What have been the annual outlays of the company on advertising during the past 25 years, and what proportions of this advertising expense have been (a) industry or "institutional" advertising? (b) product advertising? Compare with practices of competitors.

4. Over the past 25 years what have been the trends in selling expense as a percentage of total sales (tendency to creep up, stabilize, come down)? How has that trend compared with that of competitors?

5. What is the significance of the following elements in the distribution of your product:

   a) volume by type of brand?
      i. factory brand (any subdivisions?)
      ii. private label
   b) volume by class of buyer?
      i. wholesalers
      ii. direct-buying retailers
      iii. industrial users (different types?)
      iv. governmental agencies

6. (If selling a consumer product) what is the part played in your merchandising program of (a) second factory brands? (b) private labels? With what types of manufacturers' output does each of these brands compete most closely?

7. Is it the policy of the company to expand its own wholesale or retail distributional outlets (through ownership, agencies, or special agreements)?

8. Do the terms or kinds of contractual arrangements vary with the size of the users or distributors? Are any practices peculiar to your company? (Check impact of Robinson-Patman Act.)

9. What has been the record of profitability of distributors of the company's products?
What has been the annual rate of turnover of distributors of the company's products?

10. Are quoted prices strictly adhered to in your industry

   a) by type of company?
      i. by all companies
      ii. by large companies only
      iii. only by companies with well-established brands
   b) Do the answers to (a) differ when sales are slow?
   c) What company usually changes prices first in your industry?

11. Do realizations change materially from time to time (and under what conditions) because of (a) varying relation of actual prices to quoted prices? (b) varying proportion of volume in long margin and short margin items?

12. In general, what is the pricing policy of the company? Do you

   a) build prices on your own costs and standard margin?
   b) keep them level with those of certain competitors?
   c) keep them in a definite relationship to those of other competitors? (Who sets the prices, who changes them, in your company?)

13. Does the company lead or follow in the establishment of new price structures in the industry?

14. How do prices charged for the same or similar products differ

   a) by types of buyers—wholesalers, chain stores, industrial users, etc.?
   b) by brand? (What effect has the Robinson-Patman Act had on these practices?)

15. Have you worked a better average realization in your major product lines than have your competitors? What has made this possible? (Better mix of items, fewer concessions, etc.)

16. What has been the trend in the degree of price fluctuation, for the principal commodities sold by the company during the past 25 years?

What part has the company had in stabilizing either (a) prices or
(b) margin over material costs for the industry?

17. What uses have been made of market research as a basis for sales
policies? (How are findings of technological research unit transmitted
to the sales force?)

18. In what aspects of your merchandising program do you appear to
have an advantage over

    a) other large firms in the industry?
    b) small firms in the industry?

[Ascertain whether the company has an individual merchandising
program which differs from that of other large firms in the industry;
from that of small firms in the industry.

Also determine whether variety of the company's offerings influence its merchandising program, or vice versa.]

Price Recommendation Form, U.S. Steel

SECTION I—COMMERCIAL INFORMATION

Increase ☐   Price Base ☐

Decrease ☐   Extra ☐

New ☐   Other ☐

TO: COMMERCIAL DEPARTMENT   Number _____

UNITED STATES STEEL CORPORATION   Date _____

Submitted by: _____

Product: _____

Summary of Recommendation:

[This is supported by documentation in three parts incorporating: pricing history and competitive information; impact on specific accounts or industries; and detail of recommendation.]

Numerical Preference Rating:

ROUTING	Responsibility	Signature	Date

Comments

_____

APPROVED _____

DATE _____

SECTION II—FINANCIAL INFORMATION

TO: COMMERCIAL DEPARTMENT
UNITED STATES STEEL CORPORATION

Number _____
Date _____

From: _____

Grade and/or Product: _____

Recommendation _____

	Normal Annual Shipments	Present, per Ton				Proposed, per Ton					
		Cost	Sales Proceeds	Net Profit or Loss Before Taxes	% Profit or Loss	Sales Proceeds	Amount Increase or Decrease	% Increase or Decrease	Net Profit or Loss Before Taxes	% Profit or Loss	Annual Increase or Decrease
Product Price Group											
Total											
Public											
Specific Product Affected (Total)											

Data Based on 3 Months Ending _____

Extra Depreciation Included in Above Cost _____

Cost and Statistical Data Prepared By _____ Chief Accounting Officer

298

Definitions Applying To Section II

Product Price Group—Product classification primarily for financial purposes—
usually one digit grade and two digit product code.
Total—Sum of Public and Interdivision Shipments.
Public—Public Shipments only.

Specific Product Affected—That portion of the product, the price of which is
directly affected by this price recommendation. These figures on a total
basis only; i.e., the sum of the public and interdivision shipments.

Present
Cost—Includes Standard Cost, all variances, S.G.&A. and extra depreciation.
Sales Proceeds—The net mill proceeds as shown on SR 7 statements.
Net Profit or Loss—The difference between the Sales Proceeds and the
Total Cost.
% Profit or Loss—The percentage relationship of present Net Profit and
Loss to Sales Proceeds.

Proposed
Sales Proceeds—The proposed net mill proceeds.
Amount Increase—The difference between the proposed Sales Proceeds and
the present Sales Proceeds.
% Increase—The percentage relationship of Amount Increase to present
Sales Proceeds.
Net Profit or Loss—The difference between proposed Sales Proceeds and
Total Cost.
% Profit or Loss—The percentage relationship of proposed Net Profit or
Loss to proposed Sales Proceeds.

All above figures are on a per ton basis.

Normal Annual Shipments—The annual shipments of the product that can be
normally expected expressed in Net Tons.

Annual Increase or Decrease—The product of the Normal Annual shipments
multiplied by the Amount Increase or Decrease expressed in dollars.

Pricing Systems, E. I. du Pont de Nemours and Company

The du Pont company employs a variety of pricing systems ranging from f.o.b. mill plus freight at one pole to completely uniform delivered pricing (postage stamp pricing) at the other. F.o.b. pricing usually applies to bulk industrial chemicals, postage stamp pricing to consumers' products like antifreeze. The range is indicated in the following summary of representative pricing systems used in the main product departments of the corporation.[1]

Ammonia Department. Shipments from stock points or warehouses are generally f.o.b. freight collect and shipments from works are on a delivered price basis. Thus "Uramon," a fertilizer compound, is sold at a delivered price on a two-zone basis, minimum order 30 tons. Cylinder ammonia at the filling point has a delivered price on a four-zone basis and from most stock points is f.o.b. freight collect. Methanol has a delivered price on a two-zone basis, but in the western zone less than carload lots are usually f.o.b. warehouse cities. Ammonium carbonate and ammonium bicarbonate have freight equalized with a competitor on carload lots.

Electrochemical Department. This department has a range of products and price systems. In general some form of a delivered price is used, but there are many exceptions: e.g., f.o.b. for below-minimum orders (carbon tetrachloride); limited freight allowed for less than carload lots (hydrogen peroxide); freight equalized with several points (formaldehyde); only part freight paid for Pacific Coast orders (copper anodes); and f.o.b. mill (sodium and sodium cyanide products).

Explosives Department. Explosives in general are on some form of zone price basis. High explosives are priced f.o.b. magazine; others, such

[1] The basis for this summary is an over-all review of its product pricing which du Pont made in 1948 following the court decision in the Cement Case with respect to basing points and delivered price systems.

as blasting powder and fireworks powder, have a delivered price with various minimums depending upon the zone. More than 96% of du Pont sales of sporting powders are to four companies on a delivered price basis for large orders; all other sales are on a form of zone pricing unless below minimum orders. Time bombs and torpedoes are sold at a delivered price in zones; the price includes a service. Chemicals and miscellaneous products are usually f.o.b. mill, freight equalized with one or more points. For instance, nitrocellulose and sodium nitrite salt are f.o.b. mill, freight equalized with Parlin, N.J. nitrocellulose and Solvay, N.Y. (sodium nitrite salt).

Fabrics and Finishes Department. Coated fabrics have delivered prices for most of New England, metropolitan New York City, and a few individual accounts. For the rest of the country f.o.b. mill pricing is used. Mine supplies and rug anchor are on zone pricing, while tontine has freight prepaid to 127 basing points where competition maintains branches or warehouses.

Industrial finishes have delivered prices with a few exceptions. Sales to dealers and wholesalers are in zone prices, freight prepaid or allowed. Automotive finishes have delivered prices on orders of 100 pounds or more, except for shipments to the West Coast for which rail freight is allowed only to Kansas City, Missouri. Refinish prices are delivered for above minimum orders. For "No. 7" chemical specialties, prices are generally delivered with extra charges for below minimum orders.

Grasselli Chemicals Department. Most acids and heavy chemicals, such as technical sulfuric acid and sodium nitrite, are priced f.o.b. mill, freight equalized with nearest competitor's producing point. Some are delivered free within certain metropolitan areas and others are f.o.b. mill. With a few exceptions, industrial specialty products are sold f.o.b. mill. Slab zinc for all grades but the Intermediate is an exception, selling f.o.b. at a base point which is not the shipping point.

Most agricultural chemicals are f.o.b. mill or nearest warehouse, minimum freight allowed or prepaid to common carrier destination on 96 pounds or over. Others are f.o.b. mill, freight equalized with nearest competitor. Sales to retailers are at a delivered price.

Organic Chemicals Department. Dyestuffs are f.o.b. shipping point with minimum transportation allowed. Intermediates are, with some exceptions, f.o.b. Carney's Point, New Jersey. Almost all fine chemicals are f.o.b. mill or warehouse, minimum transportation allowed, with a small extra charge for the two western zones. Prices of rubber chemicals are f.o.b. mill and Cleveland, Ohio, minimum transportation allowed, except for neoprene, which is f.o.b. mill. On most other products freight is allowed: "Cel-O-Glass" has a postage stamp price, tetraethyl lead compound is in effect sold at a delivered price (additional charges for tank truck and drum shipments), and both ethyl alcohol and camphor (sold only to contract customers) have a delivered price.

Photo Products Department. Most prices are f.o.b. mill and warehouse, freight frequently equalized with other points. Motion picture film and X-ray products, for example, have a delivered price in New York City, Chicago, Los Angeles, and part of northern New Jersey for X-ray products only, Rochester and Philadelphia also.) For the rest of the country shipments are f.o.b. mill or warehouse, freight equalized with the nearest of the above cities (and San Francisco for X-ray products only). Film base is f.o.b. mill.

Pigments Department. Freight is allowed on titanium and lithopone except on the West Coast, where there is a freight differential, and less than carload lots are f.o.b. warehouse. In the northern states east of the Mississippi River, pigment colors have a delivered price; in the rest of the country various differentials are applied.

Plastics Department. Most products are f.o.b. mill but are delivered within a 25 mile radius of the plant in Arlington, N.J. In cases such as nylon molding powder, where more than one mill produces the same product, sometimes the freight may be equalized with the nearest plant.

Rayon Department. Acetate, nylon, and rayon prices are f.o.b. mill. Cellophane viscose film is f.o.b. mill, freight equalized with the nearest du Pont plant that has ever made the specific product. Transportation is allowed on cellulose sponges (prepaid) and cellulose bands.

Tables

TABLE 1. *Average Prices of Steel Products and Average Steel Capacity Operated, 1948-55*[a]

Year	Finished Steel Composite Price[b] (Cents per Pound)	Cold Rolled Sheets Price[c] (Cents per Pound)	Steel Industry Operating Rate (Per Cent of Capacity)
1st half of 1948.........	3.2	3.5	92
2nd half of 1948.........	3.7	3.9	96
1st half of 1949.........	3.7	4.0	96
2nd half of 1949.........	3.7	4.0	66
1st half of 1950.........	3.8	4.1	96
2nd half of 1950.........	3.9	4.1	98
1st half of 1951.........	4.1	4.4	101
2nd half of 1951.........	4.1	4.4	101
1st half of 1952.........	4.1	4.4	83
2nd half of 1952.........	4.3	4.5	88
1st half of 1953.........	4.4	4.6	99
2nd half of 1953.........	4.6	4.8	91
1st half of 1954.........	4.6	4.8	72
2nd half of 1954.........	4.8	4.9	71
1st half of 1955.........	4.8	5.0	92
2nd half of 1955.........	5.2	5.3	94

[a] *Iron Age* (Jan. 5, 1956), pp. 286, 291.
[b] The "finished steel composite price" is a weighted average of the base prices of ten major steel products, which account for the majority of finished steel shipments, weighted by the percentage that each of these products is to the total finished steel shipments during the base period. The products are hot rolled bars, structural shapes, plates, rails, pipe, wire, and hot and cold rolled sheets and strip.
[c] At Pittsburgh.

TABLE 2. *Price of Primary Aluminum Ingot (99 per cent), 1919-56*

Date	Price per Pound[a]	Date	Price per Pound[a]
Ingot		Ingot	
Mar. 1, 1919	$.33[b]	July 10, 1934	$.21[d]
Aug. 10, 1920	.35	April 1, 1935	.19
Oct. 1, 1920	.33	Mar. 1, 1937	.20
Dec. 20, 1920	.285	Mar. 25, 1940	.19[e]
July 15, 1921	.25	Aug. 1, 1940	.18
Nov. 15, 1921	.20	Nov. 18, 1940	.17
Sept. 26, 1922	.22	Oct. 1, 1941	.15
Nov. 1, 1922	.23	June 28, 1948	.16
Nov. 22, 1922	.25	Oct. 11, 1948	.17
Feb. 14, 1923	.26	May 22, 1950	.175
Nov. 13, 1923	.27	Sept. 25, 1950	.19
Mar. 10, 1924	.28	Aug. 4, 1952	.20
Oct. 22, 1925	.29	Jan. 23, 1953	.205
Jan. 1, 1926	.28	July 15, 1953	.215
July 1, 1926	.27	Aug. 5, 1954	.222
Jan. 15, 1927	.26	Jan. 13, 1955	.232
Oct. 20, 1927	.25	Aug. 1, 1955	.244
Dec. 21, 1927	.243	Mar. 29, 1956	.259
June 26, 1930	.233[c]	Aug. 10, 1956	.271

[a] F.o.b. Producing Plant (1918 to July 15, 1921); f.o.b. Selling Point-C/L freight allowed (July 15, 1921 to 1956).
[b] 100,000 lb. base.
[c] No base-price for any quantity.
[d] 30,000 lb. base.
[e] 10,000 lb. base.

TABLE 3. *Ingot and Wholesale Price Indexes, 1926-56*

Year	Month	Aluminum Ingot Index[a] (1947–49 = 100)	Year	Wholesale Price Index[b] (1947–49 = 100)
1926	January	175.9	1926	71.5
	July	169.7		
1927	January	163.3	1927	67.2
	October	157.1		
	December	150.8		
1928		150.8	1928	66.4
1929		150.8	1929	65.5
1930	June	144.5	1930	60.9
1931		144.5	1931	53.6
1932		144.5	1932	50.2
1933		144.5	1933	50.9
1934	July	132.0	1934	56.0
1935	April	119.4	1935	55.7
1936		119.4	1936	56.9
1937	March	126.0	1937	61.0
1938		126.0	1938	58.4
1939		126.0	1939	58.1
1940	March	119.4	1940	59.4
	August	113.1		
	November	106.8		
1941	October	94.3	1941	63.7
1942		94.3	1942	68.3
1943		94.3	1943	69.3
1944		94.3	1944	70.4
1945		94.3	1945	71.3
1946		94.3	1946	78.3
1947		94.3	1947	95.3
1948	June	100.6	1948	103.4
	October	106.8		
1949		106.8	1949	101.3
1950	May	109.9	1950	105.0
	September	119.4		
1951		119.4	1951	115.9
1952	August	125.6	1952	113.2
1953	January	128.8	1953	114.0
	July	135.1		
1954	August	139.5	1954	114.5
1955	January	144.5	1955	117.0
	August	150.8		
1956	March	163.1	1956	122.2
	August	169.7		

[a] Index based on ingot prices supplied by Alcoa. See Table 2.
[b] Includes all commodities other than farm and foods. U.S. Bureau of the Census, *Statistical Abstract of the United States 1956*; U.S. Department of Labor, Bureau of Labor Statistics, *Monthly Labor Review* (June 1957), p. 787.

TABLE 4. *Indexes of Prices and Volumes of Shipments of Fine Gauge Screen Wire*

Price		Shipments	
Date	Index (1948 = 100)	Date	Index (1948 = 100)
Jan. 1, 1948..............	100.0	1948....................	100
Sept. 29, 1950............	103.0	1949....................	138
Feb. 15, 1952............	98.0	1950....................	251
Jan. 23, 1953............	104.0	1951....................	234
July 20, 1953............	103.0	1952....................	258
Dec. 20, 1953............	101.5	1953....................	371
Aug. 11, 1954............	102.3	1954....................	368
Jan. 18, 1955............	104.0	1955....................	314
Mar. 23, 1955............	102.3		
Aug. 1, 1955..............	104.0		
Jan. 3, 1956..............	102.6		
Aug. 10, 1956............	102.6		

TABLE 5. *Chevrolet 6-Cylinder, 4-Door Sedan, Selected Models, Advertised-Delivered Prices, 1947-57*[a]

Year	Model One-Fifty[b]		Model Two-Ten[c]		U.S. Wholesale[d] Price Index
	Price	Index (1947–49 =100)	Price	Index (1947–49 =100)	
1947............	$1,205	91.5	$1,280	92.0	95.3
1948............	1,276	96.9	1,345	96.6	103.4
1949............	1,471	111.7	1,550	111.4	101.3
1950............	1,450	110.1	1,529	109.8	105.0
1951............	1,489	113.1	1,570	112.8	115.9
1952............	1,674	127.1	1,765	126.8	113.2
1953............	1,670	126.8	1,761	126.5	114.0
1954............	1,680	127.6	1,771	127.2	114.5
1955............	1,728	131.2	1,819	130.7	114.3
1956............	1,865	141.6	1,951	140.2	123.1
1957............	2,048	155.5	2,174	156.2	125.8

[a] *Automotive News Almanacs* (1948–57); *Automotive News* (Apr. 4, 1949), p. 12; *Business Week* (May 3, 1947), p. 40; U. S. Bureau of the Census, *Statistical Abstract of the United States* (1955); U. S. Department of Labor, Bureau of Labor Statistics, *Monthly Labor Review* (February 1957), p. 260.
Prices for 6-cylinder, 4-door sedan (from tables of current prices about the first of April each year and rounded off to the nearest dollar.) This is the retail price suggested by the factory, including federal tax, delivery-and-handling charges, excluding transportation costs, state and local taxes, optional equipment, or other charges that dealers may pass on to the retail buyer.
[b] Model: One-Fifty 1953–57, Styline Special 1949–52, Stylemaster 1947–48.
[c] Model: Two-Ten 1953–57, Styline Deluxe 1949–52, Fleetmaster 1947–48.
[d] Commodities other than food and farm products.

TABLE 6. *Domestic Sales of Full-Line Farm-Machinery Manufacturers and Percentages of Total Domestic Sales*[a]

(Dollar items in thousands)

Firm	1922		1929		1937		1948	
	Sales	Per Cent of Total	Sales	Per Cent of Total	Sales	Per Cent of Total	Sales	Per Cent of Total
International Harvester..........	$68,533	44.01	$137,826	28.27	$150,397	32.75	$351,511	22.79
Deere & Co.......	18,096	11.62	56,986	11.91	85,030	18.51	235,339	15.26
J. I. Case Co......	14,040	9.02	18,398	3.84	21,822	4.75	107,941	7.00
Allis-Chalmers.....	—	—	8,730	1.82	37,019	8.06	104,423	6.77
Oliver Corporation.	—	—	22,419	4.69	22,170	4.83	64,446	4.18
Minneapolis-Moline Co.............	—	—	11,956	2.50	12,358	2.69	55,742	3.63
Massey-Harris Co..	—	—	7,943	1.66	4,708	1.03	58,645	3.80
Dearborn Motor Corporation.....	—	—	—	—	—	—	156,461	10.15
Total of full-line firms..........	100,669	64.65	264,258	54.69	333,504	72.62	1,134,509	73.58
Total of short-line firms..........	55,058	35.35	214,264	45.31	125,736	27.38	407,388	26.42
Total for industry..	$155,727	100.00	$478,522	100.00	$459,240	100.00	$1,541,897	100.00

[a] Data adapted from Michael Conant, "Competition in the Farm-Machinery Industry," University of Chicago, *Journal of Business* (January 1953), p. 27.

TABLE 7. *Prices and U. S. Production of Triethanolamine and Propylene Glycol, 1929-56*

Year	Triethanolamine		Propylene Glycol	
	Price (¢/lb.)	U.S. Production[a] (MM lbs.)	Price (¢/lb.)	U.S. Production[b] (MM lbs.)
1929............	55.0	—	—	—
1930............	40.0	0.5	—	—
1931............	40.0	0.5	—	—
1932............	37.0	0.5	28.0	⎧less than⎫
1933............	37.0	0.9	28.0	⎨1 million⎬
1934............	37.0	1.3	28.0	⎩ ⎭
1935............	27.0	2.3	28.0	
1936............	27.0	2.3	28.0	1.0
1937............	22.0	3.5	18.0	2.0
1938............	20.0	3.5	15.0	2.5
1939............	17.0	4.2	9.0	3.5
1940............	18.0	5.6	9.0	2.5
1941............	18.0	7.5	9.0	4.0
1942............	20.0	8.3	14.5	10.0
1943............	20.0	8.8	14.5	11.0
1944............	20.0	9.0	14.5	9.8
1945............	20.0	8.5	14.5	13.0
1946............	20.0	13.2	14.5	35.0
1947............	20.0	15.4	14.5	50.0
1948............	21.0	15.8	13.5	80.0
1949............	24.0	12.6	15.0	85.4
1950............	26.0	13.0	16.5	79.0
1951............	27.0	16.0	17.5	88.7
1952............	27.0	14.0	17.5	90.6
1953............	27.0	17.5	14.5	59.6
1954............	24.0	16.6	13.0	50.7
1955............	25.0	21.7	13.5	69.6
1956............	25.5	20.5	13.5	65.0

[a] Carbide estimate up through 1953; 1954 to date, Tariff Commission.
[b] Carbide estimate up through 1948; 1949 to date, Tariff Commission.

309

TABLE 8. *Tank Car Prices, Selected Chemicals, 1940-56*[a]

Year	Acetone	Acetic Anhydride	Ethylene Glycol	Ethylene Oxide	(Syn.) Methanol
1940............	6.0	10.5	13.5	—	30.0
1941............	7.0	10.5	13.5	—	30.0
1942............	7.0	11.5	14.5	—	28.0
1943............	7.0	11.5	9.0	—	28.0
1944............	7.0	11.5	9.0	17.0	28.0
1945............	7.0	11.5	9.0	17.0	24.0
1946............	6.0	11.5	9.0	16.0	24.0
1947............	7.0	11.0	11.0	14.0	24.0
1948............	8.5	12.0	13.5	15.0	28.0
1949............	7.5	12.5	14.5	16.75	26.0
1950............	7.5	11.5	14.5	16.75	26.0
1951............	8.5	13.0	17.0	19.25	32.0
1952............	8.5	14.5	17.0	19.0	32.0
1953............	8.5	14.0	17.0	19.0	32.0
1954............	8.0	14.0	11.5	16.25	
1955............	7.0	14.0	13.5	15.0	
1956............	8.0	14.0	13.5		

[a] As of July 1st. *Oil, Paint & Drug Reporter.*

TABLE 9. *Average Revenue and Dollar Receipts of Plain and Moistureproof Cellophane, 1924-50*[a]

| Year | Average Revenue (Per Pound) | Dollar Sales | | Total |
		Plain	Moistureproof	
1924.............	$2.508	$1,306,662	$ —	$ 1,306,662
1925.............	1.927	1,942,373	—	1,942,373
1926.............	1.713	2,982,542	—	2,982,542
1927.............	1.431	2,869,014[b]	—	2,869,014
1928.............	1.211	3,131,608	603,222	3,734,830
1929.............	1.066	4,228,777	1,990,843	6,219,620
1930.............	.863	4,306,440	6,588,489	10,894,929
1931.............	.643	4,918,294	11,149,513	16,067,807
1932.............	.556	5,052,422	10,325,539	15,377,961
1933.............	.504	4,981,306	11,686,804	16,668,110
1934.............	.481	5,359,327	13,459,023	18,818,350
1935.............	.431	5,126,685	13,581,480	18,708,165
1936.............	.413	6,012,868	16,674,063	22,686,931
1937.............	.415	6,204,768	18,850,063	25,054,831
1938.............	.416	5,907,989	19,667,671	25,575,660
1939.............	.398	6,561,206	22,778,550	29,339,756
1940.............	.380	6,721,422	24,327,492	31,048,914
1941.............	.382	8,960,865	31,013,706	39,974,571
1942.............	.396	4,535,340	30,115,596	34,650,936
1943.............	.404	4,297,047	34,937,420	39,234,467
1944.............	.419	5,006,154	34,350,852	39,357,006
1945.............	.416	4,453,135	35,361,199	39,814,334
1946.............	.401	4,984,310	37,665,221	42,649,531
1947.............	.419	7,741,573	47,598,053	55,339,626
1948.............	.460	9,483,247	64,255,320	73,738,567
1949.............	.483	8,234,870	77,701,608	85,936,478
1950.............	.490	9,330,776	89,850,416	99,181,192

[a] *United States* v. *E. I. du Pont de Nemours & Co.*, 118 Fed. Supp. 41, pp. 82, 123.
[b] Includes 58,279 pounds of Moistureproof not reported separately in 1927.

TABLE 10. *Average Price and Annual Sales of Oxygen,*
Union Carbide Corporation, 1914-54[a]

Year	Total Oxygen Shipments (Cubic Feet)	Average Selling Price	*Selling Price as Percentage of 1914 Price*
1914	82,746,441	$1.82	*100.0*
1915	142,053,648	1.66	*91.4*
1916	304,270,090	1.46	*80.4*
1917	499,465,856	1.42	*78.0*
1918	766,063,655	1.39	*76.6*
1919	732,993,074	1.44	*79.2*
1920	851,395,206	1.45	*79.7*
1921	613,437,521	1.52	*83.6*
1922	736,773,129	1.43	*78.3*
1923	1,096,860,376	1.38	*75.7*
1924	1,035,927,623	1.34	*73.4*
1925	1,075,190,187	1.28	*70.1*
1926	1,151,847,000	1.22	*67.3*
1927	1,175,561,000	1.19	*65.2*
1928	1,257,039,000	1.14	*62.6*
1929	1,551,120,000	1.13	*62.0*
1930	1,391,733,000	1.11	*60.9*
1931	1,074,381,000	1.09	*60.0*
1932	752,484,000	1.09	*59.7*
1933	954,389,000	1.00	*54.7*
1934	1,216,035,000	.96	*52.9*
1935	1,469,418,000	.90	*49.4*
1936	2,081,126,000	.80	*44.1*
1937	2,608,597,000	.75	*41.0*
1938	1,810,743,000	.74	*40.5*
1939	2,668,629,000	.62	*34.3*
1940	3,493,759,000	.59	*32.2*
1941	5,018,696,000	.55	*30.1*
1942	7,490,259,000	.51	*27.8*
1943	9,712,970,000	.47	*25.6*
1944	10,243,039,000	.45	*24.6*
1945	8,463,954,000	.45	*24.5*
1946	6,396,325,000	.46	*25.5*
1947	8,579,402,000	.43	*23.4*
1948	10,234,768,000	.41	*22.5*
1949	9,196,525,000	.42	*22.9*
1950	11,443,854,000	.37	*20.6*
1951	13,938,036,000	.35	*19.5*
1952	13,840,682,000	.36	*20.0*
1953	15,481,463,000	.34	*18.6*
1954	13,412,406,000	.35	*19.0*

[a] The prices shown above represent a composite of pricing throughout the United States for oxygen sold through varying systems and in varying quantities. The systems involved include cylinder oxygen for industrial uses, cylinder oxygen for medical uses, bulk high pressure oxygen, and bulk liquid oxygen. The volumes purchased range from small users who consume only a cylinder or two each month (there are 244 cubic feet of oxygen in a cylinder) to very large users who consume as much as 70,000,000 cubic feet per month through a bulk liquid system.

TABLE 11. *Investment, Income, and Return on Investment,*
Selected Companies, 1947-55[a]

(*Dollar items in millions*)

Company	Invested Capital[b]	Income Before Federal Income Tax[c]	Column 2 as Percentage of Column 1	Income After Taxes	Column 4 as Percentage of Column 1
	1	2	3	4	5
—————1955—————					
Aluminum Co. of America.....	$ 863.5	$155.3	17.98	$ 87.6	10.14
American Can Company......	402.1	68.6	10.56	36.0	8.95
Bethlehem Steel Corporation...	1,548.5	361.2	23.33	180.2	11.64
Carrier Corporation..........	111.4[d]	25.7[d]	23.07[d]	8.5[d]	7.63[d]
Continental Can Company....	312.9	45.8	14.64	24.2	7.73
E. I. du Pont de Nemours & Co.	1,971.0[e]	744.6[e]	37.78[e]	431.6[e]	21.90[e]
Eastman Kodak Company.....	495.9	177.6	35.81	85.6	17.26
General Electric Company.....	1,089.7	347.9	34.40	197.6	18.13
General Foods Corporation....	287.6	83.6	29.07	39.0	13.56
General Mills, Inc...........	146.5	30.2	20.61	14.1	9.62
General Motors Corporation...	4,473.4	2,542.8	56.78	1,189.5	26.59
Goodyear Tire & Rubber Co...	633.9	108.9	17.18	59.7	9.42
Gulf Oil Corporation..........	1,714.9	325.7	18.99	218.1	12.72
International Harvester Co.....	844.0	102.3	12.12	55.5	6.58
Johns-Manville Corporation...	162.6	35.6	21.89	23.5	14.45
Kennecott Copper Corporation.	679.5	198.9	29.27	125.5	18.47
National Steel Corporation....	452.9	96.6	21.33	48.3	10.66
Reynolds Metals Company....	370.0	70.0	18.92	34.3	9.27
Standard Oil Co. of N.J.......	5,694.6[f]	824.3[f]	14.48[f]	709.3[f]	12.46[f]
Swift & Company............	379.6	40.1	10.56	22.9	6.03
Union Carbide & Carbon Corp..	1,142.9	276.6	24.30	140.8	12.32
United States Steel Corporation	2,868.7	736.1	25.66	370.1	12.90
Average percentage..........			23.58		12.66
—————1954—————					
Aluminum Co. of America. ..	791.2	82.5	10.43	46.5	5.88
American Can Company......	389.5	56.8	14.58	30.4	7.80
Bethlehem Steel Corporation...	1,232.1	251.8	20.44	132.8	10.78
Carrier Corporation..........	80.4	17.9	22.26	6.9	8.58
Continental Can Company....	275.6	38.6	14.00	20.7	7.51
E. I. du Pont de Nemours & Co.	1,788.5[e]	602.7[e]	33.70[e]	344.4[e]	19.26[e]
Eastman Kodak Company.....	453.2	139.0	30.67	69.8	15.40
General Electric Company.....	1,031.2	390.6	37.88	212.6	20.62
General Foods Corporation....	288.7	66.3	22.97	31.7	10.98
General Mills, Inc...........	138.2	26.9	19.46	12.4	8.97
General Motors Corporation...	3,572.6	1,553.0	43.47	806.0	22.56
Goodyear Tire & Rubber Co...	497.8	74.5	14.97	48.1	9.66
Gulf Oil Corporation..........	1,554.4	288.7	18.57	182.8	11.76
International Harvester Co.....	815.5	62.4	7.65	36.3	4.45
Johns-Manville Corporation...	151.1	23.7	15.75	16.7	11.05
Kennecott Copper Corporation.	637.9	124.5	19.51	77.9	12.21
National Steel Corporation....	427.1	58.1	13.60	30.3	7.09
Reynolds Metals Company....	340.8	38.6	11.33	20.3	5.96
Standard Oil Co. of N.J.......	5,237.8[f]	680.8[f]	13.00[f]	584.8[f]	11.16[f]
Swift & Company............	373.2	35.9	9.62	19.1	5.12
Union Carbide & Carbon Corp..	1,094.7	169.8	15.51	89.8	8.20
United States Steel Corporation	2,672.8	385.4	14.42	195.4	7.31
Average percentage..........			19.26		10.56

Investment, Income, and Return on Investment, Selected Companies (Continued)

(Dollar items in millions)

Company	Invested Capital[b]	Income Before Federal Income Tax[c]	Column 2 as Percentage of Column 1	Income After Taxes	Column 4 as Percentage of Column 1
	1	2	3	4	5
—————1953—————					
Aluminum Co. of America.....	714.0	99.9	13.99	48.8	6.83
American Can Company......	384.1	62.4	16.25	30.8	8.02
Bethlehem Steel Corporation...	1,163.6	294.9	25.34	133.9	11.51
Carrier Corporation..........	63.9	18.5	28.95	4.1	6.42
Continental Can Company....	263.2	29.8	11.32	15.7	5.97
E. I. du Pont de Nemours & Co.	1,664.1[e]	640.4[e]	38.48[e]	235.6[e]	14.16[e]
Eastman Kodak Company.....	419.4	128.2	30.57	50.2	11.97
General Electric Company.....	960.5	474.2	49.37	165.7	17.25
General Foods Corporation....	274.0	60.1	21.93	27.9	10.18
General Mills, Inc...........	130.6	22.6	17.30	11.2	8.58
General Motors Corporation...	2,984.5	1,593.8	53.40	598.1	20.04
Goodyear Tire & Rubber Co...	528.9	101.0	19.10	49.3	9.32
Gulf Oil Corporation..........	1,394.9	278.8	19.99	175.0	12.55
International Harvester Co.....	802.8	88.2	10.99	52.0	6.48
Johns-Manville Corporation...	147.5	29.7	20.14	19.7	13.36
Kennecott Copper Corporation.	620.6	167.4	26.97	88.8	14.31
National Steel Corporation....	418.2	118.5	28.34	49.2	11.76
Reynolds Metals Company....	353.5	35.2	9.96	18.3	5.18
Standard Oil Co. of N.J.......	4,338.2	714.8	16.48	552.8	12.74
Swift & Company............	373.5	72.8	19.49	40.1	10.74
Union Carbide & Carbon Corp..	977.1	222.5	22.77	102.8	10.52
United States Steel Corporation	2,319.1	545.1	23.51	222.1	9.58
Average percentage........			23.85		10.79
—————1952—————					
Aluminum Co. of America.....	712.9	92.1	12.92	43.5	6.10
American Can Company......	373.5	51.9	13.90	27.4	7.34
Bethlehem Steel Corporation...	1,218.0	156.9	12.88	90.9	7.46
Carrier Corporation..........	51.7	12.3	23.79	4.5	8.70
Continental Can Company....	242.6	25.2	10.39	14.4	5.94
E. I. du Pont de Nemours & Co.	1,549.1[e]	593.7[e]	38.33[e]	224.1[e]	14.47[e]
Eastman Kodak Company.....	400.5	121.3	30.29	45.8	11.44
General Electric Company.....	913.5	435.1	47.63	169.2	18.52
General Foods Corporation....	256.4	52.1	20.32	24.8	9.67
General Mills, Inc...........	121.2	22.9	18.89	11.5	9.49
General Motors Corporation...	2,729.1	1,423.7	52.17	558.7	20.47
Goodyear Tire & Rubber Co...	499.2	91.3	18.29	39.0	7.81
Gulf Oil Corporation..........	1,270.2	160.3	12.62	141.8	11.16
International Harvester Co.....	905.4	109.7	12.12	55.7	6.15
Johns-Manville Corporation...	141.3	32.0	22.65	22.6	15.99
Kennecott Copper Corporation.	600.6	140.7	23.43	86.2	14.35
National Steel Corporation....	385.0	79.6	20.68	37.6	9.77
Reynolds Metals Company....	356.9	34.5	9.67	14.7	4.12
Standard Oil Co. of N.J.......	4,062.7	654.0	16.10	520.0	12.80
Swift & Company............	349.7	41.8	11.95	22.7	6.49
Union Carbide & Carbon Corp..	854.8	218.4	25.55	98.3	11.50
United States Steel Corporation	2,197.1	260.7	11.87	143.7	6.54
Average percentage........			21.20		10.29

Investment, Income, and Return on Investment, Selected Companies (Continued)

(Dollar items in millions)

Company	Invested Capital[b]	Income Before Federal Income Tax[c]	Column 2 as Percentage of Column 1	Income After Taxes	Column 4 as Percentage of Column 1
	1	2	3	4	5
—1951—					
Aluminum Co. of America.....	483.7	115.8	23.94	39.3	8.12
American Can Company......	315.4	64.9	20.58	30.1	9.54
Bethlehem Steel Corporation..	1,093.9	268.5	24.55	106.5	9.74
Carrier Corporation..........	41.0	10.5	25.61	3.6	8.78
Continental Can Company....	242.5	31.6	13.03	15.2	6.27
E. I. du Pont de Nemours & Co.	1,379.1[e]	592.0[e]	42.93[e]	220.7[e]	16.00[e]
Eastman Kodak Company.....	383.8	127.5	33.22	49.0	12.77
General Electric Company.....	821.8	415.6	50.57	138.1	16.80
General Foods Corporation	247.7	48.8	19.70	20.4	8.24
General Mills, Inc............	122.9	21.1	17.17	9.5	7.73
General Motors Corporation...	2,532.4	1,417.2	55.96	506.2	19.99
Goodyear Tire & Rubber Co....	476.8	93.4	19.59	36.6	7.68
Gulf Oil Corporation..........	1,177.1	222.1	18.87	140.1	11.90
International Harvester Co.....	652.0	177.5	27.22	63.0	9.66
Johns-Manville Corporation...	132.2	41.7	31.54	24.5	18.53
Kennecott Copper Corporation.	578.1	155.4	26.88	91.3	15.79
National Steel Corporation....	354.6	140.3	39.57	45.3	12.77
Reynolds Metals Company....	256.1	48.1	18.78	15.8	6.17
Standard Oil Co. of N.J.......	3,736.9	695.5	18.61	528.5	14.14
Swift & Company............	340.4	25.0	7.34	12.1	3.55
Union Carbide & Carbon Corp..	734.3	261.5	35.61	103.9	14.15
United States Steel Corporation	2,150.9	582.4	27.08	184.4	8.57
Average percentage........			27.20		11.22
—1950—					
Aluminum Co. of America.....	487.3	90.9	18.65	46.9	9.62
American Can Company......	240.2	63.3	26.35	34.3	14.27
Bethlehem Steel Corporation...	977.7	245.0	25.06	123.0	12.58
Carrier Corporation..........	34.5	6.6	19.13	3.2	9.28
Continental Can Company....	206.4	24.7	11.97	14.9	7.22
E. I. du Pont de Nemours & Co.	1,250.9[e]	531.2[e]	42.47[e]	307.6[e]	24.59[e]
Eastman Kodak Company.....	356.2	117.9	33.10	51.9	14.57
General Electric Company.....	740.9	370.4	49.99	173.4	23.40
General Foods Corporation....	208.4	50.3	24.14	26.4	12.67
General Mills, Inc............	105.0	24.6	23.43	11.5	10.95
General Motors Corporation...	2,389.4	1,762.9	73.78	834.0	34.90
Goodyear Tire & Rubber Co...	355.0	70.7	19.92	35.1	9.89
Gulf Oil Corporation..........	1,083.6	175.9	16.23	111.1	10.25
International Harvester Co.....	614.6	115.2	18.74	66.7	10.85
Johns-Manville Corporation....	121.1	34.7	28.65	22.8	18.83
Kennecott Copper Corporation.	551.7	135.8	24.61	88.2	15.99
National Steel Corporation....	331.1	118.9	35.91	57.8	17.46
Reynolds Metals Company....	161.6	26.0	16.09	12.6	7.80
Standard Oil Co. of N.J.......	3,383.8	501.2	14.81	408.2	12.06
Swift & Company............	343.7	23.5	6.84	16.1	4.68
Union Carbide & Carbon Corp..	684.8	228.1	33.30	124.1	1.81
United States Steel Corporation	2,077.0	449.5	21.64	215.5	10.38
Average percentage........			26.58		13.37

315

Investment, Income, and Return on Investment, Selected Companies (Continued)

(Dollars items in millions)

Company	Invested Capital[b]	Income Before Federal Income Tax[c]	Column 2 as Percentage of Column 1	Income After Taxes	Column 4 as Percentage of Column 1
	1	2	3	4	5
		1949			
Aluminum Co. of America.....	452.8	40.7	8.99	24.2	5.34
American Can Company......	221.8	44.8	20.20	27.7	12.49
Bethlehem Steel Corporation...	903.8	165.8	18.34	99.3	10.99
Carrier Corporation..........	31.2	2.8	8.97	1.8	5.77
Continental Can Company....	204.0	17.9	8.77	12.1	5.93
E. I. du Pont de Nemours & Co.	1,116.8[e]	330.5[e]	29.59[e]	213.7[e]	19.14[e]
Eastman Kodak Company.....	318.5	75.5	23.70	49.8	15.64
General Electric Company.....	792.5	203.6	25.69	125.6	15.85
General Foods Corporation....	181.9	42.8	23.53	27.4	15.06
General Mills, Inc............	100.0	20.8	20.80	13.3	13.30
General Motors Corporation...	2,094.3	1,092.4	52.16	656.4	31.34
Goodyear Tire & Rubber Co....	329.8	30.7	9.31	20.2	6.12
Gulf Oil Corporation..........	1,022.5	110.9	10.85	100.9	9.87
International Harvester Co.....	517.4	92.4	17.86	61.3	11.85
Johns-Manville Corporation...	107.4	20.5	19.09	14.4	13.41
Kennecott Copper Corporation.	502.5	62.7	12.48	48.1	9.57
National Steel Corporation....	294.8	76.7	26.02	39.3	13.33
Reynolds Metals Company....	148.4	8.8	5.93	5.5	3.71
Standard Oil Co. of N.J.......	3,139.9	314.9	10.03	268.9	8.56
Swift & Company............	368.4	45.2	12.27	25.8	7.00
Union Carbide & Carbon Corp..	626.1	141.3	22.57	92.2	14.73
United States Steel Corporation	1,983.6	291.9	14.72	165.9	8.36
Average percentage.........			18.27		11.70
		1948			
Aluminum Co. of America.....	420.6	67.1	15.95	39.9	9.49
American Can Company......	206.9	38.6	18.66	22.9	11.07
Bethlehem Steel Corporation...	767.0	147.5	19.23	90.3	11.77
Carrier Corporation..........	29.7	4.5	15.15	2.7	9.09
Continental Can Company....	178.0	22.4	12.58	14.8	8.31
E. I. du Pont de Nemours & Co.	1,005.3[e]	249.6[e]	24.83[e]	157.4[e]	15.66[e]
Eastman Kodak Company.....	299.4	87.2	29.12	55.5	18.54
General Electric Company.....	770.0	217.5	28.25	123.8	16.08
General Foods Corporation....	169.5	38.4	22.65	24.6	14.51
General Mills, Inc............	102.5	17.8	17.37	11.7	11.41
General Motors Corporation...	1,919.4	765.9	39.90	440.4	22.94
Goodyear Tire & Rubber Co....	325.2	42.7	13.13	24.1	7.41
Gulf Oil Corporation..........	950.6	193.5	20.36	153.5	16.15
International Harvester Co.....	489.7	85.6	17.48	55.7	11.37
Johns-Manville Corporation...	100.2	23.7	23.65	15.4	15.37
Kennecott Copper Corporation.	497.7	126.9	25.50	93.8	18.85
National Steel Corporation....	268.8	73.4	27.31	40.1	14.92
Reynolds Metals Company....	92.7	14.2	15.32	9.0	9.71
Standard Oil Co. of N.J.......	2,721.0	452.6	16.64	365.6	13.44
Swift & Company............	363.1	51.3	14.13	27.9	7.68
Union Carbide & Carbon Corp..	591.2	155.7	26.34	102.3	17.30
United States Steel Corporation	1,094.6	238.6	12.53	129.6	6.80
Average percentage.........			21.19		13.09

Investment, Income, and Return on Investment, Selected Companies (Continued)

(Dollar items in millions)

Company	Invested Capital[b]	Income Before Federal Income Tax[c]	Column 2 as Percentage of Column 1	Income After Taxes	Column 4 as Percentage of Column 1
	1	2	3	4	5
1947					
Aluminum Co. of America.....	351.7	50.2	*14.27*	30.0	*8.53*
American Can Company......	196.7	31.7	*16.12*	19.3	*9.81*
Bethlehem Steel Corporation...	689.2	82.1	*11.91*	51.1	*7.41*
Carrier Corporation..........	26.3	4.2	*15.97*	2.3	*8.75*
Continental Can Company....	169.2	20.0	*11.82*	12.8	*7.57*
E. I. du Pont de Nemours & Co.	928.7[e]	184.4[e]	*19.86*[e]	120.0[e]	*12.92*[e]
Eastman Kodak Company.....	263.2	67.2	*25.53*	43.2	*16.41*
General Electric Company.....	655.4	160.1	*24.43*	95.3	*14.54*
General Foods Corporation....	159.1	28.5	*17.91*	18.3	*11.50*
General Mills, Inc...........	94.6	22.0	*23.26*	13.1	*13.85*
General Motors Corporation...	1,691.2	520.5	*30.78*	288.0	*17.03*
Goodyear Tire & Rubber Co....	313.8	42.5	*13.54*	25.5	*8.13*
Gulf Oil Corporation..........	719.2	116.5	*16.20*	95.5	*13.28*
International Harvester Co.....	456.2	74.4	*16.31*	48.5	*10.63*
Johns-Manville Corporation...	90.9	13.8	*15.18*	9.5	*10.45*
Kennecott Copper Corporation.	457.5	128.5	*28.09*	91.9	*20.09*
National Steel Corporation....	239.8	46.1	*19.22*	26.8	*11.18*
Reynolds Metals Company....	90.0	6.2[g]	*6.89*[g]	3.3[g]	*3.67*[g]
Standard Oil Co. of N.J.......	2,338.2	327.6	*14.01*	268.8	*11.50*
Swift & Company............	328.1	41.6	*12.68*	22.3	*6.80*
Union Carbide & Carbon Corp..	538.3	118.7	*22.05*	75.7	*14.06*
United States Steel Corporation	1,588.0	218.1	*13.73*	127.1	*8.00*
Average percentage.........			*17.72*		*11.19*

[a] Annual Reports to Stockholders; Standard & Poor's *Corporation Records*; Moody's Industrials; National Industrial Conference Board, *Business Record*, March 1957, pp. 106–07; December 1955, pp. 466–67; November 1954, pp. 446–47; April 1954, pp. 144–45; April 1953, pp. 146–47; December 1951, p. 478; October 1950, p. 403; July 1949, pp. 276–77.

[b] Invested capital is the sum of net worth and long term debt including long term government advances.

[c] After state and foreign income taxes (except where these taxes not segregable from federal income tax).

[d] Includes operations of Affiliated Gas Equipment, prior to merger March 1, 1955.

[e] Du Pont's invested capital figure includes investments in General Motors. In the 25-year financial record shown in the Annual Reports to Stockholders, du Pont excludes this item as well as investments in controlled but unconsolidated companies and miscellaneous other income. Its operating investment figure represents current assets plus plant and properties valued at cost (before deducting depreciation). On this basis, for 1955, income before federal income taxes as a percentage of operating investment amounts to 27.93 per cent. Income after taxes is 13.8 per cent. If depreciation ($838.5 million) were deducted from the operating investment figure, income before federal income tax as a percentage of operating investment would be 46.31 per cent; after taxes 22.95 per cent.

[f] Includes operations in Europe and North Africa.

[g] Before credit of $9.5 million representing realization of part of undistributed profits of Robertshaw Fulton Controls Company and constituents companies from acquisition date to date of sale of 50 per cent of holdings.

TABLE 12. *Sales, Income, and Return on Sales*
Selected Companies, 1947-55[a]

(Dollar items in millions)

Company	Sales[b]	Income Before Federal Income Tax[c]	Column 2 as Percentage of Column 1	Income After Taxes	Column 4 as Percentage of Column 1
	1	2	3	4	5

		—1955—			
Aluminum Co. of America.....	$ 845.0	$155.3	18.38	$ 87.6	10.25
American Can Company......	714.8	68.6	9.60	36.0	5.04
Bethlehem Steel Corporation...	2,096.6	361.2	17.23	180.2	8.59
Carrier Corporation..........	190.0[d]	25.7[d]	13.53[d]	8.5[d]	4.47[d]
Continental Can Company....	666.3	45.8	6.87	24.2	3.63
E. I. du Pont de Nemours & Co.	1,909.2	744.6[e]	39.00[e]	431.6[e]	22.61[e]
Eastman Kodak Company.....	714.4	177.6	24.86	85.6	11.98
General Electric Company.....	3,442.5	374.9	10.89	197.6	5.74
General Foods Corporation....	931.1	83.6	8.98	39.0	4.19
General Mills, Inc............	516.1	30.2	5.85	14.1	2.73
General Motors Corporation...	12,443.3	2,542.8	20.44	1,189.5	9.56
Goodyear Tire & Rubber Co....	1,372.2	108.9	7.94	59.7	4.35
Gulf Oil Corporation..........	1,895.7	325.7	17.18	218.1	11.50
International Harvester Co.....	1,165.8	102.3	8.78	55.5	4.76
Johns-Manville Corporation...	284.7	35.6	12.50	23.5	8.25
Kennecott Copper Corporation.	548.3	198.9	36.28	125.5	22.89
National Steel Corporation....	622.0	96.6	15.53	48.3	7.77
Reynolds Metals Company....	384.9	70.0	18.19	34.3	8.91
Standard Oil Co. of N.J.......	6,272.4[f]	824.3[f]	13.14[f]	709.3[f]	11.31[f]
Swift & Company............	2,404.1	40.1	1.67	22.9	.95
Union Carbide & Carbon Corp..	1,187.5	276.6	23.29	140.8	11.86
United States Steel Corporation	4,079.8	736.1	18.04	370.1	9.07
Average percentage........			15.83		8.61
		—1954—			
Aluminum Co. of America.....	708.3	82.5	11.65	46.5	6.57
American Can Company......	652.4	56.8	8.71	30.4	4.66
Bethlehem Steel Corporation...	1,656.8	251.8	15.20	132.8	8.02
Carrier Corporation..........	151.4	17.9	11.82	6.9	4.56
Continental Can Company....	616.2	38.6	6.26	20.7	3.36
E. I. du Pont de Nemours & Co.	1,709.3	602.7[e]	35.26[e]	344.4[e]	20.15
Eastman Kodak Company.....	633.5	139.0	21.94	69.8	11.02
General Electric Company.....	2,959.1	390.6	13.20	212.6	7.18
General Foods Corporation....	824.8	66.3	8.04	31.7	3.84
General Mills, Inc............	513.7	26.9	5.24	12.4	2.41
General Motors Corporation...	9,823.5	1,553.0	15.81	806.0	8.20
Goodyear Tire & Rubber Co....	1,090.1	74.5	6.83	48.1	4.41
Gulf Oil Corporation..........	1,705.3	288.7	16.93	182.8	10.72
International Harvester Co.....	994.1	62.4	6.28	36.3	3.65
Johns-Manville Corporation...	253.2	33.4	13.19	16.7	6.60
Kennecott Copper Corporation.	423.6	124.5	29.39	77.9	18.39
National Steel Corporation....	484.1	58.1	12.00	30.3	6.26
Reynolds Metals Company....	306.8	38.6	12.58	20.3	6.62
Standard Oil Co. of N.J.......	5,661.4[f]	680.8[f]	12.03[f]	584.8[f]	10.33[f]
Swift & Company............	2,510.8	35.9	1.43	19.1	.76
Union Carbide & Carbon Corp..	923.7	169.8	18.38	89.8	9.72
United States Steel Corporation	3,241.3	385.4	11.89	195.4	6.03
Average percentage........			13.37		7.43

(Dollar items in millions)

Company	Sales[b]	Income Before Federal Income Tax[e]	Column 2 as Percentage of Column 1	Income After Taxes	Column 4 as Percentage of Column 1
	1	2	3	4	5
1953					
Aluminum Co. of America.....	707.5	99.9	*14.12*	48.8	*6.90*
American Can Company......	660.6	62.4	*9.45*	30.8	*4.66*
Bethlehem Steel Corporation...	2,082.0	294.9	*14.16*	133.9	*6.43*
Carrier Corporation..........	164.4	18.5	*11.25*	4.1	*2.49*
Continental Can Company....	554.4	29.8	*5.38*	15.7	*2.83*
E. I. du Pont de Nemours & Co.	1,749.6	640.4[e]	*36.60*[e]	235.6[e]	*13.47*[e]
Eastman Kodak Company.....	633.7	128.2	*20.23*	50.2	*7.92*
General Electric Company.....	3,128.1	474.2	*15.16*	165.7	*5.30*
General Foods Corporation....	783.0	60.1	*7.68*	27.9	*3.56*
General Mills, Inc...........	487.6	22.6	*4.63*	11.2	*2.30*
General Motors Corporation...	10,028.0	1,593.8	*15.89*	598.1	*5.96*
Goodyear Tire & Rubber Co....	1,210.5	101.0	*8.34*	49.3	*4.07*
Gulf Oil Corporation..........	1,640.9	278.8	*16.99*	175.0	*10.66*
International Harvester Co.....	1,256.1	88.2	*7.02*	52.0	*4.14*
Johns-Manville Corporation...	252.6	29.7	*11.76*	19.7	*7.80*
Kennecott Copper Corporation.	476.7	167.4	*35.12*	88.8	*18.63*
National Steel Corporation....	634.2	118.5	*18.68*	49.2	*7.76*
Reynolds Metals Company....	287.9	35.2	*12.23*	18.3	*6.36*
Standard Oil Co. of N.J.......	4,137.7	714.8	*17.28*	552.8	*13.36*
Swift & Company............	2,597.2	72.8	*2.80*	40.1	*1.54*
Union Carbide & Carbon Corp..	1,025.8	222.5	*21.69*	102.8	*10.02*
United States Steel Corporation	3,853.1	545.1	*14.15*	222.1	*5.76*
Average percentage........			*14.57*		*6.91*
1952					
Aluminum Co. of America.....	577.8	92.1	*15.94*	43.5	*7.53*
American Can Company......	621.7	51.9	*8.35*	27.4	*4.41*
Bethlehem Steel Corporation...	1,691.7	156.9	*9.27*	90.9	*5.37*
Carrier Corporation..........	107.7	12.3	*11.42*	4.5	*4.18*
Continental Can Company....	476.9	25.2	*5.28*	14.4	*3.02*
E. I. du Pont de Nemours & Co.	1,602.2	593.7[e]	*37.06*[e]	224.1[e]	*13.99*[e]
Eastman Kodak Company.....	575.0	121.3	*21.10*	45.8	*7.97*
General Electric Company.....	2,987.5	435.1	*14.56*	169.2	*5.66*
General Foods Corporation....	701.1	52.1	*7.43*	24.8	*3.54*
General Mills, Inc...........	483.1	22.9	*4.74*	11.5	*2.38*
General Motors Corporation...	7,549.2	1,423.7	*18.86*	558.7	*7.40*
Goodyear Tire & Rubber Co....	1,138.4	91.3	*8.02*	39.0	*3.43*
Gulf Oil Corporation..........	1,528.8	160.3	*10.49*	141.8	*9.28*
International Harvester Co.....	1,204.0	109.7	*9.11*	55.7	*4.63*
Johns-Manville Corporation...	244.7	32.0	*13.08*	22.6	*9.24*
Kennecott Copper Corporation.	471.6	140.7	*29.83*	86.2	*18.28*
National Steel Corporation....	548.6	79.6	*14.51*	37.6	*6.85*
Reynolds Metals Company....	234.7	34.5	*14.70*	14.7	*6.26*
Standard Oil Co. of N.J.......	4,050.8	654.0	*16.14*	520.0	*12.84*
Swift & Company............	2,592.6	41.8	*1.61*	22.7	*.87*
Union Carbide & Carbon Corp..	956.9	218.4	*22.82*	98.3	*10.27*
United States Steel Corporation	3,131.7	260.7	*8.32*	143.7	*4.59*
Average percentage........			*13.76*		*6.91*

Sales, Income, and Return on Sales
Selected Companies (Continued)

(Dollar items in millions).

Company	Sales[b]	Income Before Federal Income Tax[c]	Column 2 as Percentage of Column 1	Income After Taxes	Column 4 as Percentage of Column 1
	1	2	3	4	5
1951					
Aluminum Co. of America.....	534.5	115.8	21.67	39.3	7.35
American Can Company......	570.1	64.9	11.38	30.1	5.30
Bethlehem Steel Corporation...	1,793.1	268.5	14.97	106.5	5.94
Carrier Corporation..........	80.9	10.5	12.98	3.6	4.45
Continental Can Company....	460.6	31.6	6.86	15.2	3.30
E. I. du Pont de Nemours & Co.	1,531.1	592.0[e]	38.67[e]	220.7[e]	14.41[e]
Eastman Kodak Company.....	542.3	127.5	23.51	49.0	9.04
General Electric Company.....	2,319.3	415.6	17.92	138.1	5.95
General Foods Corporation....	632.5	48.8	7.72	20.4	3.23
General Mills Incorporated....	468.9	21.1	4.50	9.5	2.03
General Motors Corporation...	7,465.6	1,417.2	18.98	506.2	6.78
Goodyear Tire & Rubber Co....	1,101.1	93.4	8.48	36.6	3.32
Gulf Oil Corporation..........	1,439.4	222.1	15.43	140.1	9.73
International Harvester Co.....	1,277.3	177.5	13.90	63.0	4.93
Johns-Manville Corporation...	238.0	41.7	17.52	24.5	10.29
Kennecott Copper Corporation.	451.2	155.4	34.44	91.3	20.23
National Steel Corporation....	618.5	140.3	22.68	45.3	7.32
Reynolds Metals Company....	215.7	48.1	22.30	15.8	7.32
Standard Oil Co. of N.J.......	3,786.0	695.5	18.37	528.5	13.96
Swift and Company..........	2,524.2	25.0	0.99	12.1	0.48
Union Carbide & Carbon Corp..	927.5	261.5	28.19	103.9	11.20
United States Steel Corporation	3,509.7	582.4	16.59	184.4	5.25
Average percentage.........			17.18		7.36
1950					
Aluminum Co. of America.....	476.2	90.9	19.09	46.9	9.85
American Can Company......	555.3	63.3	11.40	34.3	6.18
Bethlehem Steel Corporation...	1,439.8	245.0	17.02	123.0	8.54
Carrier Corporation..........	62.4	6.6	10.58	3.2	5.13
Continental Can Company....	397.9	24.7	6.21	14.9	3.74
E. I. du Pont de Nemours & Co.	1,250.9	531.2[e]	42.47[e]	307.6[e]	24.59[e]
Eastman Kodak Company.....	461.4	117.9	25.55	51.9	11.25
General Electric Company.....	1,960.4	370.4	18.89	173.4	8.85
General Foods Corporation....	589.2	50.3	8.54	26.4	4.48
General Mills Incorporated....	435.9	24.6	5.64	11.5	2.64
General Motors Corporation...	7,531.1	1,762.9	23.41	834.0	11.07
Goodyear Tire & Rubber Co....	845.1	70.7	8.37	35.1	4.15
Gulf Oil Corporation..........	1,150.1	175.9	15.29	111.1	9.66
International Harvester Co....	942.6	115.2	12.22	66.7	7.08
Johns-Manville Corporation...	203.3	34.7	17.07	22.8	11.21
Kennecott Copper Corporation.	396.9	135.8	34.22	88.2	22.22
National Steel Corporation....	537.0	118.9	22.14	57.8	10.76
Reynolds Metals Company....	166.9	26.0	15.58	12.6	7.55
Standard Oil Co. of N.J.......	3,134.6	501.2	15.99	408.2	13.02
Swift and Company..........	2,214.8	23.5	1.06	16.1	0.73
Union Carbide & Carbon Corp..	758.3	228.1	30.08	124.1	16.37
United States Steel Corporation	2,947.4	449.5	15.25	215.5	7.31
Average percentage.........			17.09		9.38

Sales, Income, and Return on Sales
Selected Companies (Continued)

(Dollar items in millions)

Company	Sales[b]	Income Before Federal Income Tax[c]	Column 2 as Percentage of Column 1	Income After Taxes	Column 4 as Percentage of Column 1
	1	2	3	4	5
1949					
Aluminum Co. of America.....	344.0	40.7	*11.73*	24.2	*6.97*
American Can Company......	468.4	44.8	*9.56*	27.7	*5.91*
Bethlehem Steel Corporation...	1,266.8	165.8	*13.09*	99.3	*7.84*
Carrier Corporation..........	46.2	2.8	*6.06*	1.8	*3.90*
Continental Can Company....	335.8	17.9	*5.33*	12.1	*3.60*
E. I. du Pont de Nemours & Co.	1,024.8	330.5[e]	*32.25[e]*	213.7[e]	*20.85[e]*
Eastman Kodak Company.....	396.2	75.5	*19.06*	49.8	*12.57*
General Electric Company.....	1,613.6	203.6	*12.62*	125.6	*7.78*
General Foods Corporation....	474.6	42.8	*9.02*	27.4	*5.77*
General Mills Incorporated....	395.8	20.8	*5.26*	13.3	*3.36*
General Motors Corporation...	5,700.8	1,092.4	*19.16*	656.4	*11.51*
Goodyear Tire & Rubber Co....	633.5	30.7	*4.85*	20.2	*3.19*
Gulf Oil Corporation..........	969.5	110.9	*11.44*	100.9	*10.41*
International Harvester Co.....	908.9	92.4	*10.17*	61.3	*6.74*
Johns-Manville Corporation...	162.6	20.5	*12.61*	14.4	*8.86*
Kennecott Copper Corporation.	246.4	62.7	*25.45*	48.1	*19.52*
National Steel Corporation....	424.9	76.7	*18.05*	39.3	*9.25*
Reynolds Metals Company....	131.9	8.8	*6.67*	5.5	*4.17*
Standard Oil Co. of N.J.......	2,891.9	314.9	*10.89*	268.9	*9.30*
Swift and Company..........	2,213.2	45.2	*2.04*	25.8	*1.17*
Union Carbide & Carbon Corp..	585.8	141.3	*24.12*	92.2	*15.74*
United States Steel Corporation	2,293.3	291.9	*12.73*	165.9	*7.23*
Average percentage........			*12.82*		*8.44*
1948					
Aluminum Co. of America.....	435.5	67.1	*15.28*	39.9	*9.09*
American Can Company......	409.5	38.6	*9.43*	22.9	*5.59*
Bethlehem Steel Corporation...	1,312.6	147.5	*11.24*	90.3	*6.88*
Carrier Corporation..........	54.5	4.5	*8.26*	2.7	*4.95*
Continental Can Company....	319.7	22.4	*7.01*	14.8	*4.63*
E. I. du Pont de Nemours & Co.	968.7	249.6[e]	*25.77[e]*	157.4[e]	*16.25[e]*
Eastman Kodak Company.....	420.8	87.2	*20.72*	55.5	*13.19*
General Electric Company.....	1,632.7	217.5	*13.32*	123.8	*7.58*
General Foods Corporation....	463.3	38.4	*8.29*	24.6	*5.31*
General Mills Incorporated....	410.3	17.8	*4.34*	11.7	*2.85*
General Motors Corporation...	4,701.8	765.9	*16.29*	440.4	*9.37*
Goodyear Tire & Rubber Co....	704.9	42.7	*6.06*	24.1	*3.42*
Gulf Oil Corporation..........	1,068.9	193.5	*18.10*	153.5	*14.36*
International Harvester Co.....	945.5	85.6	*9.05*	55.7	*5.89*
Johns-Manville Corporation...	173.5	23.7	*13.66*	15.4	*8.88*
Kennecott Copper Corporation.	348.1	126.9	*36.46*	93.8	*26.95*
National Steel Corporation....	436.5	73.4	*16.82*	40.1	*9.19*
Reynolds Metals Company....	149.2	14.2	*9.52*	9.0	*6.03*
Standard Oil Col of N.J.......	3,300.8	452.6	*13.71*	365.6	*11.08*
Swift and Company..........	2,361.1	51.3	*2.17*	27.9	*1.18*
Union Carbide & Carbon Corp..	631.6	155.7	*24.65*	102.3	*16.20*
United States Steel Corporation	2,481.5	238.6	*9.62*	129.6	*5.22*
Average percentage........			*13.63*		*8.82*

Sales, Income, and Return on Sales
Selected Companies (Continued)

(Dollar items in millions)

Company	Salesᵇ	Income Before Federal Income Taxᶜ	Column 2 as Percentage of Column 1	Income After Taxes	Column 4 as Percentage of Column 1
	1	2	3	4	5
1947					
Aluminum Co. of America.....	381.5	50.2	*13.16*	30.0	*7.86*
American Can Company......	338.2	31.7	*9.37*	19.3	*5.71*
Bethlehem Steel Corporation...	1,032.3	82.1	*7.95*	51.1	*4.95*
Carrier Corporation..........	52.9	4.2	*7.94*	2.3	*4.35*
Continental Can Company....	266.4	20.0	*7.51*	12.8	*4.80*
E. I. du Pont de Nemours & Co.	783.4	184.4ᵉ	*23.54ᵉ*	120.0ᵉ	*15.32ᵉ*
Eastman Kodak Company.....	334.6	67.2	*20.08*	43.2	*12.91*
General Electric Company.....	1,330.8	160.1	*12.03*	95.3	*7.16*
General Foods Corporation....	407.3	28.5	*7.00*	18.3	*4.49*
General Mills Incorporated....	458.5	22.0	*4.80*	13.1	*2.86*
General Motors Corporation...	3,815.2	520.5	*13.64*	288.0	*7.55*
Goodyear Tire & Rubber Co....	670.8	42.5	*6.34*	25.5	*3.80*
Gulf Oil Corporation.........	797.2	116.5	*14.61*	95.5	*11.98*
International Harvester Co.....	741.3	74.4	*10.04*	48.5	*6.54*
Johns-Manville Corporation...	133.9	13.8	*10.31*	9.5	*7.09*
Kennecott Copper Corporation.	317.0	128.5	*40.54*	91.9	*28.99*
National Steel Corporation....	329.0	46.1	*14.01*	26.8	*8.15*
Reynolds Metals Company....	129.3	6.2ᵍ	*4.80ᵍ*	3.3ᵍ	*2.55ᵍ*
Standard Oil Co. of N.J.......	2,354.9	327.6	*13.91*	268.8	*11.41*
Swift and Company..........	2,248.8	41.6	*1.85*	22.3	*.99*
Union Carbide & Carbon Corp..	521.8	118.7	*22.75*	75.7	*14.51*
United States Steel Corporation	2,122.8	218.1	*10.27*	127.1	*5.99*
Average percentage........			*12.57*		*8.18*

ᵃ Annual Reports to Stockholders; Standard & Poor's *Corporation Records*; Moody's Industrials; National Industrial Conference Board, *Business Record*, March 1957, pp. 106–07; December 1955, pp. 466–67; November 1954, pp. 446–47; April 1954, pp. 144–45; April 1953, pp. 146–47; December 1951, p. 478; October 1950, p. 403; July 1949, pp. 276–77.

ᵇ Sales are variously reported: gross sales, net sales, gross operating income, sales and operating revenues, net billings, income from manufacturing and services, etc.

ᶜ After state and foreign income taxes, except where these taxes not segregable from federal income tax.

ᵈ Includes operations of Affiliated Gas Equipment prior to merger March 1, 1955.

ᵉ Income figures include income from General Motors.

ᶠ Includes operations in Europe and North Africa.

ᵍ Before credit of $9.5 million representing realization of part of undistributed profits of Robertshaw Fulton Controls Company and constituent companies, from acquisition date to date of 50 per cent of holdings.

TABLE 13. *Price of Primary Aluminum Ingot (99 per cent),*
1939-56

Date	Price per Pound
January 1939	$.20
March 1940	.19
August 1940	.18
November 1940	.17
October 1941	.15
June 1948	.16
October 1948	.17
May 1950	.175
September 1950	.19
August 1952	.20
January 1953	.205
July 1953	.215
August 1954	.222
January 1955	.232
August 1955	.244
March 1956	.259
August 1956	.271

TABLE 14. *Price of Aluminum Pig, 1943-56*

Date	Price per Pound
October 1943	$.14
June 1948	.15
October 1948	.16
May 1950	.165
September 1950	.18
August 1952	.19
January 1953	.195
July 1953	.20
August 1954	.205
January 1955	.215
August 1955	.225
March 1956	.24
August 1956	.25

TABLE 15. *Price of 1100 F Aluminum Coiled Wire .204"-.130" Diameter, 1948-56*

Date	Price per Pound
January 1, 1948	$.260
June 28, 1948	.275
October 11, 1948	.285
May 22, 1950	.290
September 29, 1950	.315
August 4, 1952	.331
January 23, 1953	.344
July 20, 1953	.351
August 9, 1954	.365
January 13, 1955	.375
August 3, 1955	.401
March 29, 1956	.416
August 10, 1956	.438

TABLE 16. *Price of 2017 or 2014 Class 1 Aluminum Forge Stock 8″ Diameter, 1939-56*

Date	Price per Pound
January 1, 1939	$.310
March 25, 1940	.295
August 1, 1940	.285
November 18, 1940	.275
October 1, 1941	.245
October 1, 1942	.250
March 1, 1943	.210
December 16, 1946	.230
December 1, 1947	.240
January 30, 1948	.240
June 28, 1948	.255
October 18, 1948	.265
October 16, 1950	.290
December 9, 1952	.3045
March 23, 1953	.3167
July 20, 1953	.364
August 9, 1954	.381
January 13, 1955	.391
August 3, 1955	.408
March 29, 1956	.423
August 10, 1956	.450

TABLE 17. *Price of Alclad 2024-T3 Mill Finish Flat Aluminum Sheet .064" × 48" × 144", 1939-56*

Date	Price per Pound
January 1, 1939	$.440
March 25, 1940	.430
August 1, 1940	.420
November 18, 1940	.410
October 1, 1941	.390
March 1, 1943	.317
June 28, 1948	.342
October 11, 1948	.352
October 16, 1950	.387
December 9, 1952	.406
March 23, 1953	.422
October 12, 1953	.434
August 6, 1954	.448
January 13, 1955	.458
August 1, 1955	.475
March 29, 1956	.490
August 10, 1956	.514

TABLE 18. *Prices of Fine Gauge Aluminum Screen Wire Alclad 5056, 1948-56*

Date	Price per Pound
January 1, 1948	$.660
September 29, 1950	.680
February 15, 1952	.650
January 23, 1953	.688
July 20, 1953	.680
December 20, 1953	.670
August 11, 1954	.675
January 18, 1955	.685
March 23, 1955	.675
August 1, 1955	.687
January 3, 1956	.677
August 10, 1956	.677

TABLE 19. *Prices of 2024-T4 Extruded Aluminum Solid Shapes Factors 18-19, .2-.5 lbs. per ft., 1939-56*

Date	Price per Pound
July 15, 1939	$.635
March 15, 1940	.605
August 15, 1940	.595
November 18, 1940	.585
October 1, 1941	.535
March 1, 1943	.475
April 10, 1946	.515
December 15, 1946	.580
June 28, 1948	.655
October 11, 1948	.685
June 2, 1950	.695
October 16, 1950	.778
December 9, 1952	.817
March 23, 1953	.850
October 12, 1953	.866
August 9, 1954	.897
January 13, 1955	.907
August 3, 1955	.969
March 29, 1956	.984
August 10, 1956	1.040

TABLE 20. *Net Earnings on Sales and Invested Capital,*
General Electric Company, 1935-55[a]

Year	Sales to Customers (1)	Invested Capital (2)	Net Earnings (After Taxes) (3)	Earnings as Percentage of Sales		Earnings as Percentage of Invested Capital	
				Per Cent (3)÷(1) (4)	Index (1935–37 =100) (5)	Per Cent (3)÷(2) (6)	Index (1935–37 =100) (7)
	(In millions of dollars)						
1935.....	232.7	317.0	28.5	12.3	84.6	9.0	64.6
1936.....	299.1	329.2	45.6	15.2	104.6	13.9	99.8
1937.....	387.5	329.8	62.4	16.1	110.8	18.9	135.6
1938.....	292.6	332.4	27.3	9.3	64.0	8.2	58.9
1939.....	342.3	328.1	42.8	12.5	86.0	13.0	93.3
1940.....	456.5	330.7	56.6	12.4	85.3	17.1	122.7
1941.....	744.1	337.5	56.7	7.6	52.3	16.8	120.6
1942.....	964.5	347.8	44.3	4.6	31.7	12.7	91.1
1943.....	1,377.2	357.9	48.2	3.5	24.1	13.5	96.9
1944.....	1,447.1	368.1	53.5	3.7	25.5	14.5	104.1
1945.....	1,378.3	380.7	59.0	4.3	29.6	15.5	111.2
1946.....	768.9	578.7	43.0	5.6	38.5	7.4	53.1
1947.....	1,330.8	632.8	95.3	7.2	49.5	15.1	108.4
1948.....	1,632.7	734.8	123.8	7.6	52.3	16.8	120.6
1949.....	1,613.6	761.5	125.6	7.8	53.7	16.5	118.4
1950.....	1,960.4	702.9[b]	173.4	8.8	60.6	24.7[b]	177.3[b]
1951.....	2,319.3	788.4	138.1	6.0	41.3	17.5	125.6
1952.....	2,623.8	872.9	151.7	5.8	39.9	17.4	124.9
1953.....	3,128.1	932.4	165.7	5.3	36.5	17.8	127.8
1954.....	2,959.0	1,008.3	198.9	6.7	46.1	19.7	141.4
1955.....	3,095.4	1,068.9	200.9	6.5	44.7	18.8	134.9

[a] Computed from General Electric Company, *Annual Report 1949*, p. 32 and *1955*,
pp. 30–31; Standard & Poor's, *Corporation Records* (1950), pp. 7593, 8161. The figures
in the above table do not necessarily agree with those in App. Tables 11 and 12 which,
to permit company comparisons, have been compiled according to a common formula.
[b] A 2.55 per cent note issue, due 1966, and valued at $142.5 million, December 31,
1949, was completely retired in 1950.

Index

Index

A. & P. *See* Great Atlantic & Pacific Tea Company
AC Spark Plug Company, 54
acetaldehyde, 109
acetic anhydride, 118, 162n; tank car prices of, Chart, 117
acetone, 162n; effect of competition on price of, 118; tank car prices of, Chart, 117
ACSR (aluminum cable), 33
administered pricing, 257, 271–72, 282–83
Alcoa. *See* Aluminum Company of America
Allied Chemical and Dye Corporation, 108n
aluminum, pricing of, 24–39, 181, 255, 285; coiled wire, price of, Table, 324; demand elasticity, influence on, 39n; extras, 37; forge, Table, 325; ingot and pig, 31–33, 32n, 143, 145–48, Chart, 146, Tables, 32, 324; ingot and wholesale price indexes, Chart, 25, Table, 305; large buyers, effect on, 38; pigment, 37–38; primary, ingot prices, Tables, 304, 323; rolled structural shapes, competition in, 36; screen wire, 35–36, 147, Tables, 306, 326; sheet, 38, 142–43, Table, 326; solid shapes, Table, 327; substitution of, for copper, 178n; *see also* Aluminum Company of America; Kaiser Aluminum and Chemical Corporation; Reynolds Metals Company
Aluminum Company of America:
antitrust proceedings against, 26, 29–30, 142–44, 143n, 267;
company pricing policy, 142–49, 218, 255, 256, 272;
antitrust decree, influence on, 142–44, 267, 268;
and competitive relationships, 144–45, 144n, 148–49;
cross currents in pricing objective, 145–48;
goal of, 26, 26n, 142;
limit-profits policy, 26;
and market pressures, 279;
and non-integrated firms, relations with, 144n;
and stabilization of prices, 145, 146, 149, 166;
summary, 148–49;
target and realized returns, 148–49;
investment and income, Table, 213–17;
organization, pricing, 220–22;
price leadership of, 269, 270;
product pricing, 24–39;
aluminum sheets, 38;
choice of policy, basis for, 28n;

331

273–90; and administered pricing, 282–83; and character of the product, 286; comprehension and execution of policy, 276–78; and conformity in pricing, 284–86; and consistency of policy, 274–76; and independence in pricing, 278–81, 288; and market pressures, 278–80; and price-cutting, 284; and price stability, 283; and public pressures, 280–81; summary, 286–90; and types of pricing, 281–84

Smith, Paul C., 187n

Socony Vacuum Oil Company, 82, 85

Standard Brands, Inc., 215

standard costs: defined, 14n–15n; Donaldson Brown variant of, 277–78; General Motors' use of, 49, 50, 51, 55, 131–32, 134, 277; International Harvester's use of, 136, 140; purposes of employing, 15n; smaller companies' use of, 272; Union Carbide's use of, 119, 121–22, 123–25, 161–62, 164; U.S. Steel's use of, 14–16, 18–19

Standard Oil Company (Indiana), 11, 79, 157, 284;
  company pricing policy, 198–200, 218–19;
    market pressures on, 280;
    and profitability, 200;
  product pricing, 86–91;
    and local competitive conditions, 88–89, 89n, 90;
    and price changes, factors in, 89–91, 91n;
    revision of practices after World War II, 87–91, 198–99;
    rigid price formula, dependence upon, 86–87

Standard Oil Company (New Jersey). *See* Esso Standard Oil Company

Stannard, E. T., 176, 178n

steel, pricing of, 9, 13–24; and aluminum, competition between, 36; average prices and capacity operated, Chart, 20, Table, 303; basing point system, 20–21, 21n, 170, 268; cost of basic facilities, rise in, 170; extras, charges for, 14, 14n; objectives of the industry, 166; price estimation, 16, 16n; pricing studies, 13–14, 13n; and product market differences, 172–73; uniform base price for, 14; *see also* National Steel Corporation; United States Steel Corporation

Stratton, Samuel S., 13n

Sunbeam Corporation, 266

Swift & Company, 6n, 8;
  company pricing policy, 184–88, 278;
    and co-ordination of departments, 185–86;
    formula, lack of, 187;
    market pressures on, 278–79;
    meat supply and market demand, balancing of, 186–87;
  investment and income, Table, 313–17;
  organization, pricing, 239–41, 241n, Chart, 240;
  and perishability problem, 47, 185, 253;
  product pricing, 40–48;
    cut-out test, use of, 41–42;
    and livestock buying, 43–46;
    wholesale, of meat, 44, 185;
  sales and income, Table, 318–22

target return pricing policy. *See under* pricing policy, company

television sets, price shading in, 61

Temporary National Economic Committee, 70, 168, 169, 176, 222, 270, 275

terminal price (gasoline), 81, 95, 96

Texas Company, 210

TNEC. *See* Temporary National Economic Committee

triethanolamine, 162n; prices and pro-